D1458871

GOLDEN DAYS

A public schooling session at Punchestown for Jonjo O'Neill and Dawn Run before the 1986 Gold Cup

GOLDEN DAYS

Cheltenham Gold Cup Winners
from Arkle to Garrison Savannah

JONATHAN POWELL

STANLEY PAUL

London Sydney Auckland Johannesburg

Stanley Paul & Co. Ltd

An imprint of Random Century Group

20 Vauxhall Bridge Road, London SW1V 2SA

Random Century Australia (Pty) Ltd
20 Alfred Street, Milsons Point, Sydney 2061

Random Century New Zealand Limited
PO Box 40-086, Glenfield, Auckland 10

Century Hutchinson South Africa (Pty) Ltd
PO Box 337, Bergvlei 2012, South Africa

First published 1991
Copyright © Jonathan Powell 1991

The right of Jonathan Powell to be identified as the
author of this work has been asserted by him in
accordance with the Copyright, Designs and Patents
Act, 1988

All rights reserved

Set in 10/12 Sabon by SX Composing Ltd, Rayleigh, Essex
Printed and bound in Great Britain by Butler & Tanner,
Frome and London

A catalogue record for this book is available from the
British Library

ISBN 0 09 174721 X

CONTENTS

ACKNOWLEDGEMENTS

Researching and writing *Golden Days* proved to be an increasingly nostalgic journey back in time. Wherever I turned people were unfailingly helpful with background information and useful anecdotes. Sometimes there was the added bonus of seeing in retirement the valiant old horses who play such a central role in this book.

Owners, trainers, jockeys, breeders and lads involved with winners and losers all gave generously of their time. I particularly enjoyed meeting the splendid Harry Collins, owner of Woodland Venture, the winner of the first Gold Cup I attended. Well into his eighties now, Harry remembers that day with impressive clarity and still looks after his young stock at home on his own. His superb hospitality was matched by Sir John Thomson, who founded a dynasty of steeplechasers when he bought Fort Leney's dam Leney Princess so cheaply.

In the Cotswolds Jim Wilson, David Nicholson, Nigel Dimmer, Philip Arkwright and Edward Gillespie were all extremely helpful. So, too, were Jenny Pitman and Darkie Deacon in nearby Lambourn. Down in Somerset I was given a typically warm West Country welcome by Arthur Barrow, John Honeyball and Tim Handel. A pleasant winter's Sunday spent with James Hodges and his family amply demonstrated just how much fun and entertainment Ten Up has given them all in his retirement.

In Ireland, the traditional home of N.H. breeding, every trainer has a tale to tell. None does it better than merry Mick O'Toole, the trainer of Davy Lad. I am also profoundly grateful to Joan Moore, her son Arthur Moore, Francis Flood, Martin Kennelly, good-natured Jim Dreaper and John Clarke, manager of the Irish National Stud.

Michael Stone patiently unravelled for me the extraordinary sequence of events that began on a cargo ship and eventually led to the disqualification of Tied Cottage. Jim Cole of Tattersalls (Ire) and Leo Powell of Goffs both provided crucial details of vendors, purchasers, pedigrees, and sale prices. My old chum Brian Murphy from the Dunraven Arms in Adare helped me track down Jane Samuel in Canada after months of searching. From America Mrs Raymond Guest kindly supplied me with details of L'Escargot's life in retirement in Virginia. Nearer home Pip Pocock proved a constant source of encouragement.

Some of the great steeplechase jockeys of the past relived their Gold Cup triumphs as if they were yesterday. Gentle Pat Taaffe proved to be a veritable mine of information about the incomparable Arkle. My occasional tennis partner John Francome offered all sorts of fascinating background details, some of them quite unrepeatable! Tommy Carberry, as impish as ever, is surely worth a book on his own.

I am grateful, also, for the assistance of Dessie Hughes, Paul Kelleway, Graham Bradley, Robert Earnshaw, Mark Dwyer, Ron Barry, Jeff King, Tony Mullins, Jonjo O'Neill, Frank Berry, John Burke and my good friend Richard Pitman, whose boundless delight at his son's victory on Garrison Savannah helped erase the scars of his own luckless defeats in the race. Meeting Bobby Beasley again behind the bar of his pub in the Worcestershire hills was a particularly moving experience. He told his story with haunting honesty.

Visiting Sirrell and Joyce Griffiths at their farm in Nantgaredig was, quite simply, a delight – a journey into fantasy to discover Norton's Coin, the most improbable Gold Cup winner of all, with chickens clucking at his feet as he rested wearily in his box, a converted dairy.

Golden Days could not have been completed without the help of so many others, too. My thanks to them all.

Photographic acknowledgement
The author and publisher would like to thank the following for permission to reproduce their copyright photographs: George Selwyn, Gerry Cranham, Bernard Parkin, Caroline Norris, Trevor Jones, Sport & General Press Agency, The Hulton-Deutsch Collection, W. W. Rouch, Irish Field and Associated Newspapers.

INTRODUCTION

A HISTORIC DINNER IN THE HEART of London's West End late in February 1974 offered a night of delicious nostalgia for those who cherish the sport of steeplechasing. Jockeys, trainers and owners of horses who had won the Cheltenham Gold Cup were invited by the champagne house Piper Heidsieck to celebrate the 50th anniversary of this unique race.

Standing in the reception room, glimpsing famous names of the past as they arrived, was rather like spending a delightfully indulgent evening leafing through the pages of your favourite scrap-books. Small, rugged men, every one a hero, with weather-beaten faces and gap-toothed smiles, swapped memories and exchanged reminiscences long after the official function had ceased. Each one had a story to tell. Dawn was only a furlong away by the time we stumbled to bed.

Ted Leader and Evan Williams, both successful on the mighty Golden Miller, were there. So, too, were the legendary Martin Molony and Dick Black, only the second amateur to win the race.

Tom Dreaper and Pat Taaffe, trainer and rider of the peerless Arkle, travelled over together from Ireland to join his devoted owner Anne, Duchess of Westminster at the dinner. Vincent O'Brien flew back early from a trip to America. Fulke Walwyn and Ryan Price were in irrepressible form, as you would expect. Dave Dick and his great friend, the redoubtable Fred Winter, laughed uproariously together like naughty schoolboys.

No less than twenty-six jockeys who had won the Gold Cup attended the anniversary dinner that night. Eleven successful owners and ten winning trainers were there, too. They were all drawn by a shared accumulation of glory in an annual long-distance steeplechase in the Cotswolds that offers one of the most stirring images in sport.

How ironic that the Cheltenham Gold Cup at the temple of jump racing began as a flat race over three miles in August 1819, high on picturesque Cleeve Hill overlooking today's racecourse. More than a century later it became a weight-for-age steeplechase in 1924 and quickly developed into the ultimate test of excellence.

The Gold Cup has long been the accepted climax to three days of unrivalled entertainment at the Cheltenham Festival held each year in the early spring. On March 15th 1990, a total of 56,884 paying customers, the largest number since records were first kept in the fifties, squeezed into the racecourse at Prestbury Park on the edge of the town on the day that Norton's Coin won the Gold Cup at 100–1.

The meeting has become one of the peaks of the sporting year. Just to be there is an enriching experience, yet the enthusiasts who return in even greater numbers each March do so despite the frequently foul weather, the unspeakable traffic jams before and after racing and the constant battle for nourishment, both solid and liquid.

The cost of three days' racing is astronomical and the chances of recovering just some of your expenses through betting are minimal unless you happen to possess a bookmaker's licence. Even the most level-headed, knowledgeable punters are swept along on a perilous tide of enthusiasm. Common sense is invariably the first casualty of the meeting. The strain on emotions and bank balances alike is unrelenting. To survive intact at the conclusion of the Festival after eighteen races is to have overcome the most compelling examination of endurance.

Despite numerous improvements by the management team headed so ably by Edward Gillespie, the facilities for watching racing in comfort are still inadequate for the numbers involved. No matter. Regulars accept that an orderly crush is part of the meeting's charm. However much we complain we know that each March we will all be drawn back once more, united by the common bond of sharing three glorious days of jump racing at the highest level. The very fact that we return in greater numbers every year is truly a triumph of optimism over experience.

Weight-for-age races for jumpers were rare in the first part of the twentieth century. The only significant non-handicap events in the calendar were the four-mile National Hunt Chase, at Cheltenham, and the Champion Chase at Liverpool. The Festival became a three-day meeting in 1923 and the first Gold Cup followed a year later. The sound concept of a championship race for staying chasers quickly developed into a cherished tradition.

The frantic finish of the first Gold Cup run in 1924 over three miles, three furlongs, proved to be a wonderfully exciting prelude of what was to come in the years ahead. Three horses were in the air together at the last fence. Red Splash, an inexperienced five-year-old ridden by Dick Rees, made most of the running and just held on by a head from Conjuror II with Gerald L a neck away third. The winning horse, trained by Fred Withington, earned the modest sum of £685 for his owner Major Humphrey Wyndham of the Life Guards. Withington, the son of a parson, had trained both Red Splash's sire and dam.

Half a century ago racehorses were required to maintain a work rate that would cause outrage today. A fortnight after winning the 1929 Gold Cup by twenty lengths the handsome, white-faced Easter Hero, who once changed hands for £7,000, was sent to Liverpool for the Grand National, which had attracted an unprecedented total of 66 runners. Easter Hero, as befits the finest chaser of his day, carried 12 st. 7 lb. The daunting Aintree fences then were massive, upright and as solid as brick walls, a fact that Easter Hero discovered after landing perilously on the Canal Turn the previous year causing a pile-up of Foinavon proportions.

The free-running Easter Hero finished a gallant second in the 1929 Grand National, despite the handicap of spreading a racing plate. The next spring he returned to Cheltenham to win the Gold Cup again by twenty lengths but was robbed of the chance to become the first horse to achieve a hat-trick when bad weather caused the 1931 meeting to be abandoned. He ran instead in the Grand National, was hampered irretrievably at Becher's Brook on the second circuit, appeared again the very next day in the Champion Chase, and claimed a dead heat.

Easter Hero, the first outstanding horse to win the Cheltenham Gold Cup, spent his retirement in America, where he was often ridden to hounds by his owner Jock Whitney. The public did not have long to wait for a new hero. Golden Miller, who won the Gold Cup for the first time as a five-year-old in 1932, was to dominate the race for a longer period than any horse has done before or since.

Golden Miller's breeding offered precious little evidence of the great years that lay ahead. His dam Miller's Pride, who ran unsuccessfully six times, had cost £100. The advertised fee of his sire Goldcourt, chiefly used to cover hunter mares, was five guineas. The product of this mating in Ireland first changed hands for 100 guineas and was later bought for 500 guineas by the bright young trainer Basil Briscoe, an old Etonian.

Unlike the vast majority of Gold Cup horses Golden Miller won twice over hurdles as a four-year-old in January 1931. More remarkably he ran over fences for the first time a month later. When his owner Philip Carr sold all his horses later that year Golden Miller became the property of the immensely wealthy and singularly eccentric Dorothy Paget, whose curious lifestyle was the subject of endless speculation. The cantankerous Miss Paget, a fiercely ambitious owner, paid the not inconsiderable sum of £6,000 for the Miller, who had run in only five steeplechases before the 1932 Gold Cup.

That year the fences at Cheltenham were trimmed by up to six inches after widespread criticism that they were too severe. Even so there were numerous casualties over the three days. Kingsford came down in the Gold Cup. More seriously the 1931 Grand National winner Grakle, the odds-on favourite, shed his jockey Jack Fawcus as he swerved to avoid the faller. This left Golden Miller, a 13–2 chance, to win by four lengths from Inverse.

The Miller, a big, imposing horse, won a second Gold Cup the following year by ten lengths from Thomond II but unshipped his jockey on his first attempt at the Grand National. In 1934 he completed the hat-trick in the Gold Cup by six lengths from Avenger. Sixteen days later, carrying the welter burden of 12 st. 2 lb, he added a famous victory in the Grand National in a new record time. His feat of winning both races in the same season is unlikely ever to be equalled, though Garrison Savannah came tantalisingly close to matching it in 1991.

Golden Miller won a fourth Gold Cup, narrowly,

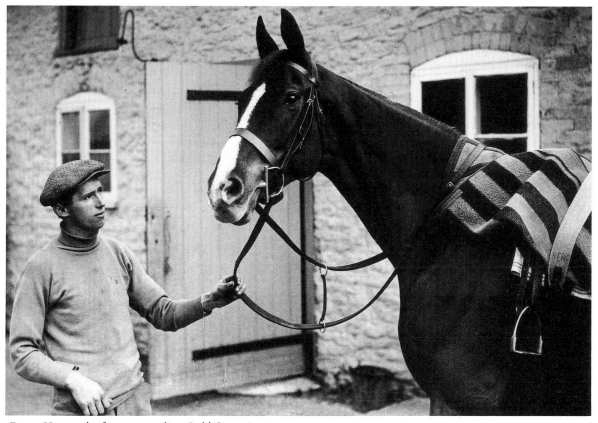

Easter Hero – the first outstanding Gold Cup winner

in 1935 after the most punishing battle of attrition with Thomond II. Many present considered this epic duel to be the finest steeplechase of all. In 1936 the distance of the race was shortened by almost a furlong but the result was the same. The Miller claimed a fifth successive victory in the race by twelve lengths, from Royal Mail. The Festival meeting was abandoned in 1937 and only the presence of the younger Morse Code prevented Golden Miller, by then eleven, winning it for the sixth time in 1938.

The Miller was, in truth, a horse apart, a colossus whose valiant achievements improved the image of steeplechasing immeasurably. The honours list of Gold Cup winners offers a rich treasury of delight. The name of Golden Miller reigned supreme for almost thirty years and his deeds became the subject of folklore. History relates that so many Gold Cup winners have died comparatively early. Mighty Golden Miller appeared at the International Horse Show at the White City in 1950 and lived to the grand

old age of thirty.

Until the fifties the Gold Cup was designed differently each year. When Dorothy Paget died she bequeathed all five of Golden Miller's Gold Cups to the Steeplechase company at Cheltenham. For three days a year during the Festival they are on display in the Royal Box. Since each one is valued at around £15,000 they spend the rest of the year locked away in the vaults of Martin & Co., the old, established Cheltenham jewellers who supply many of the trophies to this day.

The modern Gold Cup is much smaller and neater than its predecessors. It is a striking trophy comprising twelve ounces of 9-carat gold on a green Brazilian onyx base. The cup is made in London; the base is created in Torquay.

A half-size bronze of Golden Miller by Judy Boyt was unveiled by Fulke Walwyn, one of his jockeys, at Cheltenham in 1989, just over half a century after the great horse's final race. The Miller, wearing his

Over the last fence in 1935 – Golden Miller (left) and Thomond II in a finish of consuming intensity

customary bandages on his forelegs, can be found gazing inquisitively towards the paddock from his vantage point at the end of the second level of the new grandstand.

Racing in Britain was severely curtailed during the Second World War. Though the Festival meeting at first continued on a reduced scale, the Gold Cup was not held in 1943 or 1944. Less than two months before the end of the conflict in Europe Lord Stalbridge's Red Rower, the 11–4 favourite, won the 1945 Gold Cup from one of the largest field of runners ever assembled for the race.

The immediate post-war years yielded another truly outstanding chaser, Prince Regent, who took

the 1946 Gold Cup in the most majestic manner imaginable. A powerful horse, almost 17 hands with a devouring stride, he had been ridden to victory in his bumper race by his trainer Tom Dreaper, whose name would become synonymous with steeplechasing excellence. Prince Regent won the Irish Grand National in 1942, was second in it in both 1943 and 1944, and in the twilight of his career was quite superb in defeat in the English Grand National in 1946 and 1947. Had he been born in another era he might have swept the board. The war, however, prevented him from parading his enormous talent to a wider audience at the height of his powers.

The French-bred Fortina, who won at the postponed 1947 Festival meeting on Saturday, April 12th, was notable as the only entire horse to win the race. He was ridden by Dick Black, an amateur, who had been a prisoner of war. Later at stud Fortina achieved the unusual double of siring two Gold Cup winners, Fort Leney and Glencaraig Lady.

Next came the domination of a quiet, soft-spoken genius from Tipperary named Vincent O'Brien. He sent over Cottage Rake to win the Gold Cup three years running in 1948, '49 and '50. Quite small and lightly made, Cottage Rake was built more in the mould of a flat horse. Indeed he won the Irish Cesarewitch after embarking on his new career as a chaser and possessed sufficient speed to win the Naas November Handicap over one and a half miles. Before he was sent to Cheltenham two vets questioned his wind under examination. So much for expert opinion.

Tough, brave and resolute with an attractive white splash on his face, Cottage Rake was pushed to the limit by Happy Home in his first Gold Cup. Standing beside the last fence O'Brien was dismayed to see Happy Home set off up the hill with a useful lead. The trainer was quite unable to tell which horse had won until he saw his jockey Aubrey Brabazon touching his cap to acknowledge the cheers of the crowd. In 1949, when the race was held, unusually, on a Monday in April, Cottage Rake once again required all his considerable qualities of courage and endurance to withstand the determined challenge of Cool Customer.

The Rake's third victory at Cheltenham was his easiest. In 1950 he overwhelmed Lord Bicester's Finnure, until then unbeaten all season. Aubrey Brabazon's faultless riding of the Rake was immortalised in a popular Irish ditty, but a strained tendon ended any chance of Cottage Rake tackling Golden Miller's record.

Frank Vickerman, a wealthy English businessman, sent the Rake to be trained at Weyhill by Gerald Balding. The old horse, by then a faded star, was still trundling round the country meetings at fourteen.

Mont Tremblant was the first of four Gold Cup winners trained by the master Fulke Walwyn in 1952. Owned by Dorothy Paget of the mysterious nocturnal habits and gargantuan appetite, Mont Tremblant had winning form on the flat in France. Full of quality and courage, Mont Tremblant is one of a select band of horses who have achieved the notable feat of triumphing in the Gold Cup as a novice.

It was his fifth race over fences.

Vincent O'Brien claimed one more Gold Cup with Knock Hard in 1953 before departing shortly afterwards to conquer flat racing as surely as he had once ruled the world of jumping. Four Ten, formerly a point-to-pointer, won in 1954, and another pointer, the massive Limber Hill, by an anonymous sire Bassam, gained a welcome victory for the North in 1956. The gallant Kerstin, also trained in the North, became the second mare to win in 1958 after the favourite Mandarin had shed his rider at the thirteenth fence and knocked the previous year's hero Linwell out of the race.

The live-wire Roddy Owen, named after the dashing soldier successful on Father O'Flynn in the 1892 Grand National, was a lucky winner for Ireland in 1959. Saffron Tartan, the ante-post favourite, was withdrawn, coughing, at midday. Pas Seul, a brilliant horse but an alarmingly erratic jumper, only six, overturned at the last fence with victory beckoning. As he tumbled to the ground he brought Linwell to a halt. Roddy Owen, ridden by young Bobby Beasley, avoided the mêlée and scampered eagerly through the mud to claim first prize by three lengths. Thus Danny Morgan became the first man to win the race as a jockey and then as a trainer.

Crashing mistakes continued to cost Pas Seul dear but compensation awaited him in the Gold Cup the following year. Despite ploughing haphazardly through the second last fence Pas Seul, a big, robust horse, came back to challenge the much smaller leader Lochroe on the flat and gained the day by a hard-fought length. This time Roddy Owen's chance was effectively ended by the fall of Kerstin in front of him at the final fence.

Pas Seul was out of the well-related mare Pas de Quatre who, remarkably, produced two Gold Cup winners in markedly different circumstances. After giving birth to Gay Donald, winner in 1955, she became an increasingly irregular breeder. Eventually she was given away and ran in point-to-points, unsuccessfully, before giving birth to Pas Seul.

Saffron Tartan, considered by Vincent O'Brien to be the best of his ten winners of the Gloucestershire Hurdle at the Festival, was trained by Don Butchers when he beat Pas Seul in a tremendous finish to the 1961 Gold Cup. Excessive jumping mistakes by the runner-up handed the advantage to Saffron Tartan, a doubtful stayer. He was dying on his feet in the final, punishing, uphill furlong but, driven with superhuman strength and determination by the inimitable Fred Winter, he just held Pas Seul's late charge by one and a half lengths.

So to the doughtiest fighter of them all, Mandarin, who, in Fred Winter, found the most resolute ally in the 1962 Gold Cup. Pas Seul was favourite that day though he drifted ominously in the betting from 15—8 on to 9—4 against. Whatever the cause the message from the ring was unmistakable and depressingly accurate. The favourite lost his action behind after a typically shocking blunder and dropped tamely away in the final half-mile. Bob Turnell, his trainer, was convinced that Pas Seul had been doped.

Downright, old-fashioned, bulldog courage won the day for Mandarin, an eleven-year-old with a history of leg trouble. His entire life was an essay in resilience. Flat out for the final circuit as Cocky Consort, then briefly Pas Seul and finally Fortria led, the little horse simply would not be denied. His suspect legs heavily bandaged against the effects of the firm ground, the heroic Mandarin inched alongside Fortria at the final fence, refused to recognise the possibility of surrender and forced his way to the front half-way up the hill.

Fulke Walwyn, his trainer, told me years later, "You could not really describe Mandarin as a class horse. He was not the best I ever trained but I never saw a gamer or more determined one."

Mandarin was retired in the summer following his inspired victory in the Grand Steeplechase de Paris without brakes or steering when his bit broke after jumping the third fence. Already his trainer believed he had a ready-made replacement in the massive Mill House, a horse with limitless potential.

Bred in Ireland, Mill House, a strikingly heavy horse, well over 17 hands with an exceptionally deep chest and the flowing action of a Classic winner, had been broken-in by none other than Pat Taaffe, whose name was to become irretrievably linked with Arkle's. Pat had also won a point-to-point on his dam Nas Na Riogh. Mill House was trained at first by Pat's father Tom, who combined farming with training.

"I loved the horse," Pat recalls. "I thought he was everything you could ever want in a young chasing prospect and thought we had lost the finest horse we had ever seen when he was sold to England."

Mill House was bought by businessman Bill Gollings for £10,000 and moved first to Epsom with Syd Dale before joining Walwyn in the summer of 1962. Walwyn's new jockey Willie Robinson, brilliantly gifted but unusually light for a steeplechase rider, was a lifelong friend of Pat Taaffe. That autumn Taaffe wrote to Robinson in Lambourn with the good news that he would be riding the best horse that ever came out of Ireland. Yet for all his undoubted promise Mill House had fallen on his debut over fences and had run in only five steeplechases before tackling the 1963 Gold Cup as a six-year-old. Even so he started favourite and won with astounding ease by twelve lengths from Fortria and Pat Taaffe.

Mill House's ruthless dismissal of the best chasers in training inevitably sparked widespread speculation that he might be the horse to test Golden Miller's unrivalled record in the race. Those closest to him, including Fulke Walwyn and Willie Robinson, were already convinced that he was an outstanding champion. So he might have been but for the overwhelming presence of another exceptional Irish horse named Arkle, who had won the Broadway Chase at the Festival two days earlier with a flash of virtuosity.

1

ARKLE

(1964, 1965, 1966)

THE HORSE WHO RAN AND JUMPED with wings on his heels was born at 3.30 a.m. on April 19th 1957, at the Ballymacoll Stud in County Meath. His dam, Bright Cherry, a speedy two-mile chaser, had been covered on May 2nd the previous year at a cost of 48 guineas by the obscure stallion Archive, who had failed to win a single race.

Bright Cherry's subsequent mating with Straight Deal at the Ballymacoll Stud proved fruitless but the foal she produced there while waiting for his favours was to dominate steeplechasing in a manner that had only once before been witnessed. The bay colt foal whose deeds would become legendary subsequently returned with his mother to the small farm of Mary Baker at Malahow just north of Dublin. Later he was the subject of a standard gelding operation carried out on almost all young male thoroughbreds destined to race over hurdles and fences.

The unnamed young horse survived a hazardous collision with a barbed wire fence when he attempted to join some fillies in an adjoining field. Forty stitches were required to knit the wound; the scar was visible throughout his life. He was broken in, as a two-year-old, by Mary Baker's daughter Alison.

Small breeders, who are the lifeblood of the thoroughbred industry in Ireland, tend to sell rather than race the horses they produce. In 1960, when Bright Cherry's gangly, long-backed son was three, Mrs Baker, a widow, entered him in the Goffs August sale. A note on the auctioneer's catalogue indicated a reserve price of 980 guineas.

Soft-spoken Tom Dreaper, scouting as ever for fresh recruits, was immediately interested since he had trained Bright Cherry and her dam Greenogue Princess, a winner of five chases and a hurdle race. Indeed in his younger days as an amateur Tom had ridden Greenogue Princess in point-to-points. At the

sales was one of Tom's staunchest owners Anne, Duchess of Westminster, who in her youth as Nancy Sullivan had set a dashing figure across country in Co. Cork. Widowed in 1953, the Duchess kept horses with Willie O'Grady and Tom Dreaper in Ireland and with George Owen near her home in Cheshire.

Encouraged by Tom Dreaper's interest in Bright Cherry's three-year-old, lot number 148, and rather taken by the hardy bay horse as an individual the Duchess bought him at Goffs for 1,150 guineas and immediately took him home to her Eaton Hall Stud which, unhappily, closed in 1980.

Once the stud, just outside Chester, was one of the most successful breeding grounds in Europe. Twenty-eight Classic winners were produced there, including the mighty Sceptre and Flying Fox. Now the superb yard and immaculate boxes lie idle and the stud manager's office is a timeless museum containing countless treasures. Weathered gravestones in an empty paddock bear silent testimony to the great names of another age. Here, in the most peaceful setting imaginable, lie the remains of Orme, Bend Or, Shotover, Lily Agnes and Ormanent, the dam of Sceptre.

The subject of the Duchess's shrewd purchase at Goffs would rival all those immortal racehorses. Named Arkle after a mountain near her Scottish estate, he was ridden quietly at Eaton Hall in the autumn of 1960 by her much valued stud groom Bill Veal. A year later Arkle was on his way back to Ireland to join Tom Dreaper. In the early days there was scarcely any indication of the greatness to come. Like so many big horses bred for chasing Arkle was rather backward and immature when he first began the daily training routine that tended to be shorter at Greenogue than any other stable in England or Ireland. Dreaper, endlessly patient and understanding, did not believe in overworking his horses. Most mornings they would go out for only twenty-five minutes; certainly never for more than half an hour.

Arkle was fourth twice in bumper races, ridden by the stable's amateur Mark Hely-Hutchinson in December 1961. Next he ran over hurdles in a minor race for novices at Navan. Tom Dreaper supplied the favourite Kerforo, ridden by his stable jockey Pat Taaffe. The unconsidered Arkle, starting at 20–1 and ridden by young Liam McLoughlin, sloshed through the mud first with Kerforo a well-beaten third. Those clairvoyants who supported him on the Tote received a massive dividend of £6 4s. 6d.

Pat Taaffe recalls: "At the time Arkle was a great, gaunt thing. You could have driven a wheelbarrow through his hind legs. That is why I was astonished at the way he cruised past me. I could not believe it was possible."

At Naas in March it was Pat Taaffe who won on Arkle. Two defeats followed on faster ground that spring. When Arkle returned to training after a summer's break at grass he was a much stronger horse, more mature. He won twice more over hurdles in October 1962 before embarking on a new, uplifting campaign over fences.

Pat Taaffe, who became his constant ally, relates: "Arkle improved so much when he started going over fences I knew he would be a champion all right. In his younger days he could not manipulate himself too well; he was not mature enough. As he improved he was more sensible; he knew what to do. He was always a very intelligent horse and full of courage."

Even so there was an early, unexpected setback. Tom Dreaper schooled his horses constantly, until jumping became second nature to him. In addition he always gave them a brief refresher course two days before they ran. The mighty Arkle was no exception. One morning that winter he fell heavily over Dan Moore's hurdles at Fairyhouse as he warmed up before a more serious practice over fences. It was a mistake caused by over-exuberance. Mercifully, despite thrusting his front legs perilously through the bars of the hurdle, the great horse was uninjured. Pat Taaffe, more surprised than hurt, was taken to hospital, where four stitches were required in a cut above his eye.

So, fittingly, to Cheltenham, where Arkle won his first steeplechase, the Honeybourne Chase on November 17th 1962, by twenty lengths. He re-

turned to the Cotswolds in March, took the Broadway Chase again by twenty lengths from the best novices in training, then added the Power Gold Cup and John Jameson Cup before retiring undefeated for the season.

Pat Taaffe wrote again to his old friend Willie Robinson in Lambourn with the warning that Mill House could now be considered only the second-best horse ever to have come out of Ireland.

The Duke of Westminster had been a fiercely keen supporter of flat racing. His widow could not be said to display a similar interest. On a visit to Cheshire I wondered how many of her horses had won on the flat. Even her trusted aide Col Pat Smyly could not be certain. The count was brief. Brilliant Stone in the Blue Seal Stakes, Brilliant Reay and Star Burst who was taken all the way to Hamilton to win his maiden in 1980.

"Yes, just the three," answered the Colonel triumphantly.

"You are wrong," declared the Duchess with a deep, throaty chuckle, before adding a large wink for the benefit of those of us sitting in the kitchen of her lovely home, Eaton Lodge, on the Westminster estate just a few miles from Chester racecourse.

"Don't forget Arkle won at Navan."

Her memory, of course, was faultless. Just over a month before his thunderous first clash with Mill House in the Hennessy Gold Cup at Newbury in 1963 Arkle won a one mile, six furlongs all-aged maiden plate at Navan by five lengths ridden by Tommy "T. P." Burns. Those four successes tell their own story about the strength of the Duchess's involvement with flat racing, but there has never been any doubting her deep love and affection for jump racing.

The historic first encounter between Arkle and Mill House was the subject of enormous interest. In many ways it offered the flavour, passion and sheer physical involvement of a full-blooded confrontation between Ireland and England at Twickenham or Lansdowne Road to decide the fate of the Triple Crown. Eight other horses lined up with them at Newbury that misty November afternoon, but you would not have known it from the massive publicity that indicated the race was a duel between two National champions.

The giant Mill House, the title holder, carrying twelve stone, was a solidly backed favourite at 15–8. Arkle, tall, almost leggy in comparison, the much heralded challenger, was a 5–2 chance. The race proved expensively misleading for those who took the result at face value. Mill House won with astounding authority; Arkle was not even second. An incident had occurred at the third last fence largely unseen on this murky day by the massed ranks of racegoers in the stands.

Closing rhythmically on Mill House at the fence, a ditch, Arkle jumped it fluently but slipped awkwardly on landing. By the time he recovered the favourite had gone beyond recall. Mill House won by eight lengths from the lightweight Happy Spring. Arkle, believed by his admirers to be invincible, was only third.

Years later, sitting in the front room of his home a short canter from Goffs sales centre at Kill, Pat Taaffe relived that fateful moment.

"Maybe Arkle put his foot in a hole but to this day I don't know what happened. When he landed his front feet went straight on. For a long time I blamed myself. Racing one and a half lengths behind Mill House going into the fence was the wrong place to be," he reflected with characteristic modesty.

The jockey's faith in Arkle was unshaken. As he rode back at Newbury he warned Willie Robinson the result would be reversed next time. Robinson grinned in disbelief. Who could blame him? Can there have been a single Englishman at Newbury that day who did not share his conviction that Mill House was a truly exceptional champion? Didn't he win his next race, the King George VI Chase, in a canter?

Suitable conditions races for top-class chasers are scarce in Ireland. Arkle reverted to handicaps, carrying top weight of twelve stone to rousingly easy victories at Leopardstown (twice) and Gowran Park.

Battle was joined again at Cheltenham on March 7th, only the second time the Gold Cup has been run on a Saturday. It seemed as if the entire nation paused in mid-afternoon on that cold, crisp day to witness the historic showdown between two great horses. It was a mouth-watering collision of racing values. The sheer clinical power of the relentless English battleship against the poetry of the athletic Irish idol. Such was their domination that only two others turned out.

King's Nephew, winner of the Great Yorkshire Chase on his previous venture, was mildly backed from 25–1 down to 20–1. Old Pas Seul, the winner four years earlier but now eleven, was virtually ignored in the betting market at 50–1.

A fine study of the peerless Arkle ridden by Pat Taaffe

Tension increased when a brief snowstorm engulfed Prestbury Park as the two protagonists entered the parade ring. The race was delayed for five minutes until the blizzard ended. In front of the stands the betting exchanges continued with relentless fervour. Mill House, bidding for his second successive Gold Cup, was the subject of massive support from 4–5 to 8–13. Arkle drifted slightly out to 7–4.

The favourite led, as expected, from the start, jumping with a thrilling blend of boldness and accuracy in bright sunshine. Just behind him Pat Taaffe could be seen struggling to restrain Arkle from dashing impatiently to the front.

He relates: "The horse was hard to control all right. He was trained for the race and mad keen to go but I wanted to keep him back because my best chance was beating Mill House for speed up the hill. I felt if I had taken on Mill House earlier I might have come off second best."

Eventually, reluctantly, Arkle dropped in perhaps three lengths behind the leader. Though it was not obvious from the stands Pat Taaffe was confident of victory fully five fences from home.

So the two charged downhill again at a pace seldom seen in the Gold Cup or any other steeplechase at Cheltenham. Mill House still led with Arkle closing significantly as they pounded towards the third last fence. Here the leader gained a length or two with another fluent leap but within seconds Arkle was back at his girths once more. This was the moment the entire racing world had anticipated for months.

The pair were in the air together at the second last, their dark shadows dancing beside them, but as they rounded the final bend it was Willie Robinson who wielded his whip first, an act that gave a crucial clue to what ensued. A moment later Arkle showed ahead for the first time in the race, flicked eagerly over the last obstacle and sprinted clear amid a rising crescendo of acclamation. Startling powers of acceleration had won the day.

There could be no further argument now. Mill House, the champion, was overwhelmed, comprehensively beaten by five lengths. We had witnessed a stunning and ruthless display of steeplechasing at its very best. The Irish celebrated as only they can at Cheltenham. Thousands rushed to salute their hero. This time it was the Walwyn camp who greeted the result in disbelief.

Fulke Walwyn later confirmed: "I could not believe my eyes. I thought Mill House was the best chaser in the land. The ease with which Arkle beat him was astonishing. I had never seen a performance like that. I was truly shocked but foolishly hoped it might have been a fluke."

It was a judgement he would come to regret.

Returning in triumph to his homeland Arkle crowned an unforgettable season with victory in the Irish Grand National. His summers were spent with his owner, usually at her Bryanstown Stud near Maynooth, though he did return once to Eaton Hall. Anne, Duchess of Westminster believed in enjoying her horses to the full. What, she reasoned, could possibly match the pleasure of riding Arkle at home in the summer and early autumn before he resumed training? Sometimes she would ride him at exercise with Tom Dreaper's string. If anyone doubted the wisdom of this practice they did not voice it. The Duchess was a consummate horsewoman: neat, enthusiastic and fearless. Simply owning the greatest steeplechaser in training was not enough. Who could blame her for wishing to ride him at every possible opportunity?

"Oh yes, he could pull quite hard but I always felt safe on him. I felt he was looking after me," she says.

No one could doubt her depth of feeling for Arkle.

Pat Taaffe confirms, "She loved him and treated him more like a human being than a horse. He was her favourite pet."

Arkle's boundless superiority over his contemporaries led to an unprecedented alteration to the handicapping rules in Ireland. When his name appeared among the entries the handicapper was required to frame two separate sets of weights. One would be used if he ran, the second if he did not. In England his presence led to the innovation of an extended handicap. Yet even the full might of the handicapper's scales could not prevent him winning the 1964 Hennessy Gold Cup under the huge burden of 12 st. 7 lb. This time Mill House, in receipt of 3 lb, was beaten a total of thirty-two lengths in fourth place.

Next time at Cheltenham a penalty took Arkle's weight to 12 st. 10 lb in the Massey-Ferguson Gold Cup over an inadequate distance of two miles, five furlongs. Imagine the outcry today if Desert Orchid

---

CHELTENHAM GOLD CUP.   March 7th 1964.   £8,004.   *Good.*

1 Arkle	7 12 0	P. Taaffe	7–4
2 Mill House	7 12 0	G. W. Robinson	8–13 Fav
3 Pas Seul	11 12 0	D. Dick	50–1
4 King's Nephew	10 12 0	S. Mellor	20–1

5 lengths, 25.   Owned Anne, Duchess of Westminster.   Trained T. Dreaper. Bred Mrs M. Baker.   6m. 45.6 seconds.   4 Ran.   Tote win: 11s. 10d.

Arkle: b.g. 1957 (Archive–Bright Cherry)

Another historic confrontation between Arkle (left) and Mill House in 1965

were expected to carry that sort of weight. There followed Arkle's only defeat at Cheltenham. He failed narrowly and gallantly to concede 32 lb to the fine grey mare Flying Wild and 26 lb to the exciting young chaser Buona Notte. Arkle completed his preparation for his second Gold Cup with another defiant display of weight-carrying in the Leopardstown Chase, in which he was required to concede three stone to most of the runners.

Mill House, meanwhile, had been successfully exhibiting his own ability to carry excessive weight. He limbered up for Cheltenham with successive victories in the Mandarin Chase (12 st. 7 lb) and Gainsborough Chase (12 st. 5lb) which offered his supporters fresh hope for the next conflict with Arkle.

It came in the 1965 Cheltenham Gold Cup, which again yielded only four runners. Stoney Crossing, a

33–1 chance, was ridden by the adventurous Australian amateur Bill Roycroft, an Olympic event rider with extremely limited experience of racing. Even more remarkable, the Gold Cup proved to be Stoney Crossing's debut over fences in this country. Caduval, racing for the first time in twelve months, was on offer at 100–1.

In August 1964, the completion of extensive alterations at Cheltenham allowed the authorities to achieve their long cherished ambition to offer two entirely separate courses within the boundaries of Prestbury Park. Thus the Gold Cup in 1965 was held for the first time over the full new course. As a result the distance of the race was reduced by fifty-four yards to three miles, two furlongs and seventy-six yards. The belief in Arkle's infallibility was reflected cramped starting price of 30–100. This time Pat

Taaffe did not intend to restrain Arkle.

He explains: "By now he gave me the impression he knew he was better than the other one. I thought he was better, too, and decided to make all the running. We would go off at our own pace and Mill House could come with us for a while."

It proved to be a deeply one-sided affair and it was decided, just as twelve months before, after jumping the second last fence. Mill House stayed in touch until that point, vainly trying to claw back the advantage constantly claimed by Arkle's spring-heeled jumping on the firm ground. Now we saw the yawning gulf between the two horses. It proved to be deeply distressing viewing for those close to Mill House. Stretching like an Olympic athlete Arkle galloped right away from his labouring rival. He cleared the last fence with a foot to spare, increased his lead with every stride and sprinted imperiously past the winning post fully twenty lengths ahead of Mill House.

Pat Taaffe reflects: "I think he probably broke the spirit of Mill House, the poor horse, in the end. He must have known himself and asked 'Why are we running against him again?'"

Before the season ended Arkle added one more famous triumph to his ever-growing list of achievements. He returned to England at the end of April for the Whitbread Gold Cup over three miles and five furlongs, the longest distance he had ever attempted. Automatically he was required to carry top weight of 12½ st. The race provided another precious chance to marvel at Arkle's total superiority. He led throughout, brushed aside the brief challenge of the Scottish Grand National winner Brasher, in receipt of 2½ st., and won with contemptuous ease.

By now Arkle strode the stage like a colossus.

Songs, poems and eulogies were composed in his honour. Long-backed, yet wonderfully athletic with an attractive head, big ears and a bright, alert eye, he was considered a freak of nature.

Pat Taaffe reflects: "Ah, he had a terrific engine but I don't know where he got it. I rode the mare Bright Cherry and she never bred anything to touch him. She did not stay an inch more than two miles. Arkle himself had a good long stride and was very well balanced for a big horse.

"He had a very kind nature, too. Anyone could walk into his box safely. He was pleased to see visitors."

Arkle, who enjoyed a pint of Guinness in his evening feed, was proving to be the best possible advertisement for horse racing. By the sheer force of his personality, he introduced the sport of jump racing to a new generation. The miserly odds offered on his winning chance by tight-fisted bookies effectively restricted serious betting activity in his races. Yet, aware of his greatness, the public, young and old, flocked to see Arkle wherever he ran. By now most of his races were in England.

He returned to action at Sandown in November 1965, in the Gallagher Gold Cup at Sandown. Poor Mill House, in receipt of 16 lb, suffered another rout. Mill House led on the far turn but was then brushed abruptly aside as Arkle swept past. There followed another unchallenged triumph in the Hennessy Gold Cup at Newbury at the end of the month. Despite carrying automatic top weight of 12½ st. Arkle started at the remarkable odds of 1–6 that day. The bookies, eager to drum up business, introduced special place betting without the favourite.

The bold decision to pitch the brilliantly fast two-mile chaser Dunkirk against Arkle in the King

CHELTENHAM GOLD CUP.   March 11th 1965.   £7,986 10s.   *Firm.*

1 Arkle	8 12 0	P. Taaffe	30–100 Fav
2 Mill House	8 12 0	G. W. Robinson	100–30
3 Stoney Crossing	7 12 0	Mr W. Roycroft	33–1
4 Caduval	10 12 0	O. McNally	100–1

20 lengths, 30.   Owned Anne, Duchess of Westminster.   Trained T. Dreaper.
Bred Mrs M. Baker.   6m. 41.2 seconds.   4 ran.   Tote win: 5s.

Arkle: b.g. 1957 (Archive–Bright Cherry)

A rare moment of crisis for Arkle as he dives perilously through the last fence on the first circuit in the 1966 Gold Cup

George VI Chase ended in tragedy. Starting like a five-furlong sprinter, Dunkirk was a fence clear of Arkle after a mile. Over the minimum distance of two miles it might have been a race but, inevitably, the tearaway leader could not sustain the gallop. Soon Arkle caught him. As his energy drained away Dunkirk bravely tried to match strides with the challenger. He barely rose at the fifth last fence, an open ditch, crashed sickeningly through it and landed on his jockey Bill Rees.

Dunkirk died, his neck broken. A post-mortem suggested he had haemorrhaged before he fell. His jockey was carried from the course on a stretcher, his thigh badly broken. Arkle sauntered home alone, but for once the mood was sombre as he returned to unsaddle. He completed his preparation for Cheltenham with a further victory in the Leopardstown Chase.

The date of the Festival week so early in March at Cheltenham had long been a cause of anxiety for the racecourse executive. Time and again bitterly cold weather had threatened the meeting until the last possible moment. Indeed in 1947, a particularly severe spring, the Festival was postponed for a week because of severe frost and then abandoned. Instead the Gold Cup, Champion Hurdle, the Foxhunters' Cup and the National Hunt Chase were all run on the same day, Saturday, April 12th.

In the mid-sixties the eminently sensible decision was taken to hold the Cheltenham Festival a week later in March. The alteration did not meet with the approval of the directors of Aintree racecourse, who were unhappy at the proximity of the date to their own Grand National meeting, staged in those days towards the end of March. In time Aintree, however, moved their date back, too.

The 1966 Cheltenham Gold Cup was thus run a week later than usual on Thursday, March 17th. Such was Arkle's total superiority that he started at the prohibitive odds of 1–10. Fittingly, on St Patrick's Day, he carried a sprig of shamrock in his bridle, a gift from some air hostesses. This time Mill House was missing. Dormant led briefly until Arkle surged irresistibly into the lead after a mile. Quickly the race developed into an apparently carefree lap of honour.

A moment of intense drama ensued. Sailing cheerfully along in front Arkle dived recklessly through the fence in front of the stands at the end of the first circuit like a bungling novice. Slow-motion replays of the incident suggest he failed to take off at all. For an awful spine-chilling second it seemed he must fall. Then, mercifully, he was galloping gaily on as if nothing untoward had occurred. Almost any other horse would have fallen. Arkle's astonishingly quick, athletic recovery suggested we had witnessed an illusion.

Tall, leggy Pat Taaffe, a wonderfully natural horseman who rode with an extremely short stirrup length, sat like a limpet during that moment of crisis.

"Arkle was so clever. He parted the birch all right and his knees went back under him but he got his front feet out and on his second stride it was as if he had jumped the fence well.

"Maybe he was looking at the crowds in the stands. I'm not sure. Perhaps it was my fault that I did not give him a kick to go on and jump."

Approaching the next fence Michael Scudamore, some way adrift on Dormant, called out optimistically: "He might fall yet."

Arkle continued serenely on his way, jumped the remaining fences without further incident, and scampered up the hill thirty lengths ahead of Dormant to claim his third successive Gold Cup.

Pat Taaffe recalls: "I thought then we would emulate Golden Miller. I was certain of it. Sure, wasn't he only nine. Even six Gold Cups seemed possible. Time was on his side and the opposition was becoming weaker."

The mighty Miller, of course, had won a Grand National, too, but that was one race Anne, Duchess of Westminster would not consider for Arkle, despite persuasive testimony from Pat Taaffe. Her Sentina, a very good chaser, was brought down at Becher's Brook in the 1958 Grand National. Was that the reason, I wondered, that she did not wish to run Arkle in the race?

"Not really," she replied. "It's very hard to answer that because it makes me sound rather sentimental and sloppy but I was devoted to Arkle. The Grand National is a risky race with loose horses and other hazards.

"I was terrified of his being injured through no fault of his own, though Pat was certain he would win a Grand National."

The jockey confirms: "Oh, yes. I thought the Grand National would be very easy for him. He could have given the others two stone all right. He would have settled jumping those big, wide fences."

The most famous invalid in sport is surrounded by messages of goodwill as he recuperates at Kempton

The Grand National, however, remained strictly off the agenda. Far, far worse, fate decreed that Arkle would not run in another Gold Cup. A foot injury sustained at Kempton on December 27th 1966 cruelly cut short his career when he was at the very height of his powers. He came to Kempton for the King George VI Chase thirteen days after yet another sweeping victory in the S.G.B. Chase at Ascot. Frost on Boxing Day put back racing twenty-four hours. Once more Arkle was prohibitively odds-on at 2–9. Once more the opposition seemed incapable of testing him.

Arkle made most of the running and despite a mistake at the fourteenth fence, an open ditch, was soon clear again. Woodland Venture, challenging strongly, tumbled at the second last fence. Victory for the favourite seemed a formality. He jumped the final fence with a decisive advantage over Dormant but suddenly, ominously, his stride began to falter on the short run-in. Arkle tried, how he tried, to fend off the scything last thrust of Dormant but it was apparent that something was terribly wrong. Dormant caught him just before the line.

Arkle, beaten a length, hobbled back. He was distressingly lame. The powerful, flowing action that had propelled him so exultantly to a score and more of famous victories had finally foundered. It was a dreadful way for a great actor to make his final exit from his beloved stage. Yet no player ever left a favourite theatre of action trailing more glory.

Early that evening X-rays revealed that Arkle had fractured the pedal bone in his foot, possibly when he thumped the guard rail hard at the fourteenth fence. Tom Dreaper and Pat Taaffe returned, miserably, to Ireland. Arkle, the most famous invalid in the British Isles, remained at Kempton, at first under the watchful eye of Ryan Price, who proved a tower of strength in those initial grim hours.

An avalanche of mail and get-well cards engulfed Arkle during his period of recuperation at Kempton, which lasted almost two months. Though he did recover eventually, a planned comeback over hurdles at Fairyhouse's Easter festival in April 1968 was called off because the going was considered too firm. Later that year came the formal announcement that Arkle would not race again.

Sometimes in retirement the Duchess would ride him round her stud at Bryanstown. Late in 1969 Arkle, winner of twenty-seven of his thirty-five races, was the star attraction at the Horse of the Year show at Wembley. Each night he paraded to rapturous applause as the band played "There'll Never Be Another You".

Already Arkle was afflicted with arthritis in both hind feet. Drugs helped alleviate the problem but they could not cure it. His condition worsened.

When Pat Taaffe called to see his old friend at Bryanstown, Arkle scarcely bothered to move. Taaffe knew it was the end. He called the Duchess and her vet Maxie Cosgrove.

The Duchess flew over from England for a last, unhappy farewell before Arkle was put down painlessly in his box on the afternoon of Sunday, May 31st 1970. The horse with an overwhelming presence died tragically young, aged thirteen, and was buried, surrounded by daffodils, close to the house at Bryanstown.

Seven years later the new Irish Horse Museum at the National Stud requested permission to exhibit Arkle's skeleton. Though the Duchess of Westminster had sold Bryanstown by then, she gave permission for Arkle's remains to be exhumed and transported to the Museum at Tully in Co. Kildare.

There his skeleton is on display to this day with his colours and the whip carried but scarcely used on him by Pat Taaffe. Half a million visitors have passed through the museum since 1977. Many have paused, as I did in the spring of 1991, to wonder at the shape of the peerless horse who inspired a nation and brought a song to our hearts.

Even without the flesh, blood and spirit that set him apart, the bare bones of Arkle, assembled so starkly in the hushed dignity of a museum, offer an image, hint at a dream, recall distant feats of valour.

Visitors to Cheltenham, too, can gaze in admiration at a splendid bronze of Arkle, by Doris Lidner, unveiled by his owner in 1972 and now repositioned overlooking the new paddock. Nearby the Arkle Bar, too, bears testimony to his greatness.

CHELTENHAM GOLD CUP.   March 17th 1966.   £7,674 10s.   *Good.*

1 Arkle	9 12 0	P. Taaffe	1–10 Fav
2 Dormant	9 12 0	M. Scudamore	20–1
3 Snaigow	7 12 0	D. Nicholson	100–7
4 Sartorious	11 12 0	T. Biddlecombe	50–1

30 lengths, 10.   Owned Anne, Duchess of Westminster.   Trained T. Dreaper. Bred Mrs M. Baker.   6m. 54.4 seconds.   Also 33 Hunch (S. Mellor) Fell. 5 ran.   Tote win: 4s. 6d.

Arkle: b.g. 1957 (Archive–Bright Cherry)

You could almost reach out and touch the pride on Harry Collins' face as he led back Woodland Venture, followed by Fred Rimell

2

WOODLAND VENTURE
(1967)

THE SHEER CUSSEDNESS OF NATURE can foil the best-laid mating plans. When Harry Collins sent his only mare, Woodlander, to be covered by Domaha at the Ardenrun Stud near Lingfield in Surrey, the stallion would have nothing to do with her. Gerry Langford, the vet who ran the stud, was unable to contact the mare's owner so he called Collins' friend and adviser Harry Dufosee to explain his dilemma.

Dufosee suggested: "Use your other stallion Eastern Venture and I will carry the can." The result of this impromptu breeding arrangement at a cost of the £98 covering fee was Woodland Venture. Imagine the maelstrom of emotions assailing Harry Dufosee when Stalbridge Colonist, the horse he had bred and named after his own village in Dorset, was beaten a whisker by Woodland Venture in the 1967 Cheltenham Gold Cup. Dufosee had even been involved in the purchase of Woodlander. He had introduced Collins to Sidney McGregor, a sergeant in the veterinary corps in the First World War and later employed by the Government to buy horses from Ireland. McGregor had already bred the Derby winner April The Fifth. On a visit to his stud at Leamington Spa Harry Collins was taken by a sturdy young mare.

"I liked the way she sauntered past some nice two-year-olds in the paddock. She was ugly but I thought, 'I'm going to have that mare for point-to-points'," he recalled in the summer of 1990 as clearly as if it had all taken place the previous week.

Sharply alert, with bright, twinkling blue-green eyes, he chuckled: "Gerry Langford told me: 'You can't have *that*.' He thought I was quite mad." His eyes glow with delight as he recounts the story.

Woodlander proved to be an own sister to three winners and a half-sister to four more, including the very useful staying chaser Green Drill, third in the 1958 Grand National. She was five at the time of the deal and cost Harry Collins £250. Once again Harry Dufosee played a crucial role in developments. Reasoning that Woodlander was extremely well related, he advised Harry Collins to breed from her at once. Her first foal proved to be a Gold Cup winner!

Woodland Venture was big and rather backward as a young horse. Though the Collins family lived then at South Perrott in Somerset they sent him for a season's hunting to a friend in Sussex, the renowned horsemaster Roy Trigg. The horse ran three times in point-to-points as a six-year-old in 1965, fell on his debut in the Cowdray Hunt race, and was then pulled up after being baulked in the Southdown Open. But on his final outing he did show a glimpse of what was to come by finishing fifth of eleven in a competitive division of the Old Surrey and Burstow Open.

Writing in his annual that proved so essential for point-to-point enthusiasts Geoffrey Sale noted sagely: "Very promising and could develop into a useful animal".

Collins was sufficiently encouraged to put Woodland Venture, his first racehorse, into training the following autumn. Once more he turned to Harry Dufosee for advice.

He explains: "My wife's father Arthur Phillips was Harry Dufosee's closest friend. When I married Nancy I inherited Harry. He always told me what to do with horses. He said I should send this horse to a trainer with a good stable jockey, and so he chose Fred Rimell, partly because Terry Biddlecombe rode for him. When I rang up Fred he agreed to take the horse for ten guineas a week. Then his wife Mercy came on the line and said the training fee was eleven guineas!"

The trainer soon found that his new recruit was an

impossible handful; strong, powerful and at times totally unco-operative. On some days he would decline to leave the yard! In short, he was a typical young tearaway, a truly electric ride. Graham Nicholls was the man chosen to deal with Woodland Venture. A fine jump jockey in his day with Peter Cazalet and an excellent horseman, he was by then the landlord of the Royal Oak, barely a hundred yards from the Rimells' yard at Kinnersley, and kept his eye in by riding out one lot each morning. Nicholls humoured Woodland Venture and invariably rode him around on his own; the education was private, patient and certainly individual. Strict but kind, Nicholls did not break the big horse's aggressive spirit; he merely channelled it in the right direction.

Woodland Venture's early exploits with Fred Rimell were hardly inspiring. Headstrong and inexperienced, he was pulled up at Worcester then fell on his return to that course. Next he was sent to Cheltenham for another novice chase. Fred, rather disenchanted with the big horse, instructed Terry Biddlecombe: "Take this so-and-so out and just hunt him round." Perhaps the great jockey, who was the reigning champion, for once followed his orders a little too literally. Woodland Venture was staying on steadily when the presence of a jockey, Stan Mellor, lying across a fence after a spill ended his afternoon's exercise. Terry Biddlecombe sensibly pulled up, to the evident irritation of the trainer.

"I told you to go hunting, not to open every bloody gate on the way round," barked the trainer, who determined to send Woodland Venture to Cheltenham once more. Starting at 25–1 he beat the odds-on favourite Woodlawn in a tight finish. He won twice more over fences, too, before a strong late run took him into fifth place behind Different Class in the Totalisator Champion Novices Chase at the Festival. Graham Nicholls' sterling work was beginning to pay useful dividends.

He remembers Woodland Venture with great fondness: "He built himself a reputation he did not really deserve because he unloaded one or two. You would not want to go to sleep on him. He was a strapping strong horse, a big, bold sort without any vice and not half as bad as people thought," he reasons.

Woodland Venture's progress in his second season was mercurial. When he beat a Royal runner, Irish Rover, at Newbury in November 1966, Sir Martin Gilliat, the Queen Mother's loyal aide, asked Fred Rimell if Harry Collins would consider selling the horse to her. The news of this unexpected request was greeted with some derision by a close friend of the Collins family.

"Harry Collins sell Woodland Venture? He'd sooner part with his wife," was the memorable comment of Mardi Nance. Harry Collins did not have cause to regret his decision. Less than a year after winning his first steeplechase Woodland Venture was lining up against Arkle in the King George VI Chase at Kempton. Improbable as it might seem, he would have won, too, but for falling at the second last fence just as he had taken a narrow lead.

"No question, we were going best," reported Terry Biddlecombe to Harry Collins. What Woodland Venture might have achieved was naturally overshadowed by the cruel injury that day which was to end Arkle's blazing dominance.

A nasty attack of ringworm seemed to affect Woodland Venture's form in the New Year. When his price for the Gold Cup drifted out to 25–1 Harry Collins rang his local bookmaker in Yeovil and invested £80 to win and a further £20 at place odds. He raised the stake money by selling a barren heifer at Yeovil market for £99 2s. 0d.

Terry Biddlecombe, twice champion, epitomised the unquenchable spirit of jump jockeys in this most dangerous of sports. Tall, blonde and good-looking with a dazzling smile, he was utterly fearless and cut a wonderfully glamorous figure on horseback. He was, by nature, a laughing cavalier, but his legendary zest for life made his never-ending struggle with the scales all the more difficult to endure.

The day before the Gold Cup Biddlecombe damaged knee ligaments in a heavy fall. When the knee stiffened up that evening he could barely walk. Not for a minute did he consider crying off. That was not his style. The jockey turned to an old ally, Dr Bill Wilson, who agreed to give him a pain-killing injection at the start of racing the next day.

You might imagine that the regrettable absence of Arkle would have ensured a much larger field for the Gold Cup than usual. Not a bit of it. Only eight ran, and his old stable companion Fort Leney was preferred as favourite at 11–4, just a shade shorter than the redoubtable stayer What A Myth. Mill House, who had beaten What A Myth by a neck in the Gainsborough Chase a month earlier, was a 4–1 chance with Stalbridge Colonist, the perennial grey, at 11–2 and Dormant 10–1. Woodland Venture was one of the outsiders at 100–8. Foinavon, once owned by Anne, Duchess of Westminster, was dismissed at 500–1. His name would be on everyone's lips a month later after the most remarkable Grand National of all time.

It was Foinavon who set a funeral early pace for the first half of the race with Woodland Venture and Mill House racing upsides close behind. Further back Fort Leney, so impressive in the Leopardstown Chase, was moving like an old man in tight boots. He clouted the first two fences and continued to fumble his way round like a bungling novice. Mill House led at the eleventh fence with Woodland Venture in close attendance. The pair were virtually locked together until Mill House fell heavily at the final ditch, the seventeenth fence at the top of the hill.

"He put down instead of picking up and that was that," his rider David Nicholson recollects.

This left Woodland Venture in front far sooner than his jockey wanted or intended, yet the best place to be in a slowly run race is often the front and as Woodland Venture sailed gaily down the hill Terry Biddlecombe's confidence increased by the moment. Dormant was struggling after the third last, What A Myth had lost his pitch when the tempo quickened and only Stalbridge Colonist was left to mount a telling challenge. A well-timed run took him to Woodland Venture's quarters between the last two fences. Stan Mellor, small, light and ruthlessly determined, launched Stalbridge Colonist at the final fence like a ghostly white tornado and stole a precious half-length in the air. Beside them Woodland Venture jumped the obstacle well enough, but his narrow

Woodland Venture and the grey Stalbridge Colonist as one over the last fence

lead was all but gone.

As the pair set off up the hill it seemed first one, then the other would triumph. In the fierce heat of battle Stan Mellor was giving vocal as well as physical encouragement to Stalbridge Colonist but Terry Biddlecombe, the numbing pain of his knee forgotten, was riding like a man inspired on Woodland Venture, who gradually inched his way forward to claim victory by three-quarters of a length. Just behind them What A Myth rallied so effectively he was only two lengths away third.

You could almost reach out and touch the pride on Harry Collins' face as he led Woodland Venture back in triumph. That night he hosted a celebration dinner at the Queen's Hotel in Cheltenham. The bill including wine, champagne and dinner for sixteen came to £137 13s. 9d! He still has the receipt to this day. How unfortunate that Woodland Venture would never again reach such dizzy heights. He did not run at all the next season, won once more in January 1969, and later was sent for a summer's break at grass to Collins' new home near Thetford in Norfolk.

Harry Collins recalls: "That first day he stood near an oak tree in the paddock with little black flies all over his eyes, nostrils and backside. He looked so miserable I rang two vets, but they did not seem too concerned."

Woodland Venture was found dead in the paddock the next morning, May 7th 1969. The Rimells always believed he died of a rare illness known as Black's disease, but a post-mortem examination showed he had suffered a series of haemorrhages. Stalbridge Colonist outlived his Cheltenham conqueror by many years. When he lost his form at the age of twelve, his owner sent him to Ascot Sales. Harry Dufosee made the journey to Ascot to buy back the old grey, by then almost white, and immediately pensioned him off in a field below his home in Stalbridge.

When I called to see the horse shortly afterwards, Dufosee explained: "I intended to go up to 500 guineas but I was so keen he should not go to a bad home I went on until he was knocked down to me for 680 guineas."

His generous action brought a response of over one hundred cards, letters and phone calls thanking him. One punter sent a 25p postal order saying: "Please buy Stalbridge Colonist some real English carrots, not the Common Market variety"!

A second letter asked for hairs from the horse's tail and another, from Beirut, sent Allah's wishes to his favourite steeplechaser. In 1975, Stalbridge Colonist made a brief, startling comeback in a point-to-point at the age of sixteen. Ridden by Harry's grandson John Dufosee, he ran well for most of the race and was then pulled up. Harry Dufosee bred the winners of over one hundred and twenty races over jumps. Few, if any, have matched his extraordinary feat of masterminding the breeding of first and second in the 1967 Cheltenham Gold Cup.

CHELTENHAM GOLD CUP.   March 16th 1967.   £7,999 10s.   *Soft.*

1	Woodland Venture	7 12 0	T. Biddlecombe	100–8
2	Stalbridge Colonist	8 12 0	S. Mellor	11–2
3	What A Myth	10 12 0	P. Kelleway	3–1
4	Dormant	10 12 0	J. King	10–1
5	Dicky May	8 12 0	P.McCarron	25–1
6	Fort Leney	9 12 0	P. McLoughlin	11–4 Fav
7	Foinavon	9 12 0	J. Kempton	500–1

¾ length, 2.   Owned and Bred H. Collins.   Trained F. Rimell.   6m. 58.2 seconds.
Also 4 Mill House (D. Nicholson) Fell.   8 ran.   Tote win: 37s. 8d.

Woodland Venture: b.g. 1960 (Eastern Venture–Woodlander)

3

FORT LENEY
(1968)

WHEN LOT NO. 31 FAILED to fulfil her appointment in Goffs sales ring at Ballsbridge in Dublin on April 26th 1956, the assembled group of buyers and breeders missed the chance of acquiring a mare who would found an entire dynasty of top-class steeplechasers. A knee injury sustained in a fall over a wall at Punchestown prevented Leney Princess, a small, seven-year-old dark bay mare, barely 16 hands, from passing through the ring that day. Col John Thomson, so long a generous supporter of National Hunt racing, had been prepared to bid £400 for her. Now, with the help of his friend Cyril Myerscough, he bought Leney Princess in a private deal for £200 from her owner Mrs Gerald Sanderson.

The mare's form was not, in all conscience, particularly enticing. She failed to display any inherent ability in bumper races for Paddy Sleator, though she did finish a close second in a two-mile novices' chase at long defunct Rothbury in April 1955, after joining Craig Brown in Scotland. Leney Princess was hunted regularly by the Sandersons from Keltie Castle in Perthshire and had won two minor point-to-points.

Col Thomson, an eminent banker who became chairman of Barclays in 1962, had ridden in point-to-points before the outbreak of war and was the most enthusiastic racehorse owner imaginable. Now he was anxious to buy a suitable mare for breeding. He was drawn to Leney Princess by her sire Roi d'Egypte, a horse who had won the Cathcart Challenge Cup for him at Cheltenham in 1942 and was a full brother to Medoc II, winner of the Gold Cup the same year. The Colonel did not mind that her dam Biddy The Hawk had not raced. The granddam Triple Alliance, he reasoned, had won seven chases. The deal was done: Leney Princess became his property.

Leney Princess produced fourteen foals between 1958 and 1972 while lodging at the Mullingar stud of Cecil Ronaldson. One was killed by lightning and three more were put down. Two fillies did not win but proved wonderful broodmares. The remaining eight geldings were to win eighty-three races between them. Prince Tino alone won twenty-one times, the last at the age of sixteen. Lean Forward was successful sixteen times and Tuscan Prince fifteen. The best of all her foals was her first, Fort Leney, a strapping, highly-strung, dark bay gelding by Fortina, the only entire horse to win the Cheltenham Gold Cup.

Events were to show that all the produce of Leney Princess needed an unusually long period of time to reach maturity. Cecil Ronaldson believed that prospective chasers needed to learn to pick up their feet, so he took Fort Leney hunting at the early age of three. Two years later, still trained and ridden by the capable Ronaldson, Fort Leney won the Corinthian Plate, a maiden bumper, at Thurles on February 28th 1963. The reward for Col John Thomson was a modest £133. That autumn Fort Leney joined the legendary Tom Dreaper at Greenogue beside the twisty country road in Kilsallaghan not far from Dublin Airport.

Throughout his marvellous career as an unrivalled trainer of steeplechasers Tom Dreaper, of the soft voice and gentle, teasing humour, would not accept more than thirty horses in his care at any one time. Careful, studied, individual attention was his enduring theme for the inmates of Greenogue, which housed a veritable host of stars at the time of Fort Leney's arrival. He was to prove a very able deputy indeed in the immediate years that followed the abrupt departure of Arkle from centre stage. Fort Leney did not linger long over hurdles. A fine, big horse with scope and presence, he won on his debut at Naas in December 1963, and was then put straight to fences.

"This horse is my idea of the ideal Irish chaser," Tom Dreaper told his delighted owner on more than one occasion.

Ridden by Pat Taaffe, Fort Leney was second to the stable's less fancied Day Trip on his debut over fences and fell next time. His jumping and form improved notably through the season and he won both the Power Gold Cup and the John Jameson Cup after narrowly failing to hold the late thrust of the brilliant novice Buona Notte at the Cheltenham Festival.

Fort Leney's progress was so spectacular the following winter that his trainer might have been tempted to run him in the Gold Cup but for the presence of his mighty stable companion Arkle. He won the Thyestes Chase readily from an old rival Greek Vulgan despite the demanding concession of 29 lb and then, carrying the awesome burden of 12 st. 7 lb, failed honourably to hold off the redoubtable Rondetto in the National Hunt Handicap Chase at the Festival.

So to Bogside, where Fort Leney was once more asked to hump 12½ st. in the 1965 Scottish Grand National. One moment he was bounding along in the lead, jumping with his customary élan. The next he landed clumsily in the water jump and pulled himself up. Pat Taaffe was mystified by this uncharacteristic display.

"He just stopped with me without warning. I could not make out what was wrong, but he recovered within minutes," he recalls. An extensive examination revealed that the horse had strained a valve in his heart. Rest was the only cure. In addition Fort Leney, still only seven, did not have the best of legs. He was given a year off. When he returned to action it was at Newbury in October 1966. He disputed the lead for much of the way as if he had never been away but faded rather tamely in the closing stages. Pat Taaffe believes lack of effort rather than fitness was responsible for his defeat that day.

"I had instructions not to put him under pressure but I felt he would do nothing without the whip. It was not that he was a rogue or ungenuine. He was just one of those horses that needed constant encouragement," he explains.

Peter McLoughlin, using his whip effectively, won on Fort Leney next time at Navan while Pat Taaffe was away in England riding Arkle. Later when Pat Taaffe was injured young McLoughlin won twice

Pat Taaffe, winning rider in four Gold Cups

more on Fort Leney and rode him again in the 1967 Gold Cup. The dominance of Tom Dreaper's horses during that era was reflected in the position of Fort Leney as favourite at 11–4. He ran abysmally, eventually finishing sixth of the seven runners. Sleepless nights and noisy days in the busy racecourse stables might have contributed to his downfall.

Betty Dreaper, now Lady Thomson, explains: "He was within hearing distance of the course and he ran every race round his own box on the previous two days."

Fort Leney was still seeking his elusive first success in England when he returned to Cheltenham for the 1968 Gold Cup. He had beaten Greek Vulgan yet again in the Leopardstown Chase and this time a friend of the Dreapers found him peaceful quarters amid the rustic splendour of a farm in the Cotswold hills far away from the clamour of the racecourse stables. Mill House was favourite. Training problems had delayed his comeback, but when he did finally appear in the Gainsborough Chase at Sandown in February he raced with such purpose that he finished only one and a half lengths behind The Laird with Stalbridge Colonist a well-beaten third. This trio dominated the Gold Cup betting. The Laird, owned by Jim Joel and trained by Bob Turnell, was the most exciting young chaser in training at the time, good enough to win the Massey-Ferguson Gold Cup as a five-year-old and then, just turned six, to take the Stone's Ginger Wine Chase.

Leg trouble prevented the previous year's winner Woodland Venture attempting the double. What A Myth was missing, too. The paucity of top-class chasers at the time was depressingly confirmed by the fact that Bassnet was the only other runner in the Gold Cup on ground that was so unseasonably firm that Tom Dreaper seriously considered withdrawing his horse at the last minute.

Mill House, running in the race for the fifth time, set off in front, jumping boldly. A reckless leap had cost him dear a year earlier, and now it did so again. Sailing along jauntily at the head of affairs the big horse failed to take off at the fifteenth fence, the open ditch going away from the stands, ploughed through it and fell heavily. This left Fort Leney in front, closely attended by The Laird and Stalbridge Colonist. Jeff King had wanted to make more use of The Laird but Bob Turnell preferred his horses to be ridden from behind.

Surging down the hill The Laird and Fort Leney thundered towards the third fence at a heart-stop-ping pace with the grey figure of Stalbridge Colonist snapping at their heels. The outstanding equine artist Peter Biegel captured the full drama of the scene in a splendid oil painting which was hanging on the wall of Col, now Sir, John Thomson's home in the Oxfordshire village of Spelsbury when I visited him in the spring of 1991. A mistake at the second last cost Stalbridge Colonist his chance and the race now became a duel between The Laird, ridden with aggressive determination by Jeff King, and Fort Leney, partnered by the supreme horseman Pat Taaffe.

The Laird led by perhaps a neck approaching the final fence, took off with joyous abandon far, far out, and crossed it with many inches to spare. But he landed a little flat-footed, heard the crowd roaring, and lost his impetus for a vital stride or two. Beside him Fort Leney flew the fence nimbly and accurately and gained a precious length as the pair began the final daunting climb to the winning post at the top of the hill.

Though The Laird seemed to be closing again with every nerve-tingling stride, Pat Taaffe displayed a rare intensity of purpose as he drove for the line on

Over the last. The Laird (far side) just leads from Fort Leney with Stalbridge Colonist approaching the fence

Fort Leney. Even Jeff King at his forceful best could not quite close the gap in time on The Laird. For a horse with a history of a heart disorder Fort Leney battled on with the utmost courage to gain the day by a neck. Stalbridge Colonist, rallying well but all too late, was only a length behind The Laird in third place.

Jeff King recalls: "My horse put in an almighty leap at the last but landed a bit too heavy. We would have won in three more strides."

Years later Pat Taaffe reflected: "The horses kept running for us but if the stewards were enforcing the rules on excessive use of the whip as they do today the pair of us would have been suspended for two months."

Pressure of business prevented Col Thompson being at Cheltenham that day. The meeting he felt obliged to attend in London was halted briefly in mid-afternoon so that everyone present could watch the race on television. When it was confirmed that Fort Leney had indeed resisted The Laird's spirited charge a bank messenger was despatched to summon suitable supplies of champagne as a matter of urgency.

Fort Leney, Stalbridge Colonist and Mill House met again five weeks later in the Whitbread Gold Cup. Fort Leney proved best again but could not quite manage the concession of 19 lb to Larbawn in another stirring finish. A big-bodied horse whose legs gave cause for constant concern, Fort Leney broke down in the moment of victory at Fairyhouse, the following November. He did not race again. In a surprisingly brief career he ran only twenty-seven times, won fourteen races and was placed second six times.

Pat Taaffe, the man who won three Gold Cups on Arkle and another on Fort Leney, makes a telling comparison. "Fort Leney was completely the opposite of Arkle. He did not have Arkle's speed but stayed very well. That's why he used to run from the front."

Briefly Pat Taaffe looked after Fort Leney and another outstanding chaser Flyingbolt at his own stables before they left for their retirement home with Col Thomson in Oxfordshire. First Fort Leney was given a brief trial in England as a hunter. The experiment was not a success.

His owner chuckles: "The usual order was fox, Fort Leney and then the hounds, so that was not on."

Both Fort Leney and Flyingbolt lived to a great age in comfort with the very best of attention. They also enjoyed the odd day out to parade at Cheltenham or attend a Game Fair. A ride on Fort Leney was the winning prize in a raffle at one such function. When he was twenty-six Fort Leney collapsed and died one morning as he cantered gently beside his companion. Leney Princess, who began the dynasty, lived even longer with the Ronaldson family in Mullingar. When her sight began to fail the faithful Cecil Ronaldson arranged to have her put down painlessly.

By early 1991 the descendants of Leney Princess, her sons, grandsons and great-grandson, had won the quite remarkable total of 128 races. The victory of Star Cast at Punchestown on February 25th 1991 brought the total of winners trained for Sir John Thomson by the Dreapers, father and son, to the splendid figure of one hundred. Tom Dreaper supplied forty-three. His son Jim has added a further fifty-seven.

CHELTENHAM GOLD CUP.   March 21st 1968.   £7,713 10s.   *Good.*

1 Fort Leney	10 12 0	P. Taaffe	11–2
2 The Laird	7 12 0	J. King	3–1
3 Stalbridge Colonist	9 12 0	T. Biddlecombe	7–2
4 Bassnet	9 12 0	D. Nicholson	9–1

Neck, 1 length.   Owned and bred Col John Thompson.   Trained T. Dreaper.
6m. 51 seconds.   Also 2 Fav Mill House (G. W. Robinson) Fell.   5 ran.
Tote win: 22s. 6d.

Fort Leney: b.g. 1958 (Fortina–Leney Princess)

4

WHAT A MYTH
(1969)

ONE OF THE ENDURING APPEALS of steeplechasing for breeders and observers alike is the certain knowledge that it is possible to breed a top-class horse from the most obscure pedigrees. Unhappily that has not been the case on the flat for many years; but the hard-up country breeder who sends his old hunter mare to the visiting H.I.S. stallion is encouraged in his dreams by the improbable tapestry of mating arrangements that has yielded horses like What A Myth, Master Smudge, Burrough Hill Lad, Norton's Coin and Desert Orchid.

Who can possibly deny the romance in the complex events that spawned What A Myth? After breeding seven winners on the flat his dam What A Din, a grey, was taken over by Ian Muir as a bad debt for £27 10s. His sire Coup de Myth was given to Muir when a vet's examination revealed a wind problem.

The result of this unlikely mating was born early one morning in 1957 at Muir's Fawley Stud just a brisk canter from the Whatcombe Stables made famous down the years by Dick Dawson, Arthur Budgett and more recently Paul Cole. As he sat up with What A Din the wrong side of midnight awaiting the birth of what was to prove her last foal Ian Muir had already chosen the name of the lively chestnut colt which she delivered two hours later. Coup de Myth produced only one other decent chaser: the prolific hunter Baulking Green.

When What A Myth was three years old two jumping trainers turned down the chance to buy him because they considered his hocks too weak. In those days Ryan Price, known universally as the Captain, used to turn out some of his horses at the Fawley Stud in the summer. He came one afternoon, spotted the chestnut among several horses, asked for him to be trotted out and left without saying another word on

the subject. The next day the trainer rang Muir offering £1,000 for What A Myth on behalf of the partnership of Sir Archibald James and Lady Weir. A deal was struck and the raw-boned chestnut left for Price's stables at Findon, close to Worthing on the Sussex coast. When the partnership was dissolved at Ascot Sales in November 1964, Lady Weir bought him back for 4,200 guineas.

By the time of the 1969 Gold Cup, What A Myth was a veteran campaigner. The softer the going, the longer the race, the worse the conditions, the more you could be sure What A Myth would be running on dourly at the end. In short he was an old-fashioned slogger. In another life he would have been a bare-fisted pugilist, one who fought to the finish in an altogether tougher age before they limited boxers to fifteen rounds.

In his prime he had won the Mildmay Memorial Chase, the Rhymney Breweries Chase and the Whitbread Gold Cup and had finished with a typically powerful late flourish to claim third place only just behind Stalbridge Colonist and Arkle in a memorable climax to the 1966 Hennessy Gold Cup.

The horse's legs had been fired in his younger days and he suffered intermittently from back problems. In the 1967 Gold Cup he had finished an honourable third to Woodland Venture and Stalbridge Colonist. Two years later Ryan Price took the inspired decision to enter What A Myth, then twelve, in the 1969 Gold Cup. Even so, the weekend before the race he lingered among the unconsidered outsiders at 33–1. Some ante-post bookmakers unwisely dismissed him as no more than a hunter for the very good reason that late in October 1968 Ryan Price had sent him to Pauline Forsell's livery yard at Somerby in Leicestershire, where he duly qualified with eight obligatory, yet undemanding, days hunting with the Quorn.

Some hunter! After years of conceding lumps of weight to improving handicappers What A Myth proved a revelation in his unaccustomed new role. Early in March he won two hunter chases in a week with arrogant ease, ridden by the leading West Country amateur Grant Cann. At Cheltenham What A Myth was reunited with his old ally Paul Kelleway.

The 1969 Gold Cup was run on impossibly heavy going and the field of eleven runners for once in that golden decade of steeplechasing seemed rather lacking in quality. The wet spring continued through to Cheltenham. In today's more concerned climate, when the safety of horse and rider is paramount and the views of leading jockeys are earnestly canvassed by the stewards, the meeting might not even have taken place. But race they did, and since soggy conditions are more uncomfortable than dangerous who could argue against that decision?

The Laird started joint favourite at 7–2 with the tall black chaser Domacorn, barely more than a novice and perilously inclined to take on a fence if he met it wrong. The exceptionally handsome Playlord, the first good chaser trained by Gordon Richards, was a 4–1 chance. Stalbridge Colonist, bred, like Domacorn, by that canny Dorset yeoman Harry Dufosee, was next in the betting at 9–2 with the elderly hunter What A Myth steady in the market at 8–1.

When Paul Kelleway reached Cheltenham on Thursday his chief fear was that the race might be abandoned.

"Oh yes, I fancied him so much I even backed him. He was almost unbeatable in those conditions," he confessed with disarming candour twenty-one years later.

Lolloping along at the rear of the pack, What A Myth was lucky to survive an early moment of crisis when Dicky May fell heavily and unexpectedly in front of him at the eighth fence, bringing down The Laird. Jeff King, displaying an acute sense of urgency, was about to remount The Laird and set off in hot pursuit when he noticed that the horse's shoulder had been punctured deeply by an errant hoof. Their race was over. Two fences later Stalbridge Colonist came down, too, and once more What A Myth was forced to scramble sideways to avoid horse and jockey lying in a tangled, muddy heap.

"It was a bit like a battlefield out there so I decided to move up out of the way," recalls Kelleway. Passing the stands with a circuit to travel, King Cutler led

from What A Myth and Playlord, with Domacorn struggling after a series of errors.

What A Myth was considered a nightmare ride by some jockeys. Blunders of earthquake proportions were his speciality. They would come once, sometimes twice in a race without warning. Over the years he had sent several jockeys into orbit, including the rugged, granite-jawed Kelleway, but the pair eventually reached an understanding, albeit at times an uneasy one. The trick, reflects Kelleway laconically, was to stay with him.

"The old horse was never easy," remembers Kelleway. "But for him I might have been a backroom boy all my life. He got me going. You could never relax because if he was wrong he would gallop straight on. He could hit a fence harder than any horse I knew and find a leg somehow. You just had to hope you came out on him on the other side. You had to keep asking him up at his fences and keep chasing him.

"Because of the way he jumped I was always looking for daylight on this horse. It was self-preservation. I had to have a clear view of a fence on him. It was the only way."

So it was that dramatically and uncharacteristically What A Myth swept into the lead in the 1969 Gold Cup fully a mile from home. King Cutler briefly challenged him again before a blunder at the twentieth fence ended his active participation in the race.

With Kelleway pushing him on like a man possessed, What A Myth was clear on the run downhill for the final time until Domacorn emerged as the last and most serious challenger. He had closed to within perhaps a length of the leader when he barged recklessly into the second last fence, an act that all but dislodged poor Terry Biddlecombe. Showing an acrobatic degree of balance born of survival the jockey somehow clawed his way back into the saddle but in the process his whip was lost and with it went any remaining chance of victory.

Biddlecombe returned claiming that he would have won with a whip to encourage Domacorn but there were plenty of those present, including Paul Kelleway, who would disagree. Even though What A Myth was desperately tired he pricked his ears as he struggled towards the last fence with a lead of barely three lengths. He jumped it well, more on instinct and memory, and landed a bit steep as Domacorn began to close once more, with his jockey slapping his loose reins urgently down the horse's shoulder. Years later, in a similar predicament in a flat race in

Out in front – What A Myth and Paul Kelleway at the final fence

France, Lester Piggott snatched another jockey's whip, won the race and was then suspended for his initiative. Unhappily for Biddlecombe there was no one in sight to hand over a spare stick.

Kelleway recalls: "It was so deep on the run-in my horse could not find his action. We were virtually walking by then."

What A Myth, leaning wearily right-handed, was almost joined by Domacorn half-way up the hill, but stamina and courage had always been the leader's finest qualities and now they ensured that he became only the second twelve-year-old to win the Chelten-ham Gold Cup. At the line his advantage over Doma-corn was one and a half lengths. Fully twenty lengths further back Playlord, at the point of exhaustion, just won the struggle for third place with Arab Gold. King Cutler was the only other horse to finish. The enormity of What A Myth's achievement was not lost on his exhausted jockey.

"It was quite a feat to win the Gold Cup with a horse like that . . . a bit like a plater winning the Derby," insists Kelleway. "The horse was a chal-lenge to the Captain. He had his training problems over the years. At first he could not complete his

Two gallant old soldiers in retirement – What A Myth and the inimitable Ryan Price

races and he started off in handicaps with ten stone."

The Gold Cup was What A Myth's twenty-first success in nine years of supremely honest endeavour and took his total of prize money to £40,000. Ryan Price and his owner Lady Weir at once announced that he had run his last race. He would not be going to Liverpool for another assault on the Grand National. So the big, brave chestnut with the distinctive white blaze on his face returned to a life of peaceful retirement at Findon with other ageing heroes trained by Ryan Price.

The public image of the tough, buccaneering, wartime commando Captain only partially disguised his very real affection for his horses. An inspirational trainer with an unrivalled understanding of his horses, he conquered every peak over jumps before becoming equally successful on the flat.

Ryan Price was a showman. Centuries earlier he might have been a swashbuckling pirate. Outrageous, irascible, at times quite impossible, generous of spirit, utterly fearless and wonderfully entertaining; he was all of these things and more. The Captain faced every challenge head-on and expected his horses to do the same.

Most days when his hectic schedule allowed Ryan Price would spend some time with his retired horses in a paddock on the Downs above Findon at his splendidly named Soldiers Field stables. One autumn afternoon in 1979 I joined him on a visit of delicious nostalgia. Persian Lancer was there with the jet black Major Rose. So, too, were Le Vermentois and Charlie Worcester. What A Myth, his coat shaggy and his mane in tangles, wandered across to nuzzle his master.

"These are my friends, real men," declared the Captain in those inimitable rasping tones. "They were athletes, every one of them. How could I let them go to a bad home? What! Not bloody likely. They ran their hearts out for me. If it had not been for

them who would have heard of me?"

When Ryan Price retired from training at the end of 1983 he, too, remained at Soldiers Field. How unfair that he died so soon – on his birthday in August 1987 – and was unable to enjoy the lengthy retirement in comfort that he had ensured for his old warriors. What A Myth lived to the grand age of thirty-three under the watchful eye of Ryan's widow Dorothy and was put down painlessly among familiar surroundings on the morning of January 30th 1990.

CHELTENHAM GOLD CUP.   March 20th 1969.   £8,129 10s.   *Heavy.*

1	What A Myth	12 12 0	P. Kelleway	8–1	
2	Domacorn	7 12 0	T. Biddlecombe	7–2 J. Fav	
3	Playlord	8 12 0	R. Barry	4–1	
4	Arab Gold	8 12 0	P. Buckley	25–1	
5	King Cutler	6 12 0	B. Fletcher	22–1	

1½ lengths, 20.   Owned Lady Weir.   Trained H. Price.   Bred D. J. Muir.
7m. 27.2 seconds.   Also 7–2 J. Fav The Laird (J. King) B. Down, 9–2 Stalbridge Colonist (S. Mellor) Fell, 22 Dicky May (P. McCarron) Fell, 50 Kellsboro' Wood (A. Turnell) P.U., 100 Furtive (Mr W. Roycroft) Fell, and Castle Arbour (F. Dever) P.U.   11 ran.
Tote win: 22s.

What A Myth: ch.g. 1957 (Coup de Myth–What A Din)

5

L'ESCARGOT
(1970, 1971)

SELDOM HAS A RACEHORSE been so misleadingly named as L'Escargot, one of only two horses ever to conquer the mountainous twin peaks of the Cheltenham Gold Cup and the Grand National. Even he would not match the peerless Golden Miller, who won both great races in the same year, 1934, during a purple patch when his accumulation of glory included the unrivalled total of five consecutive successes in the Gold Cup.

L'Escargot proved to be the very opposite of a snail – though, to be sure, he was bred for stamina rather than speed, being out of What A Daisy, a three-parts sister to the Grand National winner Mr What. He was bred, like Mr What, by Mrs Barbara O'Neill near Mullingar in Co. Westmeath, a large, open region north-west of Dublin with the best grassland imaginable for stock. Here you will find an exceptionally high percentage of thoroughbred mares to the acre. To this day many small farms there continue the time-honoured Irish tradition of running a mare or two with their cattle and sheep on nourishing pasture interrupted by wind-blown hedges, old, crumbling walls or lines of ancient, gnarled trees.

Irish breeders are invariably dealers too. L'Escargot proved to be a rather wishy-washy chestnut as a foal. His dam, What A Daisy, had not raced. His sire Escart III won seven races in his native France, including the Prix de Madrid, and was then bought as a lead horse for a Classic hope owned by Sir Adrian Jarvis, but soon broke down. Later he ran once over hurdles before a move to Ireland as a stallion at Frank Latham's Blackrath Stud. What A Daisy's first foal Havago, by Richard Louis, proved a brilliant young racehorse whose six wins included the Gloucestershire Hurdle at Cheltenham. With the benefit of hindsight busy Mrs O'Neill certainly sold L'Escargot cheaply as a foal to Jimmy Brogan for 950 guineas.

Poor Jimmy, trainer, jockey and proud farmer of two hundred acres at Rathfeigh, died soon afterwards in February 1965, aged forty-four. Just over a year later his widow Elizabeth sold L'Escargot, by then three, for 3,000 guineas at Ballsbridge. The buyer was the B.B.A. (Eire)'s astute Tom Cooper, a gentle, kind man, much missed since his death in 1990. He was acting for Raymond Guest, the American Ambassador to Ireland, who had already experienced one Derby success with Larkspur in 1962, the year when seven runners fell, and would enjoy another with Sir Ivor in 1968, both trained by Vincent O'Brien. Over the years the myth that Raymond Guest was an exceptionally lucky owner was converted into fact by English and Irish racing writers eager to develop a story line. It was a description that irritated the usually genial Ambassador.

"I don't like to be told I'm a lucky son of a b . . . ," he would insist. "I don't mind being called a s.o.b, that puts me in very good company. But lucky? Hell, no. I owned my first horse at college in 1931. I had to sell him. As soon as I did that he won for his new owner.

"My father had a jumper Koko that fell at Becher's in the Grand National in 1928 and really fouled up the whole field. My first National runner Virginius fell at the first fence, too, in 1957. So did another of my horses, the grey mare Flying Wild who was one of the favourites. Each time I swallowed my pride as though I liked it," he declared.

In a move that would continue to revive his reputation as a fortunate racehorse owner Raymond Guest sent L'Escargot to Dan Moore, a bluff, engaging character, who once rode four winners in a day at Cheltenham and on Royal Danieli had been caught on the line by Battleship in the 1938 Grand National. He had been training since 1948 with notable success.

In his early days L'Escargot was a nervous sort of horse, a little bit fragile with very flat feet. Mick Ennis, Dan Moore's loyal head lad, would spend hours soothing the new arrival in his box. It was time well spent for L'Escargot displayed precocious ability within a short time of being broken. For all his considerable wealth Raymond Guest liked nothing more than an old-fashioned punt and would go to extraordinary lengths to secure a big price about one of his fancied runners. Advised of L'Escargot's swift progress he determined to plot a coup. The man entrusted with the job of riding L'Escargot in his first bumper race at Navan in February 1967 was Dan Moore's enthusiastic assistant, slim, elegant Ben Hanbury. The gamble was landed at rewarding odds. The snail had speed to burn. Ben, who won a second bumper on the horse at Naas in October, would later turn professional in England before training with much success on the flat at Newmarket.

L'Escargot was developing into an intelligent, powerful chestnut, with lop ears and exceptional speed for a jumper. Put to hurdles he was ridden by dashing Tommy Carberry, twice champion flat race apprentice in Ireland before increasing weight turned his attention to jumping. You often wondered how such a small, slight man could hold, let alone control, the big, heavyweight chasers he rode so bravely and effectively for almost two decades. Impish Tommy Carberry was a roistering cavalier. His twinkling brown eyes, bottomless stamina, lively spirit and infectious chuckle gave a misleading impression that he approached his role as a jockey with reckless, carefree abandon. In reality he was a superb horseman and a quite outstanding jockey with an excellent record on his sorties to England.

Pitched against some useful novices, L'Escargot won on his debut over hurdles at Naas on March 2nd 1968, then captured a division of the Gloucestershire Hurdle at the Festival just over a fortnight later. When he was twice beaten subsequently, Carberry reported that the horse was making an unnatural noise in his throat. At first Dan Moore was unconvinced. The jockey persuaded him to stand close to the gallop as he rode past on L'Escargot. The sound of laboured breathing, caused by a blockage in the throat, was alarmingly loud. A hobday operation was carried out that summer to cure the problem.

Happily it proved a success, though L'Escargot always tended to carry his head rather high and to the side as if trying to inhale more air. All Dan Moore's horses ran in fluffy sheepskin nosebands. The use of one on L'Escargot helped minimise the effect of his unusual head carriage.

After a sweeping triumph in the Scalp Hurdle the next season he returned to the Festival as second favourite to the mighty Persian War in the Champion Hurdle, finished an honourable sixth and was immediately put to fences. Two brisk successes followed a creditable second to Kinloch Brae on his debut. Raymond Guest now directed that L'Escargot should race in America that summer. He believed in the concept of international racing and was prepared to run his horses wherever the opportunity arose.

"There are those who say I run the juice out of my horses," he declared at the time. "That's nonsense. If you have a top horse, that's what racing is all about: to give him a chance to see how good he is. If you can't take a licking I think you'd better stay out of it."

It was a fighting policy that ensured L'Escargot's presence in New York in June for the Meadow Brook Chase at Belmont Park. Despite his inexperience over fences he won it by a head from Rural Riot. Lameness prevented him tackling a second race a fortnight later and he returned to Ireland for an all too brief period at grass. L'Escargot flew back to Belmont Park in the autumn for the Temple Gwathmey Chase on October 17th, and finished a close third, giving 20 lb to the winner Somaten. Hardened New York critics were sufficiently impressed to elect the visiting Irish horse as the American chaser of the year.

There was precious little respite for the globetrotting chestnut. Exactly a month later second place at Punchestown was enough to qualify him for the Wills Premier Chase Final, which he won impressively from the strongest possible field of novices at Haydock in January. That was over two and a half miles. Doubts about the hard-working L'Escargot's stamina increased after he was a well beaten second under a big weight in the Leopardstown Chase. Dan Moore envisaged a crack at the Two-mile Champion Chase or possibly a two-and-a-half-mile race. The ambitious Raymond Guest dictated otherwise. As ever, he believed in an aggressively attacking policy. L'Escargot, only seven, would go for Gold.

In the summer of 1991 the delightful Joan Moore,

An all-Irish finish. French Tan is about to be overtaken by L'Escargot (noseband) at the end of the 1970 Gold Cup

Dan's widow, now energetically managing Punchestown racecourse, recalled: "Dan felt the horse was still very much a novice and was concerned about his stamina in the early days. Later we discovered he was very idle in front."

L'Escargot's presence in the field for the 1970 Cheltenham Gold Cup barely caused a ripple of interest. He was ignored in the betting, at 33–1. Most of Ireland seemed to believe in the invincibility of the Duchess of Westminster's imposing new star Kinloch Brae, who jumped fences with breathtaking speed and had won his last four races with complete authority. He was backed down to 15–8 favourite on the day.

Another strong Irish contender was Archie Watson's French Tan, successful at Ascot a month earlier. English hopes largely rested on the handsome head of Spanish Steps, bred, owned and trained by charming Edward Courage, who despite the handi-

cap of suffering an attack of polio as a young man, lived a full life and proved to be a wonderfully generous supporter of the Injured Jockeys Fund. A leading novice the previous season, Spanish Steps had thrashed strong opposition in the Hennessy Gold Cup in November and had later won the Benson & Hedges Gold Cup before beating The Laird decisively in the Gainsborough Chase. Titus Oates, the pride of the North, had confirmed his class with a hard-earned victory over Flyingbolt and The Laird in the King George VI Chase.

It was Titus Oates who led briefly at a smart pace over the first few fences until joined by Larbawn. The Dikler, going well in midfield, fell at the eleventh fence and a moment later Kinloch Brae rushed irresistibly ahead, jumping with a thrilling blend of boldness and accuracy. French Tan, Spanish Steps, Freddie Boy and L'Escargot comprised the chasing group as they breasted the rise at the top of the hill on the far side of the course.

Tommy Carberry was prepared to wait as long as he dared on L'Escargot: "He was a horse you had to give a chance to. He jumped big over the first fences but after a mile he had started to get the hang of it. He was always very careful not to take a fall," he relates.

Just ahead of him the wily Pat Taaffe, on the more experienced French Tan, was preparing to play his cards as soon as possible.

"Kinloch Brae had been allowed to have his own way for too long. I thought, 'I am going to see how good this lad is', and took him on racing towards the third last fence. The pace we were travelling, one of us was going to fall," Pat recalled twenty-one years later, speaking so softly, almost apologetically, that you marvelled at such patent disregard for his own safety as he launched French Tan like a missile at this trickiest of all Cheltenham fences.

Perhaps unsettled by the challenge Kinloch Brae ploughed headlong into the fence and plunged to the ground as French Tan swept by. L'Escargot side-stepped the prone figure of Timmy Hyde with the agility of a ballet dancer, but moments later Titus Oates, too, came down at the fence, bringing down Herring Gull. Photographs at Timmy Hyde's home, the Camas Park Stud, deep in Co. Tipperary, show Kinloch Brae bursting through the birch low down as though it had no more substance than a paper bag.

To this day he insists, "We would certainly have won. Kinloch Brae was the best horse in Ireland since Arkle."

Pat Taaffe's audacious tactics had removed one serious threat to French Tan, but as they headed towards the final fence, another arrived alongside like a winged assassin in the athletic shape of L'Escargot. The pair were in the air together but French Tan was quite unable to withstand the blistering pace of his rival on the flat. Scampering up the hill, his chestnut mane neatly plaited, his head held unnaturally high in the manner that would become his trademark, L'Escargot won well by one and a half lengths from French Tan. Spanish Steps, surprisingly outpaced, was fully ten lengths away in third place ahead of Freddie Boy and The Laird.

The unconsidered outsider who won the 1970 Gold Cup was allowed a full summer's rest, this time in Ireland, before returning to action – unusually, in a flat race, the Irish Cesarewitch in October. He ran once more on the flat, this time over a mile and a half, before returning to America for a much vaunted new steeplechase, the Colonial Cup at Camden in South Carolina. He finished fourth. Defeat followed heavily on defeat that season; on the flat, in America, back over hurdles in Ireland in the Sweeps Hurdle at Christmas and then, disastrously, over fences at Punchestown when Tommy Carberry was unseated by a particularly monstrous mistake. At last L'Escargot gave some cause for optimism with an encouraging third in the Leopardstown Chase under 12 st. 2 lb.

L'Escargot now embarked on his annual March visit to Cheltenham, where heavy rain overnight and throughout the morning ensured exceptionally

---

CHELTENHAM GOLD CUP.   March 19th 1970.   £8,103.   *Good.*

1	L'Escargot	7 12 0	T. Carberry	33–1
2	French Tan	8 12 0	P. Taaffe	8–1
3	Spanish Steps	7 12 0	J. Cook	9–4
4	Freddie Boy	9 12 0	R. Pitman	40–1
5	The Laird	9 12 0	J. King	40–1
6	Gay Trip	8 12 0	K. B. White	50–1
7	Larbawn	11 12 0	M. Gifford	25–1

1½ lengths, 10.   Owned R. Guest.   Trained D. L. Moore.   Bred Mrs Barbara O'Neill.
6m. 47.5 seconds.   Also 15–8 Fav Kinloch Brae (T. Hyde) Fell, 10 The Dikler
(G. W. Robinson) Fell, and Titus Oates (S. Mellor) Fell, 33 Herring Gull (J. Crowley) B.D.,
50 Arcturus (P. Buckley) U.R.   12 ran.   Tote win: 107s. 6d.

L'Escargot: ch.g. 1963 (Escart III–What A Daisy)

demanding going that put a premium on stamina in the Gold Cup. One horse who would have relished the conditions was the previous year's third, Spanish Steps, but a distressing error by his trainer's wife Mrs Hermione Courage prevented him taking his chance. Poor Mrs Courage declared a stable companion instead of Spanish Steps at the start of the week. By the time the mistake was discovered declaration time had passed. Spanish Steps, impressive winner of the Stone's Ginger Wine Chase at Sandown under top weight, could not be reinstated. He would have to stay in his box at Edgcote in Oxfordshire during the Festival.

The flamboyant Kinloch Brae was absent, too. He had suffered leg trouble soon after the previous year's Gold Cup and was later sent by the Duchess of Westminster to England to join Toby Balding, whose stables were then close beside the A303 at Weyhill just west of Andover. Kinloch Brae was patched up sufficiently for one trial run at Wincanton late in February, won narrowly from Foxtor, but finished lame. His season was over. Injury, too, ruled out French Tan, while Titus Oates, winner of the Gainsborough Chase, was pulled out when the rain continued to fall.

The Dikler, however, was back with a new rider, Barry Brogan, a brave but flawed jockey ultimately destroyed by excesses of betting and alcohol. Brogan was immensely strong and utterly fearless, qualities which proved invaluable on The Dikler, a massive horse who could pull like a runaway train. Into View was the leading hope of England. Starting at the realistic odds of 50–1 he had begun his life as a racehorse with an improbable defeat of Salmon Spray in the Oteley Hurdle before developing into a consistent, high-class chaser. His trainer Fred Winter and jockey Paul Kelleway came to the Gold Cup fresh from winning the Champion Hurdle with Bula the previous day.

Once again the Irish were strongly represented. Tom Dreaper's new star Leap Frog, narrowly beaten by Into View at Ascot, had taken the Wills Premier Chase Final with impressive ease. Glencaraig Lady, trained by Francis Flood, had won the S.G.B. Chase at Ascot and was remembered as the unluckiest loser at the previous year's Festival when falling in front at the final fence in the Totalisator Champion Novices' Chase. She had subsequently finished second to a stable companion in the Irish Distillers Grand National. In a particularly open betting market

L'Escargot, Into View and Leap Frog were joint favourites at 7–2.

Leap Frog and then Royal Toss led early on until Glencaraig Lady swept to the front after the first mile. Jumping boldly in the cloying ground she still held a useful advantage running downhill for the final time, but fell at the third last fence just as Kinloch Brae had done twelve months earlier. What might have been does not pay the bills, but both her jockey Bobby Coonan and trainer Francis Flood remain convinced that the tumble robbed her of victory. Glencaraig Lady's sudden departure left L'Escargot and Leap Frog in front, but once again Tommy Carberry was determined to delay making his move.

"My lad was going well enough at the time the mare fell. He was a deceptive horse to weigh-up and would always find a bit more. I waited a while because he was better off with company," he relates.

With the remaining runners struggling far behind Carberry coolly and clinically restrained L'Escargot until jumping the last fence. Only then did he ask his horse to go and win his race. The response was emphatic. Squelching through the mud L'Escargot came home ten lengths in front of Leap Frog with The Dikler a further fifteen lengths away third. To this day L'Escargot remains the only horse since Arkle to win the Gold Cup twice.

The time of the 1971 Gold Cup, 8 minutes 0.7 seconds, was one of the slowest on record, more than seventy seconds longer than L'Escargot had taken in 1970. Conditions were so unspeakable on the day that the stewards decided the race should be started from a new position on the old course. As a result the runners were required to jump twenty-three fences, one more than usual. Those who doubted the value of the form of L'Escargot's second Gold Cup were given sound cause to reconsider three weeks later when he came tantalisingly close to winning the Irish Distillers Grand National, carrying the crushing burden of 12 st. 7 lb.

In the years to come L'Escargot would visit the Festival four more times. He finished fourth in the next two Gold Cups after losing vital ground by running right-handed down the second last fence on both occasions. Beating the best at level weights was now beyond him. So to Liverpool for the first time in 1972 for the Grand National where he was violently knocked out of the race at the fearsome first ditch, the third fence. The following season the versatile

L'Escargot and Tommy Carberry complete a famous double in the 1971 Gold Cup

L'Escargot is ridden in retirement in Virginia by Raymond Guest's son Achille

L'Escargot finished a creditable but distant third in the epic 1973 Grand National, still remembered for Crisp's valiant, heart-breaking defeat in the shadow of the post by Red Rum achieving his first success in the race.

Despite his hectic racing schedule over the years L'Escargot remained a wonderfully sound horse. Like so many wise old horses he sometimes kept a bit back for himself; but in the mood, given a chance by the handicapper, he was still a formidable racehorse. All distances came alike to him. Back at Cheltenham in March 1974, aged eleven and sporting a hood for the first time in England, he was a worthy runner-up in the Cathcart Chase over two miles and was then second to Red Rum in the Grand National.

The old horse came back to the Festival for the eighth successive year in 1975. It was to be his last hurrah at Cheltenham. He had not won a race of any description since the 1971 Gold Cup four years earlier and though he stayed on well enough in fifth place in the Two-mile Champion Chase he never threatened to end that dismal losing sequence.

Tommy Carberry was delighted with that run. He felt it had put L'Escargot just right for Liverpool, where he had at last been given a serious chance by the handicapper in the Grand National in which Red Rum was seeking an unprecedented hat-trick.

L'Escargot all but fell at the seventh fence, the most innocuous obstacle on the course that comes after Becher's Brook. Carberry reported: "I was nearly gone and was left hanging round his ears praying for that old head to come back up."

By the second Canal Turn only five were left in the hunt and L'Escargot, just behind Red Rum, could be seen going better than any horse should normally be after three and three-quarter miles over Aintree's daunting fences. A moment later he eased alongside Red Rum, whose jockey Brian Fletcher looked across in dismay before calling out "Go on Tommy, you've won five minutes."

It may have been a slight exaggeration but when Carberry did allow L'Escargot his head the old horse seemed to sprint up the long, pitiless run-in. At the line he was fifteen lengths in front of Red Rum. It was a heart-warming triumph after four barren years. Outside the weighing-room Dan Moore, pink with delight, explained just why he was so pleased to win the Grand National. Since his narrow defeat on Royal Danieli he had endured the galling experience of finding, training and then selling two horses, Team Spirit and Freebooter, who were to go on and win the race.

"You know, when Mr Guest asked me to find him a Grand National winner I told him we already had one in L'Escargot. Though he had then won his Gold Cups he took a bit of time to prove us right," he said.

The proud owner related: "My family has been trying to win this thing for half a century and I have wanted it all my life. The Good Lord gave it to me this year. I'll not try again. I was a little emotional, quite shaken, and I have to admit it was the most satisfying win I'll ever have."

Wanting a permanent record of his busy chaser Raymond Guest had commissioned a film company to follow L'Escargot intermittently over several years. The old horse's rousing success at Aintree provided the perfect finale. The documentary, entitled *The Snail, the Diplomat and the Chase*, was later shown on BBC television.

As the celebrations drew on into the night after his Grand National Triumph the decision was taken that L'Escargot would not run again. He was given to Joan Moore for the rest of his days. The old horse had run sixty times in nine seasons of shining endeavour, winning two Gold Cups, a Grand National and a total of fourteen races. His versatile record would stand the most searching examination.

Less than six months later Raymond Guest, by then living at his family estate Powhatan Plantation in Virginia, was surprised and not a little annoyed to hear that his famous warrior had run one more time at Listowel, where he had been beaten in a photo finish in the Kerry National. Clearly there had been a misunderstanding. L'Escargot's welfare was the prime concern of Joan Moore and her family at all times. Sensing that the old horse was missing the thrill of the chase she had entered him at Listowel to give him a bit of fun; but Raymond Guest was not amused. Soon L'Escargot was on his way to permanent retirement at Powhatan, where he was sometimes ridden by his owner's daughter Virginia and his son Achille. In 1976, reunited with Tommy Carberry, he took part in a celebrity parade before the Colonial Cup.

In his later years Raymond Guest liked nothing more than showing his great horse to visitors to Powhatan, approximately an hour's drive from Washington. Powhatan's pastures are deep within the woods. You approach the estate on a dirt road that winds through the pines, down a hill, over a stream and up a steep rise to the top of a knoll where a broad, lush green panorama reaches out to greet you. Two carved wooden Indian figures stand sentry at the entrance to the stables. Inside the main house ivory tusks from elephants shot in Kenya form an archway to the room dominated by L'Escargot's Cheltenham and Grand National trophies.

Here, in the peaceful surroundings of his owner's lavish farm, L'Escargot died suddenly in his paddock on June 5th 1984, aged twenty-one.

CHELTENHAM GOLD CUP.   March 18th 1971.   £7,995.50   *Very heavy.*

1	L'Escargot	8 12 0	T. Carberry	7–2 J. Fav
2	Leap Frog	7 12 0	V. O'Brien	7–2 J. Fav
3	The Dikler	8 12 0	B. Brogan	15–2
4	Into View	8 12 0	P. Kelleway	7–2 J. Fav
5	Fortina's Palace	8 12 0	P. Jones	33–1
6	Herring Gull	9 12 0	H. Beasley	33–1

10 lengths, 15.   Owned R. Guest.   Trained D. L. Moore.   Bred Mrs B. O'Neill.
8m. 0.7 seconds.   Also 7 Glencaraig Lady (R. Coonan) Fell, 10 Royal Toss (E. P. Harty)
Fell.   8 ran.   Tote win: 60p.

L'Escargot: ch.g. 1963 (Escart III–What A Daisy)

6

GLENCARAIG LADY
(1972)

Many fine jockeys spend a lifetime trying to win a race at the Cheltenham Festival. Frank Berry, a fresh-faced refugee from the flat, won the greatest prize of all on his very first ride over the famous course on the brave mare Glencaraig Lady in 1972. It was a triumph laced with controversy, following the first objection in the history of the race.

The result was in doubt for many anxious minutes after a complaint against the winner by Nigel Wakley, the rider of the fast-finishing runner-up, Royal Toss. The stewards' deliberations were further confused by a second objection against Royal Toss by Barry Brogan, the rider of the third horse, The Dikler.

It was the first time that Glencaraig Lady had completed the course at Cheltenham, in three attempts. Small at barely 16 hands, but very athletic, she had fallen at the last fence in front with certain victory in her grasp in the 1970 Totalisator Champion Novices' Chase and was still going strongly in the lead when she came down three fences from the finish in the following year's Gold Cup.

Francis Flood, frequently amateur champion jump jockey of Ireland, was the man who spotted Glencaraig Lady, then an unnamed three-year-old, at the Goffs Sales. With him that day was Patrick Doyle, an auctioneer looking for a young racehorse.

"She's the one for you," suggested Flood. However, the filly by Fortina out of Luckibash was led out unsold at a price Patrick Doyle believed was much too inflated. The breeder James Hogan wanted 1,500 guineas. Doyle was prepared to pay 600 guineas. After some spirited haggling outside the ring, the filly who was to win a Gold Cup became the property of Doyle for 800 guineas. Two days later she joined Flood, who was just starting to train after a lengthy period working and riding as an amateur for the legendary trainer Paddy Sleator.

Glencaraig Lady's early promise was cut short when she chipped a bone in her knee on her second start in a bumper race at Dundalk. It was an injury that would be a source of concern for the rest of her days as a racehorse. After her unlucky fall as a novice at Cheltenham she ended her first season over fences with a spirited second to Garoupe in the Irish Distillers Grand National. The following season another fall probably robbed her of victory in the 1971 Gold Cup.

Francis Flood asserts: "Oh yes, she would definitely have won that time by a long way. The thing about her was that she always kept going. She had great heart and was better then than the year she did win."

The mare's lad Larry Dunne ensured that she was given extensive roadwork in the autumn of 1971. Usually the pair would be out from 8.30 until midday, walking and trotting along the peaceful roads and country lanes near Grangecon in Co. Wicklow where meandering cattle and sheep on sharp bends still offer an unexpected hazard for visiting drivers.

Glencaraig Lady's soundness was a constant problem that final season when she carried a new jockey, Frank Berry. Small, quiet and a natural horseman, he had won the Irish St Leger as an unknown eighteen-year-old apprentice on the President of Ireland's headstrong Giolla Mear, a notoriously difficult ride. Berry rode only fifteen winners on the flat before increasing weight turned his attention to jump racing. All the glamorous appeal of jumping seemed justified as he stormed to victory on his first ride on Glencaraig Lady at Fairyhouse in December 1971. After a subsequent failure behind The Dikler in the King George VI Chase the bouncy little mare ploughed through the mud to another success in the P. Z. Mower Chase at Thurles early in March.

The Dikler leads over the final fence from the winner Glencaraig Lady (right) and Crisp. Royal Toss is almost hidden behind the leader

By now Glencaraig Lady had developed into a formidable racehorse, displaying perhaps more quality than substance, but various problems with her knee and joints ensured that the final days before Cheltenham were anxious ones for Francis Flood and his staff.

Frank Berry recalls: "There was a floating chip in her knee that could not be removed. Francis could not give her all the work he might have wanted but her action improved once she warmed up."

On the morning of the Gold Cup Berry, still with precious little experience over fences, rode Glencaraig Lady in a sharp spin with L'Escargot and Tommy Carberry, winners of the race in the two previous years. It was a dispiriting experience for the mare's supporters.

"We worked over four or perhaps five furlongs and L'Escargot left us for dead," relates Berry.

Despite his superb record at Cheltenham, L'Escargot was not favourite for the 1972 Gold Cup, sponsored for the first time by Piper Heidsieck champagne and worth a record £15,255 to the winner. He had not won a race for a year and like Glencaraig Lady had been soundly beaten in the King George VI Chase.

The spectacular jumping Australian champion Crisp headed the market at 3–1 on the strength of his decisive defeat of The Dikler at Kempton three weeks earlier. L'Escargot was joint second favourite at 4–1 with young Jim Dreaper's hope Leap Frog, the game winner of the Massey-Ferguson Chase over the course under top weight in November. Glencaraig Lady, heavily bandaged on both front legs, drifted from 9–2 to 6–1 as stories of her training problems circulated. The Dikler was freely available at 11–1 with the handsome, immaculately turned out West Country hope Royal Toss at twice those odds.

Royal Toss, trained by Tim Handel, a wholesale butcher, at his farm at the delightfully named village of Hatch Beauchamp, was the last foal sired by Royal Challenger in Ireland before his sale to Japan. His dam Spinning Coin cost only £215 and once won eight point-to-points in a season. One of the greatest admirers of Royal Toss was an unknown young amateur Martin Pipe, who rode out for Tim Handel. The son of a local bookmaker and already an obsessively keen racing enthusiast he compiled a detailed analysis of the career of Royal Toss while lying in hospital with a broken thigh. Later Martin Pipe would make his own indelible mark on the pages of racing history.

Royal Toss was a splendid example of what is widely described as an old-fashioned type of chaser, big and powerful enough to pull a plough and very sound, with short legs, hairy heels and abundant stamina. On the Handel farm he was often required to herd and drive cattle.

Since there was a lingering doubt about Crisp's stamina in the rain-softened ground his trainer Fred Winter decided Richard Pitman should employ waiting tactics on him. Normally a happy, flamboyant, free-running horse, Crisp resented restraint and sulked in the rear when he was not given his head. So, unexpectedly, Gay Trip, winner of the 1970 Grand National, took the field along for almost two and a half miles, with Glencaraig Lady in close attendance. The Dikler, who had been travelling comfortably just behind them, was then dashed into a clear lead by Barry Brogan at the top of the hill in a premature bid for glory.

Glencaraig Lady was almost swamped as the cavalry set off in pursuit, but she clung on tenaciously. Beside her L'Escargot appeared to be cantering, Crisp closed up menacingly, and Spanish Steps was still moving sweetly. Much further behind, Royal Toss was at last beginning to make some progress from the rear.

Crisp's effort was short-lived. Forcibly prevented from bowling along, he lost interest when asked a serious question. The fire had gone out of him. L'Escargot's challenge, too, effectively ended as he ran sharply right-handed down the second last fence, losing vital momentum. He would not be completing his hat-trick. Glencaraig Lady, who had been struggling to hold her place, was reducing the gap again and as The Dikler veered out from the rail on the final bend she switched nimbly inside him.

The Dikler's lead had dwindled to less than a length as the pair landed over the final fence. Fully six lengths behind, Royal Toss was finishing best of all. The Dikler, by now very tired, continued to hang steadily right-handed as Barry Brogan called for one last supreme effort. Seventy-five yards from the line the gallant little mare had drawn level; then, slowly, inexorably, she edged ahead, but the effort cost her dear. Her stride faltered and she, too, began to lean right-handed away from the rail. At the same moment The Dikler, wandering like a drunken sailor, changed tack again and lurched towards her.

In a finish of consuming intensity Royal Toss suddenly rushed between the two with the speed of a five-furlong sprinter but his inspired charge was just too late. Glencaraig Lady, who pulled up lame, had held on by three-quarters of a length from Royal Toss with The Dikler a head away third. The drama, however, had only just begun. Nigel Wakley insisted on objecting to the winner for taking his ground on the run-in. Barry Brogan quickly added his contribution to the uncertainty by claiming that Royal Toss had bored into The Dikler.

Frank Berry recalls: "I was surprised about the inquiry because the only other horse I had seen was The Dikler and there was a lot of room between us."

Tim Handel took himself off to the nearest bar to await the stewards' verdict. Years later, sitting round the kitchen table in his farmhouse, we discussed that fateful finish again.

"If my jockey had ridden to orders he would have won anyway," declared the forthright farmer. "I asked him to be breathing down their necks at the second last and he was still six lengths behind at the last. So it was marvellous to get so close," he beamed.

Fifteen years after her greatest triumph Glencaraig Lady is pictured at the Coolmore Stud in 1987 with her last foal by Carlingford Castle

The inquiry into the brace of objections lasted twenty minutes. All three jockeys were quizzed at length and the film of the finish was viewed several times before the jockeys were ushered from the room while the stewards debated the evidence. Clearly first and third had wandered off a true line in the closing stages, but had there been sufficient room for Royal Toss to mount his scything late challenge or had he been prevented from completing his run? A large crowd gathered outside the weighing-room door awaiting the outcome. The announcement that the placings remained unaltered was greeted by a sustained roar of approval. Those of us later allowed to see the head-on patrol film agreed that justice had been done. Crucially at no stage did Nigel Wakley have to snatch up Royal Toss.

Frank Berry reflects: "Glencaraig Lady did nothing to justify disqualification. She was very short in front but had marvellous power when she jumped. She was a very, very game mare, who never knew when she was beaten. Her courage won her the Gold Cup."

Fog hampered the return to Ireland of the victorious trainer and jockey. Their plane to Dublin was delayed, then diverted to Shannon. Dawn was only a furlong away by the time they reached home in a borrowed car. Whatever the triumphs and disasters, the racing caravan rolls inexorably onward. Four hours later Frank Berry set off for Limerick, where he rode another winner. It was further confirmation that a shining new talent had emerged at Cheltenham. In the years ahead Frank Berry would become champion jockey of Ireland a remarkable ten times.

Glencaraig Lady did not race again. In truth Francis Flood had done wonderfully well to nurse her for so long. She was lame once more after the Gold Cup and it was felt her fragile legs and injured knee could no longer stand the strain of serious training. A fresh life at stud beckoned but unfortunately Glencaraig Lady has proved frustratingly barren, with only four foals in twenty years. At first, believing he should introduce more speed, Patrick Doyle sent her to flat race sprinters such as Yellow God and Sandford Lad.

Glencaraig Gem, a filly by Sandford Lad, is her only winner. Trained by Francis Flood, she was successful over hurdles in 1981 and over fences the next year. When Glencaraig Lady proved barren several years in succession Doyle gave her back to James Hogan, her breeder, and his son Tom at the Fattheen House Stud in Co. Tipperary. Later they agreed a

share deal with Peter Magnier, who runs the jumping wing of Coolmore's mighty stud empire. At Coolmore Glencaraig Lady produced a colt foal by Carlingford Castle in 1987. Sent to Goffs August National Hunt sale in 1990 he was led out unsold at 18,500 punts after failing to reach his reserve.

Time was running out for Glencaraig Lady in 1991. The oldest surviving Gold Cup winner, she was barren again to Supreme Leader in 1990 and at the grand old age of twenty-seven was covered, probably for the last time, by Executive Perk in 1991. Nature has its own way of balancing life. How unfortunate that the wonderful toughness of spirit exhibited by this fine racemare has been passed on so sparingly at stud.

CHELTENHAM GOLD CUP.   March 16th 1972.   £15,255.   *Soft.*

1 Glencaraig Lady	8 12 0	F. Berry	6–1	
2 Royal Toss	10 12 0	N. Wakley	22–1	
3 The Dikler	9 12 0	B. Brogan	11–1	
4 L'Escargot	9 12 0	T. Carberry	4–1	
5 Crisp	9 12 0	R. Pitman	3–1 Fav	
6 Spanish Steps	9 12 0	W. Smith	10–1	
7 Bighorn	8 12 0	D. Cartwright	33–1	
8 Gay Trip	10 12 0	T. Biddlecombe	35–1	
9 Titus Oates	10 12 0	R. Barry	40–1	

¾ length, head.   Owned P. Doyle.   Trained F. Flood.   Bred J. F. Hogan.
7m. 18 seconds.   Also 4 Leap Frog (V. O'Brien) Fell, 40 Young Ash Leaf (T. Stack) P.U., 66 Dim Wit (D. Mould) P.U.   12 Ran.   Tote win: £1.05.

Glencaraig Lady: ch.m. 1964 (Fortina–Luckibash)

Objection by the rider of the second to the winner for "taking my ground on run-in" was overruled. A further objection by the rider of the third to the second for boring in last 150 yards was also overruled.

7

THE DIKLER
(1973)

STABLE LADS CAN MAKE or break horses. None has a finer record with strapping steeplechasers than Darkie Deacon, a neat little sparrow of a man with outsize, sturdy hands, a steady gaze and a devotion to his job that has been a byword in Lambourn for thirty years.

On a memorable March day in 1973 Deacon, a Prince among stable lads, was responsible for two runners in the Cheltenham Gold Cup: The Dikler and Charlie Potheen. Years of riding a brace of the strongest, hardest-pulling and most difficult horses in the business have not noticeably lengthened his arms or affected his nerve.

The Dikler, from the hunting field, was enormous, well over 17 hands, large enough to be mistaken for one of those hairy-heeled giants that used to pull ploughs before the days of mechanisation. He was a strong-willed devil, too, and had a nasty habit of kicking people, normally poor Darkie Deacon. The Dikler had a mouth like iron. On a going morning on the gallops high above Lambourn an entire chain gang would not have restrained him in full, awesome flight.

Charlie Potheen at 16.2 hands was not quite as big but he was an even tougher ride at home. He leaned rather than pulled, all the time, until his rider's arms were exhausted. Then he would tug at his bit even harder. In his early days he would whip round without warning on the downs and try to set off back to his stable. If Darkie Deacon remonstrated with him a battle of wills ensued and the long-suffering lad was invariably the loser.

Tim Forster, who has trained three Grand National winners, was offered The Dikler as a five-year-old, but later sent him back to his owner Mrs Peggy August, suggesting that a season's hunting might help him mature. John Honeyball had broken in The Dikler with commendable patience and now volunteered to take him hunting with the South Oxfordshire. One day, in unfamiliar territory, they jumped a high stone wall and found themselves in a boggy meadow complete with crosses, wreaths and trees of remembrance. They had landed in the grounds of a crematorium! The horse proved a revelation as a point-to-pointer in 1969 as a six-year-old. He won twice from the front before running out in the lead at the South Oxon, breaking the ankle of his rider Brian Fanshawe as he darted through the wing of the fence.

The Dikler, by the prolific Vulgan out of an un-raced mare Coronation Day, was bred in Co. Meath by Joseph Moorhead. Neither mother nor son stayed in his possession for very long. Once Coronation Day, by then aged twelve, was covered again by Vulgan she was sold for a modest 200 guineas at Goffs in November 1963. Her large foal, the next lot in the ring, was led out unsold and later bought for £500 by an agent, Charlie Rogers, and turned out to mature at the Ballymacoll Stud.

Peggy August had inherited The Dikler in unusual circumstances. On a visit to the Ballymacoll Stud her uncle Edward Bee, owner of the Cotswold Stud, had agreed to pay £3,000 for the horse as a three-year-old, subject to a favourable vet's report. This duly took place satisfactorily a fortnight later, but by the time the formalities were completed Edward Bee had died from a sudden heart attack. So the exceptionally tall young horse became the property of his two nieces Peggy August and Katherine Gregory, though neither of them wanted a racehorse.

Peggy August confirms "I rang up the vendors in Ireland hoping they would cancel the sale in the circumstances but they were adamant. We must take him. When he came over he looked like a great big giraffe."

The two sisters agreed to sell their gift horse. They found a buyer and agreed a price, but to their dismay another vet failed the youngster's wind. A little later Peggy August bought out her sister's share. Through the paddock at Edward Bee's farm at Lower Slaughter ran a tiny stream, the Dikler. Hence his name, though Peggy August called him Tuppenny because at first she felt he was not worth tuppence.

Following The Dikler's display of brilliance in point-to-points Peggy August determined to put him in training with Fulke Walwyn, a veritable master with steeplechasers. Darkie Deacon, with jet-black, wavy hair as his nickname implies, was chosen to look after the massive new recruit. Once a fitter's mate at Aldermaston, he weighed barely eight and a half stone and seemed far too light to handle let alone control such a hulking great beast.

"I loved the big sod," Darkie reflects without a trace of sentimentality. "He could bolt, oh yes, he would run with you all right and when you put his saddle on he could kick you harder than any horse alive. He also tried to rear over backwards on me some mornings."

At times The Dikler was like a runaway car without steering or brakes. Darkie chuckles as he concedes: "The Dikler was the only horse that ever ran away with me. Oh yes, he used to cart me regular. Holding him was a matter of confidence, not strength. I always tried to keep him in behind a lead horse . . . when I could," he chuckles again. Darkie's long-suffering wife Joyce did not share his enthusiasm for his heavyweight charges and expressed her views one day to Fulke Walwyn's wife Cath.

"It's all very well expecting my Darkie to look after these difficult horses, but he is no good to me when he comes home at night," she declared in forthright tones.

The Dikler possessed so much raw talent that Walwyn took him to Cheltenham for his first race over fences. It proved a rare baptism of fire for the stable jockey Willie Robinson, an outstanding horseman light enough to have ridden with much success on the flat. The Dikler bolted going to the start, tried to leave the course during the race, was still six lengths behind when he all but fell at the last fence, yet still snatched an improbable victory in a photo finish! Such was his progress in his first season that he ran in the 1970 Gold Cup while still technically a novice, starting at 10–1, but his jumping was still dange-

rously erratic and he fell at half-way.

Stan Mellor took over on The Dikler, following the retirement of Willie Robinson, but he was not always available, and so Barry Brogan, a talented but at times wayward jockey, came down to Lambourn one morning to school the big horse over fences. The Dikler duly scorched over three fences before disappearing into the mist at a million miles an hour with his new jockey powerless to check him. General amusement at Brogan's discomfort turned to anxiety when the pair failed to return. Walwyn hurriedly arranged a posse which eventually found horse and rider still in one piece. Despite that alarming experience Brogan rode The Dikler in the 1971 Gold Cup but the horse had run up rather light after a busy season and finished a distant third to L'Escargot. The Dikler was such a massive, raw-boned horse he was only then finding his strength. The best was yet to come.

The next season the admirable Darkie Deacon took over a second high-class but headstrong prospect, Charlie Potheen, who had also run out when leading in a point-to-point. Despite testing the strength and endurance of his jockeys and lad to the limit he soon won three chases for Walwyn. The Dikler's victory in the 1971 King George VI Chase at Christmas suggested he was still improving. He beat Spanish Steps in a stirring duel, with Titus Oates, L'Escargot and Glencaraig Lady well behind. It is the view of Darkie Deacon that Barry Brogan's premature move for the lead cost him certain victory in the 1972 Gold Cup.

"I knew the moment he took it up at the top of the hill he would not win. He was there far too soon, left them all for dead down the hill and had shot his bolt jumping the last," he laments.

Even so The Dikler still led for most of the run-in and stayed on doggedly for third place barely a length behind Glencaraig Lady.

A year later Darkie Deacon was back at Cheltenham with two fancied Gold Cup runners. In his second season Charlie Potheen had already fulfilled all his undoubted promise by winning the Hennessy Gold Cup and the Great Yorkshire Chase in his only two starts to date. He was ridden at Cheltenham by Terry Biddlecombe and at 9–2 was preferred in the betting to his stable companion now preparing to run in his fourth consecutive Gold Cup. The Dikler had been soundly beaten by the brilliant Pendil at Kempton in the King George VI Chase at Kempton

Sensation is seconds away as Pendil clears the last fence pursued by The Dikler (left) and Charlie Potheen

and few could see any good reason why he should reverse that form at Cheltenham. The dual Gold Cup winner L'Escargot was a 20–1 outsider this time.

Pendil, lean and light, shaped like a greyhound, was completely dwarfed by The Dikler and Charlie Potheen. He was, in short, a freak, with a pair of tiny horns on his forehead and an exhilarating, spring-heeled jump that set him apart. He had won the Arkle Chase in scintillating manner the previous year and approaching the 1973 Gold Cup his unbeaten

run extended to eleven races. He had given 27 lb and a comprehensive beating to the easy Mackeson winner Red Candle at Sandown and later outgunned specialist two-milers Inkslinger and Tingle Creek at Newbury.

Once he was fit Pendil became extremely aggressive. The scars on the hands of his lad Vince Brooks bear testimony to the sharpness of his teeth, and he once took a fleshy chunk out of the nose of his travelling companion Paddy's Road House on the way to the races. Walking briskly back from the gallops Pendil would often display an exaggerated goose-step, his head thrust out low and his front feet swinging above his ears. Adaptable and exceptionally athletic he was equally effective at any distance between two and three miles and was unquestionably the best steeplechaser in the country, a fact that was fully reflected by his prohibitive starting price of 6–4 on.

Barry Brogan's abrupt departure to be dried out, once more, at an acoholics' hospital in Dublin left Walwyn searching for a new jockey for The Dikler. His choice was Ron Barry, a tall, dynamic Irishman based in Cumbria, poised to become champion jockey for the first time. Before the race Barry came down to Lambourn to school The Dikler. Darkie Deacon, on foot, showed the first fence to the big horse, who proceeded to jump it from a standstill to his new jockey's surprise!

Ron Barry, who sometimes gave the impression of eating iron filings for breakfast, was nursing a broken collar-bone before Cheltenham. Most jockeys would have taken an obligatory rest for three weeks to allow the break to knit. Not Ron Barry. After a few days off he came back to ride Dark Sultan to victory in a valuable hurdle at Chepstow on the Saturday before the Festival; but in doing so he aggravated the injury and promptly gave up three more rides that afternoon. The stricter medical supervision of the eighties and nineties would have prevented Ron Barry riding The Dikler in the Gold Cup. He chose not to make a drama out of a crisis and kept his injury secret, though he was increasingly concerned at the problem of holding such an intractable horse on the way to the start.

Darkie Deacon watched the 1973 Gold Cup through a red haze of pain. As he prepared to lead up The Dikler in preference to Charlie Potheen the big horse kicked him with such brutal force that he feared his thigh was broken. The time-honoured cure of a bucket of cold water and a sponge brought the gallant stable lad round but he was barely able to walk and still feels the injury to this day. Out on the course Ron Barry and The Dikler had arrived safely at the start but the jockey was in trouble as soon as the race began.

"I was certain there would be a good gallop with Charlie Potheen and Clever Scot in the race, but going to the first my horse took such a grip I could not hold him as my broken collar-bone was hurting like hell. Because I could not fight him he went to sleep, dropped his bit and settled beautifully like a sensible old hunter," he remembers. The crisis was over.

Charlie Potheen, racing as keenly as ever, led at a furious pace on unusually fast going for most of the journey and was still in front running downhill for the final time with Pendil, who had been jumping with breathtaking precision and at times, pulling too freely for his own good, moving ominously well just behind. A little further back The Dikler was closing, too, until his progress was briefly, but crucially, hindered by his stable companion as they raced towards the second last fence. Ron Barry wanted to go on Terry Biddlecombe's inside and shouted for room, but Charlie Potheen, as usual, was hanging left onto the rail and stopped him.

Barry recalls: "I had to pull back and round and that cost me ground at a vital stage of the race."

While the two Walwyn heavyweights were jostling each other, Pendil swept into the lead with another extravagant leap at the second last fence. Quickening away, he had established an advantage of fully three lengths as he approached the final fence. He jumped that well, too, but froze momentarily and fatally on landing.

Richard Pitman explains: "Pendil was a horse that could come up further away from a fence than any horse I ever sat on, but because we were clear and I wanted to be sure I sat for the last three strides into that fence instead of really going for it as I would normally do in company. He just seemed to lose his momentum for a second on landing."

The Dikler was galloping flat out as he reached the fence. He met it on a long stride, threw his strapping frame through the air like a giant missile and gained precious yards in the air. Pendil was still clear but his head came up and his ears flicked back and forth as if he was startled by the crashing waves of sound assailing him from all sides. Suddenly the gap was closing rapidly. The next few moments were ghastly ones for those who so badly wanted Pendil to win.

Charging ferociously uphill, The Dikler caught the leader with fifty yards to run and galloped on relentlessly towards the line. Then gloriously, but all too late, Pendil was responding to the challenge like the champion we believed him to be. One second The Dikler was almost half a length ahead. The next the little horse with his head raised like a gazelle was cutting him back. They surged past the post locked together and though Pendil was back in front a stride or two later the judge confirmed that The Dikler had gained a stunning victory by the shortest possible margin.

Looking back on the race in the autumn of 1991 the winning jockey concluded: "Pendil was a brilliant horse, much better than mine but he tied up badly on the hill. He did not stay as well as mine."

Richard Pitman begs to differ: "Pendil was really running at the end. He stayed very well. He loved competition. The moment The Dikler passed him he ran on like a lion."

Down on the lawn, watching in agony, his damaged thigh turning blacker by the moment, Darkie Deacon limped towards the winner's enclosure while he waited nervously for the result to be announced. He knew that Charlie Potheen had finished an honourable third but could not be certain The Dikler had prevailed.

"The big sod was a horse and a half," he reflects. "When you rode him he felt as though he could walk and gallop on eggs. But when he kicked . . . . "

The cruel defeat of Pendil was engraved on the hearts and bank balances of those who were still convinced he was the finest steeplechaser of his generation. That evening a party developed at the Queen's Hotel to celebrate The Dikler's triumph. When I arrived clutching a copy of the photo finish print Ron Barry, whose stamina in these matters was legendary, was generously holding court at the bar.

As the pace quickened, a combination of extreme pain from his collar-bone and a surfeit of champagne

Fulke Walwyn (right) admires The Dikler, who obscures the head of his faithful lad Darkie Deacon

eventually proved too much even for him. The next afternoon back in Fleet Street I was surprised to read a Press Association report from Uttoxeter stating, "Ron Barry, fresh as paint after his success in the Gold Cup, won the opening race here today."

Half an hour later there was a not entirely unexpected postscript . . . : "Ron Barry is feeling unwell and will not ride again today"! Seldom has a hangover been more richly earned.

Pendil and The Dikler would have a return match in a year's time. Indeed The Dikler was to run in a total of seven consecutive Gold Cups before his retirement to his owner's home near Burford. In the

twilight of his career he won the Whitbread Gold Cup in 1974 and finished fifth in the 1975 Grand National and sixth the following year aged thirteen.

The old warrior enjoyed a busy retirement: he was ridden by his owner's step-daughter Jackie Ellis at various times out hunting, in hunter trials and events. The once barely controllable great chaser was even spotted performing elegant dressage tests. During his final years he lorded it over his owner's young horses in a field beside her home. He developed a back problem, perhaps brought on by arthritis, and was put down in September 1984, aged twenty-one.

CHELTENHAM GOLD CUP.   March 15th 1973.   £15,125.   *Good.*

1	The Dikler	10 12 0	R. Barry	9–1	
2	Pendil	8 12 0	R. Pitman	4–6 Fav	
3	Charlie Potheen	8 12 0	T. Biddlecombe	9–2	
4	L'Escargot	10 12 0	T. Carberry	20–1	
5	Garoupe	9 12 0	F. Berry	50–1	
6	Spanish Steps	10 12 0	P. Blacker	10–1	
7	Red Candle	9 12 0	J. Fox	50–1	

Sh. head, 6 lengths.   Owned Mrs D. August.   Trained F. Walwyn.
Bred J. F. Moorhead.   6m. 37.2 seconds.   Also 22 Clever Scot (D. Mould) Fell.
8 Ran.   Tote win: 87p.

The Dikler: b.g. 1963 (Vulgan–Coronation Day)

8

CAPTAIN CHRISTY
(1974)

LIFELINES COME IN MANY FORMS. Bobby Beasley's appeared in the chunky shape of the hard-pulling, arm-wrenching Captain Christy, potentially the best chaser since Arkle. Just occasionally down the years a race, a game, a result can transcend the narrow theatre of sport and touch a much wider audience. Who could possibly fail to be moved by the toughness of spirit exhibited by Bobby Beasley after he emerged from dark, wasted, abandoned months in a hundred anonymous bars? His gritty comeback against apparently insuperable odds reached an unforgettable climax with victory on Captain Christy in the 1974 Cheltenham Gold Cup. It was a triumph over extreme adversity that reached the very core of our senses.

Bobby Beasley's problems were, perhaps, self-inflicted, though he will tell you to this day that alcoholism is an illness. Whatever the cause Beasley, a graceful and gifted horseman, had won the 1959 Gold Cup on Roddy Owen, the 1960 Champion Hurdle on Another Flash and the 1961 Grand National on Nicolaus Silver before falling victim to the demon drink. By the spring of 1969 he was at his wits' end. He rode his last winner Rimmon for Fred Winter at Fontwell on May 7th that year then drifted out of racing, a sad and increasingly isolated figure, old before his time as he continued his self-destructive journey towards obscurity.

Fred Winter, that great and generous man, promised Beasley his job would remain open till the day he recovered. It was a gesture the fallen jockey felt unable to accept in his self-pitying state at the time. His once glittering career apparently at an end, he became, briefly and uncomfortably, an insurance salesman. One of his first customers was Richard Pitman, the man who was riding many of his old horses for Fred Winter. Purely out of pity Pitman agreed to buy an inexpensive policy. When Beasley later began riding again Pitman tried in vain to cancel that agreement. By 1991 it was worth £11,000!

Bobby Beasley hated himself and his new role as a salesman. He spent one forlorn week holed up in lodgings in the Midlands morosely watching the 1970 Cheltenham Festival on television. The sight of horses winning that were once his rides by right had a profound effect on him.

"An oldish woman was watching the races with me. I made a promise that if I could get myself together I was going back to Cheltenham one day to have one last crack just to prove that the booze could be beaten," he relates. Many alcoholics in their cups have made similar grandiose pledges. Few have fulfilled them as gloriously as Bobby Beasley.

He returned to his native Ireland in despair, uncertain if he wanted to ride, unsure if anyone would give him the chance.

"I had lost the one thing in life that gave me a purpose and expression. I felt the self-disgust of what I'd done. Somehow I knew I was not finished . . . but something was stopping me trying again. It was the blues. An illness. When you go to rock bottom your illusions go, too.

"If I could make a stand and do something about it, instead of just accepting it and fading away I felt I could show that drink could be beaten."

Weeks, sometimes entire months, drifted by in a blur. Grotesquely flabby at around 13 st. and still drinking ferociously, he began riding again on some mornings for a friend, Stuart Barratt, who trained a small team of horses near Portmarnock. Once the weight dropped sufficiently he nervously accepted a ride for Barratt on a moderate hurdler, Gordon, at Limerick on December 28th 1970; he carried 4 lb overweight at 11 st. 3 lb and finished fourth.

When the chance came to ride for another loyal ally, Paddy Murphy, Bobby Beasley took the most difficult step of all by agreeing to the request of his friend Nicky Rackard to attend Alcoholics Anonymous. Salvation had arrived, though the torment was to continue for many months. On February 20th 1971, Bobby Beasley, his face the colour and texture of parchment, rode to victory on Norwegian Flag in the Stillorgan Hurdle at Leopardstown. After almost two empty years he was on his way back.

Irish racing at the time offered the curious spectacle of a former Army officer Major Joe Pidcock, in his sixties, perched precariously on the back of a hard-tugging hurdler named Captain Christy, who was by the French-bred sire Mon Capitaine out of an unraced mare, Christy's Bow. The volatile young hurdler did not appear to possess any brakes or steering.

Tom Nicholson, a noted judge of young stock, had bought him as a foal for 290 guineas at Ballsbridge from his West Cork breeder George Williams, who revealed that Christy Cut, the dam of Christy's Bow, had once changed hands for two shillings!

The genial Nicholson relates "I never saw Captain Christy until he came into the ring. Then I just took a fancy to him. He turned out to be a mad horse to break, real tough and slow to learn. I think he put more than one man in hospital.

"He would throw his riders off his back or run under a tree to get rid of them. He proved to be a machine, all right, but he was so wayward."

Captain Christy exhibited the same spirit on the racecourse. After the wilful young horse had won two bumper races Tom Nicholson sold him to the intrepid Major. Nicholson remembers receiving £15,000. The purchaser reported at the time that he paid £10,000. For a while Major Pidcock, small and eccentric, mentioned in despatches, owned, trained and rode Captain Christy. They made, it must be said, an odd couple even by the delightfully unconventional standards of Irish racing. Usually they would travel much further than the others in a race, and at Limerick they ran right off the course; but at Baldoyle, with the help of a constant running rail, they won a maiden hurdle.

Eventually Captain Christy was sent to be trained by Pat Taaffe, but after another embarrassing experience in a race at Kilbeggan the major decided to sell him. Pat Samuel, an entrepreneur from New Zealand, bought the horse for his wife Jane for £10,000.

The following season Captain Christy's form was a revelation. When Bobby Coonan was unable to ride him in his second race Pat Taaffe chose Bobby Beasley as his replacement. The young tearaway and the wise old jockey proved an irresistible combination, winning five times, usually from the front, including the Irish Sweeps Hurdle, and also finished a close third in the 1973 Champion Hurdle.

"We were advised you could not make all the running at Cheltenham but half-way round I realised I had not gone fast enough," recalls Beasley.

Captain Christy then embarked on a hair-raising career over fences. He won twice, jumping fast but sometimes alarmingly low, and was all set to beat Bula at Ascot when he ploughed through the second last fence, decanting Bobby Beasley. After two doughty runs over hurdles carrying lumps of weight he blundered expensively again at the second last fence at Haydock with the valuable Wills Premier Chase Final his for the taking.

Beasley explains: "He was the most athletic horse, so active, like something on springs, but he could not fiddle his fences. He would either gallop through a fence or . . . ", his voice tails off at the memory of those costly tumbles at Ascot and Haydock.

Pat Samuel, an inveterate punter, had already backed Captain Christy at long odds for the Gold Cup. Trainer and jockey now determined on an intensive period of schooling to improve the horse's jumping. He won twice more at Punchestown and Thurles.

"He blundered badly at Thurles and his head was on the floor but he made ground doing it," remembers Beasley.

When Captain Christy travelled to Cheltenham again for the 1974 Gold Cup he had run in only six steeplechases and had shed his jockey in two of them. Pat Taaffe advised the eager Samuel: "He's no certainty to get round but if he does I think he will win."

Bobby Beasley was guardedly optimistic, too, as destiny beckoned.

"I was burning to have one last crack at Cheltenham and I believe it was fate that Pat put me on the horse eighteen months earlier. He believed I could still do it and made me believe I could.

"Captain Christy would launch himself at his fences. He was very highly strung, a hypersensitive horse. So he would anticipate your movements in the saddle and early on it was difficult to organise him going into a jump."

A year previously bookies had offered odds of only 7–1 against the precocious Killiney, a gentle giant, winning the 1974 Gold Cup. Tragically he had been killed in his next race at Ascot in April.

The betting for the 1974 Gold Cup was again dominated by Pendil, an automatic choice as favourite, at 8–13, after beating The Dikler by no less than thirty-two lengths in the King George VI Chase. The Dikler was next in the betting, at 5–1, with Captain Christy supported from 8–1 to 7–1 despite his woeful lack of experience over fences. Inkslinger was a useful second string from Ireland. Charlie Potheen was back again, but Terry Biddlecombe was now riding the Queen Mother's Game Spirit on his final day as a jockey. Terry's brother-in-law and fellow champion Bob Davies was on a notoriously risky jumper, the 100–1 shot High Ken, a faller already three times that season.

A death threat to Pendil greatly added to the tension among Fred Winter's team in the final twenty-four hours before the Gold Cup. Vince Brooks, his devoted lad, told the trainer he would rather the horse did not run if there was the slightest chance of his being harmed. Pendil was not alone for a second. Brooks slept outside his box on the night before the Gold Cup. At the races two burly policemen plus Mick Cullen, Winter's tough travelling head lad, provided constant cover. The first Richard Pitman knew of the problem was in the paddock when Brooks implored him to withdraw the horse at the start.

Just as he had done the previous year Charlie Potheen made much of the running in the 1974 Gold Cup. His nearest pursuer, Inkslinger, fell at the awkward downhill fence first time, caught Captain Christy with his legs as he did so and nearly brought him down. High Ken took over from Charlie Potheen after a circuit with Pendil in close attendance, once more running keenly, and Captain Christy, settled towards the rear, jumping soundly. Running downhill to the third last, the most tricky fence on the course, the field began to bunch. Pendil, so fresh he was still pulling his jockey's arms out, had been tracking High Ken, but Richard Pitman, aware of the leader's reputation, had been pulling out of his slipstream as each fence approached.

Now, alarmingly, he found his escape route blocked. Suddenly The Dikler, Captain Christy and Game Spirit smothered him as they thundered towards the danger fence.

"I'd committed myself to a position I could not leave and remember thinking 'God, let me get over this one safely'," relates Pitman.

It was not to be. In one of the most dramatic and violent moments in the history of the Gold Cup, High Ken fell heavily. Poor Pendil, who jumped the fence superbly directly behind him, took one step before his legs were whipped from under him as if by a hidden trip-wire. He sprang up and cantered off shaking his head in bewilderment. It was the only time in his life that Pendil came down and it was through no fault of his own. As High Ken tumbled upside-down, one of his feet caught the left stirrup iron of Bobby Beasley on Captain Christy.

He recalls: "I had moved to the outside because I did not want to land on top of anything at that fence. It was one of those instinctive things. I suppose by the age of thirty-nine you have those feelings of what might happen."

The Dikler was left in the lead by the abrupt departure of the favourite, but a quick, fluent jump took Captain Christy alongside him at the second last fence, much sooner than his jockey wished or intended. Galloping on strongly, Captain Christy rushed headlong towards the final fence, victory beckoning. So far he had jumped like an experienced handicapper but now he all but threw away a famous triumph with a ghastly blunder that would have unshipped many a jockey. Diving through the fence, Captain Christy pitched perilously on to his nose.

"He was looking around at the crowd, lost concentration and though he met it spot-on just did not get high enough," relates Beasley. "It would be very hard to get him to fall. The biggest problem was staying with him. He was so short in front his head would disappear and there was not a lot of shoulder in front of you to sit on."

Displaying a wonderful degree of balance the jockey remained securely in the saddle and did not even lose his irons in the moment of crisis that left The Dikler once more in front. Despite setting off again almost from a standstill Captain Christy, remarkably, was running so powerfully within a few yards that he bounded past The Dikler and swept to a truly heart-warming success by five lengths. So many in the vast crowd had wanted Pendil to win; but now they rushed to salute a great horse and his brave jockey, whose comeback against all odds had received its finest reward.

On his return to the weighing-room Bobby Beasley

ordered a case of champagne for his fellow jockeys and calmly sat in a corner sipping a glass of lemonade as he reflected on the crucial moment of the race.

To this day he insists: "I was forced to go on sooner than planned by events in the race. If Pendil had stood up I would have won more easily. He would have given me the lead I needed going to the last."

Naturally Richard Pitman disagrees. He apologised to Fred Winter and said Pendil should have won two Gold Cups. Winter, whose character shone through in the many difficult and painful moments every trainer endures, replied "Never mind, Richard, he will win it next year."

"But will I still be riding him then?" asked the jockey anxiously.

"Of course," replied the trainer, patting the disconsolate jockey on the back.

Horse and rider never did get the chance to set the record straight. Pendil was soundly beaten by Cap-

tain Christy in the King George VI Chase at Christmas and broke down badly at Kempton shortly before the 1975 Gold Cup. He came back twenty-two months later and quickly registered a hat-trick. Once more fate intervened. When another horse ran into him during roadwork in Lambourn, Pendil became entangled in metal fencing beside the road. The damage to his neck and back took months to heal; even worse, the legs that had propelled him so thrillingly over the most daunting fences were a constant worry.

Pendil was hunted for a while by an army officer in Dorset before returning briefly into the care of Richard Pitman. Later he became the property of Bob Champion and featured as a runaway horse on the gallops in the film *Champions*. When Bob moved to Newmarket, Pendil remained in Wiltshire with me, and spends much of his time in a paddock gently bullying a small pony.

Injury cut short Captain Christy's meteoric career,

Captain Christy lurches dangerously through the final fence like a bungling novice. But Bobby Beasley sits tight and they recover to beat The Dikler

too. He ran in only one more Gold Cup, when exceptionally soft ground proved his downfall, then suffered persistent leg trouble. Though Pat Taaffe had become only the second man in history to win the Gold Cup as a jockey and trainer the Samuels, rather ungraciously, transferred Captain Christy to Francis Flood. But the problems remained and he was retired to his owner's home at the Ballinakill Stud, Kilfinny, near Limerick, where he spent his retirement in the company of an old donkey. There he was put down painlessly in 1979 shortly before Jane Samuel sold the stud.

Her affection for him remains undimmed by the passage of time. "In my book he was brilliant; but like many brilliant people he was a little unpredictable. In retirement he was not a sociable horse and certainly not the old favourite that you could pat and give a sugar lump. He was remote. He and the donkey would stand together under a tree and watch the other horses playing but never joined in," she relates.

Bobby Beasley believes Captain Christy's potential was limitless. "All things being equal, with different owners, and if he had stayed sound this horse would have been on a par with Arkle. He was a freak.

He did not look like a chaser and he did not act like one. He was a hurdler, really. He took time to learn how to jump fences and was just becoming a good ride."

Beasley retired from riding for the second time within a few months of his uplifting triumph at Cheltenham. Later he returned to England, married again, and began training racehorses first at Lewes then at a small yard on the Wiltshire Downs above Ogbourne Maisey where Sir Gordon Richards lived for many years. When he gave up training in 1988 he became, of all things, a landlord of a pub, the Baking House, in a remote corner of Worcestershire! When I called to see him there I wondered if his new role might not provide tantalising temptations.

"Not at all. I'm stronger against drink than ever," he replied, chain-smoking incessantly as he talked with haunting honesty of the lost years when he was kidnapped by alcohol.

"Once the booze was boss. Now that I've changed the roles around and sell it, I'm the boss. Instead of it using me I'm now dispensing it in a rational way as part of my life. There is no temptation."

CHELTENHAM GOLD CUP.   March 14th 1974.   £14,572.50.   *Soft.*

1	Captain Christy	7 12 0	H. Beasley	7–1
2	The Dikler	11 12 0	R. Barry	5–1
3	Game Spirit	8 12 0	T. Biddlecombe	20–1
4	Charlie Potheen	9 12 0	W. Smith	33–1

5 lengths, 25.   Owned Mrs Jane Samuel.   Trained P. Taaffe.   Bred George Williams. 7m. 5.5 seconds.   Also 8–13 Fav Pendil (R. Pitman) B. Down, 11 Inkslinger (T. Carberry) Fell, 100 High Ken (B. R. Davies) Fell.   7 Ran.   Tote win: 75p.

Captain Christy: b.g. 1967 (Mon Capitaine–Christy's Bow)

9

TEN UP

(1975)

FOLLOWING IN THE FOOTSTEPS of a master craftsman must be one of the most unenviable tasks in sport. If you are young and inexperienced the odd mistake you make along the way will inevitably fall under public scrutiny. Happily Jim Dreaper, quiet, intelligent with a delightful sense of humour, came through those difficult early years intact. Pitched into training at the age of twenty, long before he intended or planned, he was soon plundering the major prizes at Cheltenham and elsewhere with such outstanding success that he topped the trainers' list in Ireland in each of his first four years.

Declining health forced Tom Dreaper to retire at the end of 1971. His name will always be linked with that of Arkle, whose fortunes he guided with a telling blend of patience and instinct. Arkle was certainly the best he ever trained but he was one of a veritable army of top-class steeplechasers nurtured so skilfully by Dreaper. Flyingbolt, Fortria, Prince Regent, Royal Approach, Fort Leney, Olympia, Kerforo . . . the list is endless. He also won the Irish Grand National a record number of times.

Since licences in Ireland are issued annually, Jim Dreaper became a racehorse trainer on New Year's Day 1972. He would not be twenty-one for another month, and apart from working for his father since he left school at seventeen had spent barely a fortnight as a teenager in the French training centre of Lamorlaye. In a rare appearance in England as an amateur jockey Jim had come agonisingly close to winning the 1971 Grand National on his father's Black Secret in a tight finish with Specify.

Among the young horses he took over in 1972 at the family farm, Greenogue, barely fifteen minutes from Dublin Airport, were Brown Lad, Colebridge and Ten Up, who would all feature prominently in Gold Cups in the seventies. Ten Up had won a bumper race on his racecourse debut at Leopardstown on December 27th 1971, ridden by the man who would become his trainer five days later. A big, lengthy, dark gelding by Raise You Ten, a Cup horse on the flat, out of Irish Harp, a mare who won over hurdles and fences in Ireland, he was bred by Joe Osborne. He was bought for 5,500 guineas at Goffs Sales as a three-year-old by Tom Dreaper for Arkle's owner Anne, Duchess of Westminster. Later he was broken in by Pat Taaffe before joining Dreaper. To this day Jim Dreaper trains much as his father did for so many years.

"Certainly that is true when they are fit. Dad would have his horses out for no more than half an hour a day and I do much the same," he confirms.

Ten Up tended to resemble an under-nourished greyhound throughout his career, once he was racing fit. He simply could not hold condition. If he looked well and burly he invariably ran below form. Traditionally horses at Greenogue that are bred for chasing do not waste too much precious time over hurdles. Ten Up ran only six times over hurdles in a period between December 1972 and May 1973, winning three including the Osberstown Hurdle at Naas and being placed in a further two. He proved to be a very keen racehorse, so headstrong that he frequently led from the start. His jockeys preferred to give him his head rather than fight him.

Put to fences in the autumn of 1973 he was an extremely slow learner at the business of crossing an obstacle at racing pace. Those who had witnessed his hesitant schooling sessions at home did not rush to take the miserly odds of 2–5 available for his first attempt over fences in the Neill's Gorse Chase at Punchestown in November. Ten Up duly won by three-quarters of a length from Canta King, despite slowing almost to a walk at most fences and clambering awkwardly over them.

The memory of that abject display still haunts Jim Dreaper. "I was so ashamed of his jumping," he admits readily. "It was appalling. He would lose four lengths going into each fence and a further four coming out."

Like his father, Jim Dreaper believed in regular and thorough jumping practice at home. Constant schooling helped improve Ten Up's jumping eventually. Ridden with dash and determination by the apparently carefree Tommy Carberry he developed into a safe, rather than flamboyant jumper, was beaten only once from six starts that season and ended his campaign triumphantly in the Sun Alliance Chase on the opening day of the Cheltenham Festival on the same afternoon that his massive stable companion Brown Lad took the Sun Alliance Novices' Hurdle with ease.

When Ten Up returned to England the following February for the Whitbread Trial it was clear he had developed into a serious Gold Cup contender. On going that was exceptionally heavy even by Ascot's standards Ten Up, carrying 11 st. 6 lb, made most of the running, was clear entering the final mile and, galloping on tirelessly through the mud, claimed victory by twenty-five lengths from the spring-heeled American horse Soothsayer trained by Fred Winter.

The eternally wet spring of 1975 almost put paid to the entire Cheltenham Festival. The first day's racing was lost when the stewards considered the course waterlogged and the remaining two days were in jeopardy until the last moment, even though the programme was hastily rearranged to preserve the major prizes. Eight races, including the Champion Hurdle and Two-mile Champion Chase, were held on Wednesday in the sloppiest conditions imaginable. Jim Dreaper had brought his brilliant young chaser Brown Lad over for the Sun Alliance Chase, but aware that might be lost, he let him run first in the Lloyds Bank Hurdle on Wednesday. Brown Lad won easily.

As the rain continued to tip down on Thursday, conditions were so critical that two fences were omitted. Pendil, twice so unlucky in the Gold Cup, had been ante-post favourite once more until finishing lame at Kempton in February. In his absence Fred Winter was double-handed with Bula and Soothsayer. John Francome, the emerging star, expected to be on Soothsayer but, much to his surprise, replaced the stable jockey Richard Pitman on Bula, a 5–1

chance. So Pitman rode the 28–1 outsider Soothsayer.

Captain Christy was the 7–4 favourite despite the substantial weight of evidence that heavy going did not suit him. Racing with tremendous zest in more benign conditions he had dismissed Pendil ruthlessly in the King George VI Chase at Kempton but had subsequently failed under top weight in the

Leopardstown Chase run on heavy going. He was now ridden by Bobby Coonan, seven times champion jockey of Ireland. Ten Up was heavily supported for the Gold Cup at 2–1. The Dikler, back again at the age of twelve, was an outsider this time and High Ken, whose fall had changed the shape of the race so dramatically a year earlier, was dismissed in the betting at 33–1.

The 1975 Gold Cup proved to be less a horse race, more a battle of survival in the most testing conditions imaginable. The starter used a flag to send the field on its way. Glanford Brigg, an habitual front runner, led over the first three fences before High Ken briefly took over. By the sixth fence Ten Up had

Ten Up crosses the last fence ahead of the mud-spattered stable companions Bula (left) and Soothsayer

pulled his way irresistibly to the front after winning his brief struggle for supremacy with his jockey Tommy Carberry.

"After a few fences I felt he was going to break my heart or I was going to break his so I let him go," recalls the jockey, his brown eyes twinkling merrily.

"This lad would maul you all the way if you let him. Riding him was like tugging at a barn door in a gale. Once he got in front that day no one was too anxious to take him on. So I just lobbed round trying to save a bit for the end."

Carberry's light frame disguised strength of steel. Was it harder for a small jockey to control such a powerful, aggressive horse in these conditions?

"Well I was never very keen on a horse dragging me all the way. I'd prefer to go on if I could. Ten Up was a strong devil to ride, he attacked everything he faced and his jumping was good by then. He could go a right gallop and keep it up," he reflects.

The pace set by Ten Up found out all the opposition. Captain Christy, Bruslee and The Dikler were all out of the race soon after half-way, and coming down the hill for the final time Fred Winter's pair were struggling to stay in touch with the leader. Just before the bend John Francome on Bula moved upsides Richard Pitman on Soothsayer. In a brief, but breathless, discussion they agreed to share the prize money if either managed to catch Ten Up, who lost precious ground with a mistake at the second last fence.

Ten Up, however, was the only one to meet the last fence as his jockey would have wanted and though patently tired landed safely with the race won. Just behind him both Bula and Soothsayer ran into the bottom of the fence, hit it hard and landed in a tangled heap alongside each other. Somehow both stayed upright but by then Ten Up had gone beyond recall and was on his way to victory by six lengths. The weary Soothsayer, who had been headed by Bula on the final bend, fought his way past his exhausted stable companion to claim second prize by half a length.

A few moments after Ten Up had received the traditional Irish greeting reserved for their country's heroes at Cheltenham the rest of the meeting was abandoned. Jim Dreaper and Tommy Carberry would not have the chance to add a further success with Brown Lad.

Dreaper, winning his first Gold Cup at the age of twenty-four, proudly insists "In my opinion Ten Up gave 101 per cent that day. His guts won the race. He gave everything and for days at home afterwards he was gone. I don't think he was ever as good again. I often felt he might have strained something in the Gold Cup. When you dig that deep into the reserves of a horse you never know."

Happily Tom Dreaper lived to see his fine young son train a Gold Cup winner. Old Tom, one of the legends of Irish racing, died just over a month later.

The next season Ten Up began breaking blood vessels. Probably for this reason he never again reached the same peak of achievement. He did win at Limerick Junction in March at 8–1 on, then was withdrawn sensationally at the last minute at Cheltenham before the 1976 Gold Cup. He fell in the Irish Grand National a month later and again broke a blood vessel.

Ten Up ran three more times the following winter but when the same problem recurred it seemed his racing career had reached a premature end. The Duchess gave him as a hunter to her godson, James Hodges, at the time a tall, rather burly young captain in the King's Troop, the Royal Horse Artillery. The eager new owner picked up his gift horse at a pre-arranged rendezvous at a lay-by near Worcester in the autumn of 1977. The captain lived in barracks at St John's Wood. Within a month Ten Up had moved there to join him. At once he gave the impression of being bombproof by walking sedately through heavy traffic at Swiss Cottage.

In the next two years the Gold Cup winner and his enthusiastic young rider could be seen exercising regularly nearby on Wormwood Scrubs. It was not the ideal place to gallop a big, long-striding old racehorse but then training-grounds are in rather short supply in NW8. Ten Up proved to be an exciting and natural hunter.

"He was so keen with the Quorn that I would run him round a field about three times after jumping a fence to take the gas out of him before the next hedge," relates James Hodges. Soon he asked his godmother if she would object if he ran the old horse in point-to-points. She did not. He then rang Jim Dreaper to ask if he felt a return to to racing would put the horse under sufficient pressure to cause him to break blood vessels again.

The trainer replied, memorably: "James, I doubt if you will ever get him going fast enough to find out."

So, three years after his finest triumph at Cheltenham, Ten Up, aged eleven, appeared in a two-horse

Some retirement. Ten Up canters eagerly past H.M. prison at Wormwood Scrubs, ridden by his new owner James Hodges

point-to-point at Tweseldown on March 1st 1978, and readily overcame his sole opponent, to the evident relief of his new rider. The tote dividend to a 10p stake was 11p! The alert Secretary of Sandown's Grand Military meeting at once wrote to Hodges urging him to run the old horse in the Grand Military Gold Cup there nine days later.

Hodges takes up the story: "The horse was not one-quarter fit at Sandown and I could not hold one side of him. We zoomed round in the lead for a circuit and then he, or maybe it was me, blew up and we finished fifth. He was such an exhilarating ride."

Hodges readily accepted Tim Forster's generous suggestion to bring the horse to Letcombe Bassett for the occasional gallop. Early in April horse and rider won the Royal Artillery Gold Cup by twenty-five lengths. Twice in one season James Hodges survived

painful and sudden damage to his tack. At Sandown, when his leather broke at the first fence, he kicked his other foot out and rode like a man inspired to claim second place. Bruisingly aware of his discomfort on that occasion he chose to keep his other foot in its stirrup when an iron broke at Cheltenham. Reliable Ten Up kept straight at his fences and claimed third prize.

The old horse's unexpected revival continued happily until 1982 when, aged fifteen, he won the R.A. Gold Cup again, two more hunter chases and a point-to-point. He was trained for two seasons by Tim Forster and in his final year's racing by Mick McNeill at a livery yard barely a furlong from the home of Hodges' parents near Andover.

In the winter of 1990–91 Ten Up was still going strong, ridden each morning by Hodges' mother Ann

Anne, Duchess of Westminster gives Ten Up a well deserved pat on the neck

who, I trust, will forgive me for mentioning that she is over seventy. For several years she delivered the local parish magazine to the more remote parts of the village of Quarley from Ten Up's back. At weekends James Hodges hunts him with the R.A. and often takes his eldest daughter Larch alongside on her leading-rein pony.

Retirement proved more hectic than his earlier life for Ten Up. He ran fifty-nine times between 1971 and 1982, won twenty-seven races, and was placed in a further nineteen. He still looked in superb condition when I rode him briefly on a crisp morning in the spring of 1991. In his wildest dreams James Hodges could not have wished for a better present or a safer schoolmaster.

PIPER CHAMPAGNE CHELTENHAM GOLD CUP.   March 13th 1975.   £17,757.50.   *Heavy.*

1	Ten Up	8 12 0	T. Carberry	2–1
2	Soothsayer	8 12 0	R. Pitman	28–1
3	Bula	10 12 0	J. Francome	5–1
4	Glanford Brigg	9 12 0	S. Holland	25–1
5	High Ken	9 12 0	B. Brogan	33–1

6 lengths, ½.   Owned Anne, Duchess of Westminster.   Trained J. Dreaper. Bred J. Osborne.   7m. 51.4 seconds.   Also 7–4 Fav Captain Christy (R. Coonan) P.U., 12 Bruslee (A. Turnell) P.U., 20 The Dikler (R. Barry) P.U.   8 Ran.   Tote win: 25p.

Ten Up: b.g. 1967 (Raise You Ten–Irish Harp)

10

ROYAL FROLIC
(1976)

TIMING IS SO OFTEN THE KEY to success in life. You cannot protect a promising sportsman or racehorse forever from the harsh reality of competition in the most demanding arenas of the world. Yet pitching a burgeoning young talent against the best too soon can destroy his confidence for ever. There is only one way to gain experience at the highest level of sport, and those who pamper a runner, a player or a racehorse of rich promise too long often find that they have been shielding a paper tiger.

This was the very dilemma that faced Fred Rimell before the 1976 Gold Cup. He trained a particularly exciting young chaser, Royal Frolic, only seven at the beginning of the year and with notably limited experience of racing. As the entry date for the Gold Cup approached, Royal Frolic had run in only eight steeplechases and twice over hurdles. Normally Fred Rimell would not have considered the Gold Cup at such an early stage of a horse's career, not even one of Royal Frolic's extreme potential, but his elderly owner Sir Edward Hanmer was in failing health. Aged eighty-two, Sir Edward had first become a steward at Haydock in 1929 and had owned a number of useful horses on the flat including Moneybox, winner of the Manchester Cup, and Fury, successful in the Park Hill Stakes.

When Rimell rang to suggest entering Royal Frolic in the Gold Cup Sir Edward responded that he felt it might be a year too soon. The trainer, a naturally open and friendly man, replied as diplomatically as possible: "But aren't we running out of time?"

There was a brief silence while Sir Edward considered the implications of that leading question before he retorted: "Perhaps you are right." Thus the fateful decision was made to enter Royal Frolic in the 1976 Cheltenham Gold Cup. Mind you, his chance was not immediately obvious to the men who frame the ante-post odds. He had been beaten fully ten lengths into third place carrying a light weight in the Massey-Ferguson Gold Cup in December and had fallen next time at Haydock. It was shortly after he won a minor handicap at Wolverhampton on firm ground in January that he was entered in the Gold Cup.

One firm of bookmakers advertised Royal Frolic's Cheltenham odds at 500–1, a price that proved all too tempting for Rimell's astute wife Mercy and the stable's bright young assistant Kim Bailey, who would later train the 1990 Grand National winner Mr Frisk. They each invested £5 each way. Even before he ran for the final time before the Festival, odds of 200–1 were available about Royal Frolic. They dropped dramatically when he won the Greenall Whitley Breweries Chase at Haydock in record time on March 6th, ridden by Sam Morshead in place of his usual jockey John Burke, out of action with a broken collar-bone.

Burke, a quiet, intelligent man, the son of a schoolteacher from the village of Nobber in County Meath, was a naturally gifted horseman with God-given hands that could tame a raging bull. Anxious to be back in time for Haydock, he rode Royal Frolic at home the day before the race, was dropped when the horse whipped round at the bottom of the gallops, and watched in pain and mounting horror as the horse ran loose for fully twenty minutes.

"That was a desperate morning," he recalls cheerfully. "We all knew the horse could go to the top and there he was charging round like a lunatic just over a week before Cheltenham."

Like so many good racehorses Royal Frolic had been full of spirit as a youngster, at times almost wild. When he arrived at Rimell's yard at Kinnersley as a backward three-year-old the horse was given a goat as a companion in his box to help calm him. The next morning the goat was dead. That first season Royal Frolic proved a frustratingly finicky eater and became so wound up he could not hold any condition. He was a keen, clean-winded horse who did not require much work. Usually he was ridden each morning by John Burke or Basil Jones, another tenacious jockey.

"He was very exciting to sit on, quite an electric ride," relates Burke laconically. "He was very flighty, almost unmanageable at first and would whip round on a sixpence. You could not relax for a moment on him."

Royal Frolic's pedigree did not offer any serious clues to his undoubted brilliance. His sire Royal Buck, a hardy stayer on the flat, was the winner of thirteen races and later the sire of useful chasers like What A Buck, The Pilgarlic and Flitgrove. His dam Forward Miss was unplaced on the flat and over hurdles and fences in a thoroughly undistinguished career as a racehorse, and for many years was no more successful at stud. While carrying Royal Frolic at the grand age of twenty she was bought for 290 guineas at Goffs in November 1968 by Jack White for his brother-in-law Jack Powell, an experienced vet who owns the Wellington House Stud in County Tipperary.

"We saw this fine mare walking round the ring, a real old-fashioned type with legs like oak trees. She was for nothing," relates Powell, who quickly passed her on to a neighbour John Seymour on the condition that he had first refusal of the resulting foal.

Jack Powell paid £400 for the foal, Royal Frolic, who duly won a championship at the Royal Dublin Show as a yearling. An English agent then agreed to buy him for £1,250, but backed out of the deal when he studied the dam's pedigree. Another sale at three, to an English trainer, also foundered. Jack Powell is a director of Doncaster Sales and it was there that Fred Rimell bought Royal Frolic as a three-year-old for 5,100 guineas in August 1972.

Royal Frolic ran once over hurdles at Worcester as a four-year-old in January 1973, but a problem with his liver was diagnosed afterwards, so his trainer wisely gave him a year off to strengthen and develop. When he raced again in November 1974, he won at the first time of asking and was then switched, at once, to fences.

"He was the most tremendous galloper but a right boyo," relates John Burke. "Not difficult for the sake

of it. Just a playful character. He had been known to whip round at a full canter."

The field for the 1976 Gold Cup was seriously depleted by the absence of Captain Christy and Ten Up, winners in the previous two years. Though we did not know it at the time, the Captain's meteoric career was virtually over after a series of towering performances culminating in the ruthless dismissal of Bula in the King George VI Chase at Christmas by a quite remarkable thirty lengths. In mid-February the bleak news filtered through from Ireland that he had strained a tendon. He would not be returning to Cheltenham.

Ten Up was an intended runner in the Gold Cup despite some indifferent displays on the few occasions he raced. He had begun to break blood vessels, a problem that might have been the result of the severe strain of victory in the atrocious conditions at Cheltenham twelve months earlier. Ten Up was a distant last of four to Captain Christy at Punchestown, failed to concede lumps of weight to Spanish Tan at Naas but, starting at 8–1 on exactly a week before the Gold Cup, did beat a solitary opponent at Limerick Junction. In Ireland Jim Dreaper was able to give Ten Up a coagulant, Estro, quite legitimately to help prevent him bleeding. The rules were much more strict in England, though Dreaper admits with disarming honesty that he gave another of his runners Lough Inagh a coagulant in the stable yard at the Festival meeting a year earlier before he won the Two-mile Champion Chase.

"Yes, I did it and simply did not say anything," he confirms.

Secrecy was impossible in the case of Ten Up in the 1976 Gold Cup because his problems were so well chronicled. Sensibly Jim Dreaper advised the Cheltenham authorities of his intention to give Ten Up medication before the Gold Cup. The stewards reminded the young trainer that under rule 180(ii) the horse was liable to disqualification if traces of any non-normal nutrient showed up in the horse's post-race dope test. They further warned Dreaper that his licence could be in jeopardy if the test proved positive. Jim Dreaper had no alternative but to withdraw Ten Up on the morning of the race and suffered the indignity of being required to pay a fixed-penalty fine of £125 for doing so.

He reflects: "It made sense to tell the stewards. Because of all the hype they would have looked for traces of a drug anyway."

Despite Ten Up's sensational late withdrawal Dreaper was still two-handed in the Gold Cup with Colebridge and Brown Lad, winner of the Irish Grand National in 1975. An unusually dry spring had left the ground at Cheltenham far too firm for Brown Lad, a massive, plain, round-chested chaser who was naturally lazy but in a field rather short of class he started a well-backed second favourite of 13–8.

Bula headed the market at 6–4, largely on the strength of his comfortable defeat of The Dikler, by then thirteen, at Sandown. Twice winner of the Champion Hurdle with a swooping late run, he was bidding to become the first horse to complete the elusive double in the Gold Cup. Bula had jumped hurdles for so long that he tended to be too flat over fences and invariably hit one or two hard in each race. He certainly had the class to win a Gold Cup but his style of jumping remained a subject of concern.

Bula's stable companion Pendil was out for the season and Soothsayer, who used to be trained by Fred Winter, raced only once for his new trainer Toby Balding before suffering a setback. The Dikler, running in the Gold Cup for a remarkable seventh successive time, was ignored in the betting at 33–1. Royal Frolic's odds tumbled in the final fortnight to 14–1.

Money Market and What A Buck set a fierce pace from the start on unseasonably fast ground officially described as firm. The headstrong Glanford Brigg, usually a front runner, took over briefly at the twelfth fence and led again at the fifteenth with Royal Frolic, Colebridge and The Dikler moving up.

John Burke recalls: "Royal Frolic was always going well. He flew the water, another great jump at the ditch put him in the race and we nearly hit the front when he outjumped Glanford Brigg at the top of the hill."

A moment later Royal Frolic, a large white splash

A soaring leap at the last fence by Royal Frolic

Royal Frolic and John Burke return in triumph followed by the horse's trainer Fred Rimell

on his nose, dashed eagerly into the lead. It was an advantage that was never to be fully threatened. As Glanford Brigg fell away Bula and Colebridge began to close but a wholesale blunder at the twentieth, three from home, effectively ended Bula's brief challenge.

Royal Frolic's escape was complete by the last bend and he soared over the final fence like a fleet-footed gazelle with at least a foot to spare. Brown Lad, some way behind after labouring throughout the race, finished with his customary dash.

"I had given up hope at the top of the hill," recalls his jockey Tommy Carberry. "The next thing he started running, passed a few then flew from the last fence."

Brown Lad overtook his stable companion Cole-

bridge on the flat but was still five lengths behind Royal Frolic at the line. Money Market, who often needed oxygen after his races, was fourth, Bula a weary sixth and The Dikler eighth of the nine finishers in his last Gold Cup.

Fred Rimell's enterprise in entering Royal Frolic had gained its due reward. How unfortunate that persistent leg trouble in future years would prevent the horse fulfilling the glowing promise offered by his superb victory.

"Royal Frolic's career was just starting but when he came back after injury he never showed the same spark as that day," relates John Burke.

"You could always depend on him. If you attacked a fence blindfold and gave him a kick you knew he would come up. I loved him, really. He was a smashing horse and but for his problems could have been one of the greats."

Happily Sir Edward Hanmer lived to see his colours carried to victory in the Gold Cup. He was not well enough to travel to Cheltenham, but watched the race on television at his home Bettisfield Park with mounting pride. The decision to run Royal Frolic had been gloriously justified. If owner and trainer had decided to wait twelve months with the horse it would have been too late for Sir Edward Hanmer. He died on January 1st 1977.

Just over two weeks after the Gold Cup Fred Rimell and John Burke shared a second famous victory with Rag Trade in the Grand National. When Fred died suddenly in the summer of 1981 Mercy Rimell, his wife, friend and companion in a wonderfully successful partnership, bravely and predictably determined to carry on. Within two years she became the first woman to train the winner of the Champion Hurdle.

John Burke left racing for a while when he gave up riding but in 1990, cheerful as ever, he returned to Kinnersley to act as head lad to the freshly installed trainer Simon Christian.

Leg problems, the bane of all steeplechasers, severely restricted Royal Frolic's programme in later years but he ran with distinction in two more Gold Cups and carried John Burke into sixth place in the 1979 Grand National under top weight of 11 st. 10 lb. He raced for the final time in 1981 in a hunter chase at Cheltenham, aged twelve.

Royal Frolic's retirement was divided between Bettisfield Park, where he was looked after by Betty South, and The Mere House at nearby Hanmer with Sir John Hanmer, who inherited his father's title. The old horse proved a lively hunter, ridden by Sir Edward's grandson Guy with the Wynnstay Hounds, though on some days he even consented to stand still when gates had to be opened. When his heart was damaged by a nasty attack of colic Royal Frolic was put down on October 14th 1983 to save him from further suffering.

PIPER CHAMPAGNE CHELTENHAM GOLD CUP.   March 18th 1976.   £18,134.50.   *Firm.*

1	Royal Frolic	7 12 0	J. Burke	14–1
2	Brown Lad	10 12 0	T. Carberry	13–8
3	Colebridge	12 12 0	F. Berry	12–1
4	Money Market	9 12 0	R. Barry	33–1
5	Glanford Brigg	10 12 0	M. Blackshaw	50–1
6	Bula	11 12 0	J. Francome	6–4 Fav
7	Otter Way	8 12 0	G. Thorner	50–1
8	The Dikler	13 12 0	A. Branford	33–1
9	Roman Bar	7 12 0	P. Kiely	50–1

5 lengths, same.   Owned Sir Edward Hanmer.   Bred John Seymour.
Trained F. Rimell.   6m. 40.1 seconds   Also 16 Flashy Boy (D. T. Hughes) Fell and What A Buck (J. King) P.U.   11 Ran.   Tote win: £1.02.

Royal Frolic: b.g. 1969 (Royal Buck–Forward Miss)

11

DAVY LAD

(1977)

IN A SUSTAINED SPELL OF EXCELLENCE between 1975 and 1981 merry Mick O'Toole of the laughing eyes and lightning repartee trained at least one winner at the Cheltenham Festival each year. The first of them was a resolute mudlark, Davy Lad, who took the Sun Alliance Hurdle in 1975 with eye-catching ease on atrocious going that would have tested the endurance of a marauding band of marines. Two years later he gained an unexpected but utterly decisive victory in a Gold Cup that will for ever be remembered for the tragic death of the former Champion hurdler Lanzarote.

Mick O'Toole is a man of fun. Though it is not immediately obvious from his rounded, jolly figure these days, he once rode in point-to-points and bumper races before switching his interest to greyhound racing. In 1965 he became the first Irishman to train the winner of the greyhound Oaks at Harringay. The lure of horse racing proved too strong and for a while he trained both racehorses and greyhounds at Ashtown just a couple of furlongs from Phoenix Park racecourse.

Nothing was impossible for the ambitious trainer, whose eternally cheerful banter does not entirely conceal the razor-sharp mind lurking behind. If there was a stroke to be pulled, a gamble to be organised or a deal to be done, Micko was yer man. For him the intrigue and the plotting were almost more important than the result. To this day when Mick O'Toole wins everyone celebrates. Even those on the peripheral edges of his company are swept along irresistibly by the sheer force of his personality.

When his stables at Ashtown were overflowing with horses he bought a larger yard named Maddenstown, close to the Irish National Stud, with scope for expansion. He is, you will perceive, the very opposite of a cautious man. His routine at the time was to buy batches of horses and not begin to think of selling them on until they were broken, being ridden and displaying a glimpse of potential. It was a system that required an iron nerve, convincing powers of persuasion and a particularly friendly bank manager.

Dessie Hughes, O'Toole's stable jockey and loyal lieutenant for so many years, relates: "Only when he saw a spark in a horse would he consider finding an owner. If the horses were no good he would get rid of them, often five or six at a time, in one lot, to a horse dealer."

Breeding purists who spend days, even weeks, agonising over the mating arrangements of their broodmares will be dismayed at the eccentric methods employed by Kathlyn Westropp-Bennett and her husband when they came to choose a stallion for Davy Lad's dam Chateau.

Though Chateau was a half-sister to Majority Rule, winner of the 1963 King's Stand Stakes over five furlongs at Royal Ascot, Mrs Westropp-Bennett had bought her cheaply from her uncle. She decided to send the mare to be covered at Martin McEnery's stud in Kilkenny, which housed two stallions, Polyfoto and David Jack, at the time. Polyfoto's fee was cheaper, but Liam Westropp-Bennett chose David Jack to mate with Chateau for the perfectly understandable reason that he had a cousin of that very name in England.

Kathlyn chuckles "My husband told Martin we would not have Polyfoto even if he offered us a free service!"

It proved an uncannily sound decision. David Jack was a high-class stayer on the flat, winner of the Magnet Cup and Ormonde Stakes, and he passed on his bountiful stamina to Davy Lad who was sent to Goffs by Mrs Westropp-Bennett as a yearling with a reserve of 2,000 guineas. Imagine her profound disappointment when he was led out unsold. Outside the sales ring Maura Hanley, the breeder of the Irish Grand National winner Olympia, agreed to pay 700 guineas for Davy Lad.

"He had no pedigree whatsoever and was quite small but he was a good looker and a good walker," she recalls.

"In the two years we had him at home near Neenagh he was not a very pleasant person. He had his own ideas about life all right," she adds.

In the summer of 1973 Mick O'Toole called in briefly at the Goffs sales complex while taking one of his owners, Benny Schmidt-Bodner, to Dublin Airport. He was particularly keen on the unbroken hardy bay submitted by Maura Hanley and bought him for 5,000 guineas before completing his journey.

"I assumed I would pass him on to Benny by the time we reached the airport and had the money already spent in my mind, but I could not persuade him," he recalls.

So the unnamed three-year-old followed the pattern of so many raw young horses bought by Mick O'Toole and broken in by the tireless Dessie Hughes. Though he kept him for several months the trainer's patience was amply justified by the promising manner of the horse's work at home. John Mulhern, a high-powered businessman who later became a trainer too, introduced O'Toole to a friend, Joe McGowan, a wealthy property dealer, who bought a three-quarter share in the David Jack colt, now called Davy Lad, for his gorgeous wife Anne Marie. He was her first racehorse.

O'Toole recalls: "I kept a quarter of him and sold the rest of him for a good bit of money."

On one of the first occasions when Dessie Hughes schooled Davy Lad over hurdles the pair turned upside-down, yet the horse exhibited precocious ability on the Curragh gallops from a very early stage. He won two bumper races readily but was beaten, surprisingly and rather fortuitously, when an odds-on favourite in a maiden hurdle at Leopardstown in March 1974, as a four-year-old. This allowed him to start the following season as a novice.

Davy Lad won six hurdle races in 1974–75, injured his hock badly in mid-winter, was confined to his box for six weeks and only recovered in the nick of time for the Sun Alliance Hurdle at the Cheltenham Festival, a meeting Mick O'Toole had been visiting religiously every year since the heady day

that he saw Arkle win the Broadway Chase in 1963.

He explains: "The place consumes me. You plan, scheme and dream all year in the hope that you might just have one good enough to bring over for this meeting."

In boggy ground that some faint-hearts considered unraceable, Davy Lad, the 5–2 favourite, sloshed home first by three lengths from the Queen Mother's massive Sunyboy. Davy Lad returned to Cheltenham a year later, attempting to complete a rare double in the Sun Alliance Chase, but already he was displaying signs of the idleness that would eventually make him an impossibly hard ride. He reacted to the application of a hood by whipping round as the tapes rose, proved unable to recover the lost ground and finished fifth behind Tied Cottage, who was making the first of many splendid appearances over fences at Cheltenham.

Davy Lad's form as a seven-year-old did not readily advertise his chance as a Gold Cup contender. He ran frequently, won only one minor prize early in the season and was regularly and easily beaten, though he did seem to improve whenever he encountered extremely testing conditions. The imposing Bannow Rambler, a milk-drinking chestnut trained by Padge Berry on a remote part of the coast in Co. Wexford, was the shining hope of Ireland. He beat Davy Lad easily in the Thyestes Chase in January and then narrowly in the Leopardstown Chase a month later. Mick O'Toole's belief in his horse was unshaken.

"Sure, wasn't my lad always going to run at Cheltenham," he chuckles. "He had to. I had him backed with £500 at 40–1 with Sean Graham before Christmas."

Now stories of Mick O'Toole's betting arrangements are legendary and many of them, no doubt, have improved with the telling. Once, during a hilarious breakfast in his house at Maddenstown, I watched him invest £1,000 each way at 28–1 with a fellow guest, an English bookmaker, on his runner in the Sweeps Hurdle that very afternoon. The horse won. Even an eternal optimist like O'Toole cannot be right every time and there were many doubters in Ireland in the final month before Davy Lad landed the gamble.

"The horse was hard on himself all his life and the older he became the worse he got," relates Dessie Hughes. "Every time he ran that Gold Cup season he would be off the bridle after jumping two fences. He was dead lazy. It was me or him. That was his attitude. If his rider became tired he would be laughing. But if you could keep going he would always find a bit more. At home he was a super work horse with loads of gears. The trouble was finding them in a race."

Pendil was missing again from the Gold Cup field. He had come back at Kempton, almost as good as ever, in December 1976, and won a three-horse race at the astonishing odds of 10–1. That evening a telegram arrived from Brigadier Gerard saying "Many congratulations. Next to me you are the tops!"

He won twice more and even beat Fort Devon, one of the Gold Cup favourites, in a close finish at Kempton, but then injured his neck and back when a horse from another string in Lambourn cannoned into him as he was being led out by Vince Brooks. He would never again return to Cheltenham.

Once more tragedy enveloped his trainer Fred Winter at the Festival like an undertaker's cloak. Fred chose to run Bula on the opening day in the Two-mile Champion Chase. The brave and inspiring winner of thirty-four races, he fell heavily at the fifth fence and hit the ground so hard that he broke a bone in his shoulder. Though he was taken gently back to Lambourn, he failed to respond to exhaustive treatment. After three weeks Fred Winter and his vet Frank Mahon decided the kindest course was to put the old horse to sleep. His devoted lad Vince Brooks was riding out that morning when the trainer, grim-faced, trotted alongside on his hack and quietly told him that Bula was dead.

Brooks, who later left racing, recalls: "I was glad his suffering was over but when I went to work the next day the sight of his empty box was a dreadful thing. He was such a kind, trusting animal, a perfect gentleman in every way."

With Pendil lame and Bula lingering painfully at home in Lambourn, Winter's hopes for the Gold Cup rested with another former Champion hurdler Lanzarote, a thoroughly solid and dependable citizen, who had taken well to fences despite the misgivings of his owner Lord Howard de Walden. Lanzarote had begun the season over hurdles and only switched to fences at the end of November with a creditable and close fourth in the Colonial Cup in South Carolina. Cheltenham, however, is a course that tames lions and for all his undoubted brilliance Lanzarote came to the Gold Cup dangerously ill-prepared for the supreme test, with only three facile successes in novice company.

Royal Frolic, Brown Lad and Colebridge, the first three home the previous year, were all missing. So too was the mercurial Border Incident, so talented but injury-prone. Sore shins left him on the sidelines at Cheltenham. Bannow Rambler started a well supported favourite at 11–4 with Lanzarote next best at 7–2 and the American hope Fort Devon, trained by Fulke Walwyn, at 5–1.

Traditionally the Gold Cup start was staged in a chute below and slightly behind the grandstand. It was a highly unsatisfactory position which had become an anachronism, since those watching at home on television had a much better view than the vast majority of racegoers on the course. In 1977 Capt. Charles Toller, who ran Cheltenham briefly in the seventies, took the eminently sensible decision to move the start area to a point on the course that was visible from the stands. In the process the distance of the race was reduced by 76 yards to exactly three miles and two furlongs.

Tied Cottage, successful over the course a year earlier as a novice, set off at a spanking gallop from the new start.

Tommy Carberry, his jockey, remembers: "He went too fast for his own good. The trouble was if you organised him he'd just get thicker and thicker. I tried a couple of times to talk the horse out of it but he would be away again round another bend, down a hill seeing another fence."

Zarib was an early casualty at the fifth fence, where Davy Lad, sulking at the rear, gave every indication of his increasingly unwilling behaviour. The more Dessie Hughes pushed, shoved and cajoled his mount the less response he seemed to achieve.

The pace set by Tied Cottage claimed a notable and tragic victim. Lanzarote was lying fourth as he approached the ninth fence at the top of the hill, where horses seem to jump out into space as the ground slopes away on the landing side. Inexperience round Cheltenham at such a strong speed now proved Lanzarote's undoing. He failed to rise quite high enough, clipped the top of the fence, stumbled along for several strides, then slithered to the ground, his near hind-leg broken. Bannow Rambler, racing directly behind Lanzarote, was brought down in the mêlée. His jockey Michael Furlong swiftly remounted and gave chase for another circuit but the task was an impossible one and he finally pulled Bannow Rambler up two fences from home.

John Francome waited disconsolately until the racecourse vet arrived to put Lanzarote out of his misery. He recalls: "It was a sad day for everyone connected with the horse. When push came to shove over fences he used to jump very low. He had been hurdling so long he could not round himself properly when jumping. All he did was bend his front legs."

With the first two favourites gone, Tied Cottage sailed on at full steam ahead. Fort Devon fell when a close third at the seventeenth, and as Tied Cottage began to tire, the unconsidered Summerville jumped past him four fences from home. On his day Summerville was a high-class chaser, an exciting, athletic jumper with immense experience; but often his wayward nature clouded his very real ability. For a few heady moments it seemed that this would be his day. Ridden by Jeff King in place of his regular partner Andy Turnell, who was injured, Summerville charged downhill with victory beckoning.

Tommy Carberry confirms: "Summerville came past me running away. I could not believe it."

Far, far behind, Dessie Hughes was close to exhaustion as he continued his battle of attrition with the indolent Davy Lad.

Davy Lad passes Tied Cottage (noseband) at the final fence. Summerville, who broke down badly, is almost obscured by Tied Cottage

Anne Marie McGowan and merry Mick O'Toole united in victory with Sir Desmond Plummer

"With a circuit left I was last and going nowhere. At the fifth last I was still trailing them with the next horse six lengths in front of me. If I had not known Davy Lad I would have given up. I was almost unconscious by then but I knew he was capable of finding something if I could manage to keep riding him."

Only when Davy Lad started to freewheel downhill towards the third last fence did he begin to respond to the very physical message his jockey had been attempting to transmit for the previous two and a half miles through his legs, arms, reins and, it must be said, whip. He was fully fifteen lengths behind Summerville as he soared over that fence but then,

improbably, he was closing rapidly on the two horses still ahead of him.

Jeff King, arguably the finest jump jockey never to be champion, now experienced the anguish of seeing certain victory snatched from his grasp as Summerville broke down suddenly on his near foreleg shortly after jumping the second last fence.

"No ifs or buts. He would have won doing handsprings. He was as lame as if he had broken a leg, but I could not pull up as we were still in front," Jeff King assured me years later. One moment Summerville was winning comfortably. The next the entire complexion of the race changed in a frantic flurry of activity on the run to the final fence.

No sooner had the weary Tied Cottage rejoined poor Summerville than Davy Lad appeared from nowhere, rushed between them, threw an extravagant leap at the last fence and landed a length in front. Victory was his by six lengths from Tied Cottage. Above all it was a triumph for his jockey's supreme fitness and sustained perseverance. Twenty lengths further back Summerville, almost hobbling by then, just held third place from his stable companion April Seventh. The stewards held an inquiry into possible interference by the winner but though Davy Lad had veered towards the stands rail he had been well clear of Tied Cottage at the time.

You could not wish for a more suitable winner of the Gold Cup on St Patrick's Day, but Joe McGowan was not even present to witness the extraordinary triumph of his wife's young chaser. He had a pressing engagement in the saddle elsewhere. Joe had become a wildly enthusiastic amateur after learning to ride at the age of twenty-five and had flown back to Ireland after the first two days of the Festival to partner a warm favourite in a bumper race at Limerick on Thursday.

Davy Lad followed the depressing pattern of so many young winners of the Cheltenham Gold Cup.

He broke down quite badly after running lifelessly on several occasions the following season. He was given a long rest after his tendons were injected in an unusual attempt at a cure but there was never any question of his racing again. So Davy Lad retired at the early age of eight to a pleasantly undemanding life at the McGowans' Dollandstown Stud near Maynooth and later moved with them to their new home at the Hollywood Rath Stud close to Fairyhouse. When Davy Lad was afflicted with arthritis at the relatively young age of fourteen in 1984 the McGowans accepted the advice of their vet Paddy Kelly that he should be put down. The horse was buried at the bottom of the garden beside their much loved labrador Sheba.

Joe McGowan developed into such a proficient horseman that he won a bronze medal for the Irish team at the 1989 European Three Day Eventing championship at Burghley. He also enjoyed the luck of two more Festival winners, Parkhill and Hartstown, trained, of course, by the irrepressible Mick O'Toole.

"Davy Lad was always a character, so tough, but he became an old scoundrel," reflects Mick O'Toole. It is a statement offered with obvious affection.

PIPER CHAMPAGNE CHELTENHAM GOLD CUP. March 17th 1977. £21,990. *Soft.*

1 Davy Lad	7 12 0	D. Hughes	14–1
2 Tied Cottage	9 12 0	T. Carberry	20–1
3 Summerville	11 12 0	J. King	15–1
4 April Seventh	11 12 0	S. C. Knight	66–1
5 Fort Fox	8 12 0	F. Berry	10–1
6 Tamalin	10 12 0	J. J. O'Neill	11–1
7 Master H	8 12 0	Mr J. Weston	66–1

6 lengths, 20. Owned Mrs J. McGowan. Trained M. O'Toole. Bred Mrs K. Westropp-Bennett. 7m. 13.8 seconds. Also 11–4 Fav Bannow Rambler (M. Furlong) B.D., 7–2 Lanzarote (J. Francome) Fell, 5 Fort Devon (W. Smith) Fell, 12 Zarib (R. Evans) Fell, 50 Even Up (R. Champion) P.U., 66 Banlieu (B. R. Davies) P.U. 13 ran. Tote win: £1.09.

Davy Lad: b.g. 1970 (David Jack–Chateau)

12

MIDNIGHT COURT
(1978)

IF A WEEK IN POLITICS IS perceived as a long time, a month in racing can seem an eternity. Certainly the nature of the 1978 Gold Cup changed substantially when an unscripted and unwelcome blanket of snow enveloped Cheltenham shortly before dawn on Thursday, March 16th. After the first two absorbing days at the Festival meeting the Irish invasion force was on an unstoppable roll with six winners already, including the gallant little colt Monksfield in the Champion Hurdle. With five Gold Cup contenders led by the imposing Brown Lad on the morrow the visitors were confident of yet another famous victory as they mulled over the prospects in hundreds of noisy pubs, bars and hotels that wintry night. The weather was to prove the only winner at Cheltenham on this occasion and when we all assembled again at the course in mid-April the balance of chance had rolled unerringly against the horses that made the journey for a second time across the Irish Sea.

The busily efficient clerk of the course Philip Arkwright, formerly of the Royal Dragoons and in charge at the Festival for the first time, woke at his home near Banbury at around 3 a.m. on Thursday horrified to see snow falling heavily. He set off gallantly through the blizzard towards Cheltenham, 35 miles away, with all possible haste until he was halted by a jack-knifed lorry near Northleach.

Frustrated and increasingly anxious he alerted various disbelieving racecourse worthies from an isolated call-box before displaying sound military initiative by following a gritting lorry slowly, and sometimes hazardously, on the few remaining miles of his torturous journey to snowbound Prestbury Park. He arrived there at 6.15 to discover snow drifting up to the tops of some fences. When a lone steward Tim Holland-Martin joined the forlorn clerk of the course shortly before dawn the pair had no alterna-

tive but to abandon the final day of the Festival.

The Irish, being far more flexible about these things, just put back racing for a day or two until the weather improves. Many visitors felt that the superb card on the final day of the meeting could have been run either on the Friday or Saturday when a rapid thaw had done its job. Unhappily the heavy racing programme here dictates that we are far too rigid in these matters though the authorities are keener nowadays to preserve the better prizes lost to the weather. Four key races were abandoned that day but at least the Gold Cup and Daily Express Triumph Hurdle were added to the card on April 12th, the first of a two-day meeting at Cheltenham.

The unexpected white-out was not the only drama at Cheltenham that year. On Wednesday, just as he was preparing to leave for home after racing, John Francome, the dashing, curly-haired jockey who was to be champion seven times, was summoned by a bowler-hatted official to attend an investigation by two Jockey Club security men in the presence of his chief employer Fred Winter. Questions were asked about his association with the bookmaker John Banks, a man who had maintained a very high public profile ever since he described betting shops as licences to print money. During the interrogation the jockey readily admitted to discussing with Banks some of the horses he rode and to visiting the bookmaker's home. Inevitably the matter was referred to the stewards of the Jockey Club at Portman Square in London.

Both trainer and jockey found the interview unpleasant and embarrassing. As they left the room Francome assured Winter that he had never deliberately prevented a horse from winning a race. The great trainer, invariably at his best in a crisis, was a formidable sight when angered. His eyes would nar-

A Christmas card scene at Cheltenham on the day of the 1978 Gold Cup

row until you appeared to be facing a chilling, unforgiving gun-fighter, an assassin peering through the tiniest gun-slits.

Now he replied, memorably: "Son, if I thought anything else you would be lying there on the floor."

Until the icy weather intervened the pair held high hopes of winning the Gold Cup the very next day with Olive Jackson's emerging star Midnight Court. John Francome has always possessed the raw courage to face any challenge head-on, but that was one day he did not mind that racing could not take place.

"Yes, I was more relieved than disappointed. I did not fancy having to go back to Cheltenham to face the music," he confirms in that naturally open way of his.

A whiff of something slightly improper was in the air, though if you believed the wildly inaccurate reporting at the time you might have sensed something much graver. Fred Winter had his say two days later. Horses that have been trained for a specific target all season cannot stand idle for a month. Sensibly Fred had entered Midnight Court in a valuable race at Chepstow on the Saturday after Cheltenham . . . just in case. He ran and won there, ridden, intriguingly, by the former champion Graham Thorner. Francome, suitably chastened, was despatched instead to Lingfield for rather more humble duty. It was the trainer's way of giving his jockey a stern warning.

Francome recalls: "I was livid at being taken off Midnight Court. It never crossed my mind Fred would do it but he was obviously annoyed with me. He was all right after that though I did wonder for a while if I would be back on the horse in the Gold Cup."

George and Olive Jackson were the best possible type of owner. Generous, patient and understanding, the only instruction they issued to their jockeys was to come back safely. They had a series of good horses with Fred Winter in the seventies and early eighties. Midnight Court, an athletic bay with modest form over hurdles in Ireland, was to prove the best. He was one of an endless stream of cavalry nurtured, then exported, by that astute horse master Tom Costello at Newmarket-on-Fergus near Limerick. Bred at Tim Rogers' Airlie Stud, Midnight Court was by the Ascot Gold Cup winner Twilight Alley out of Strumpet, who won a modest mile and a half maiden race at Catterick. She cost Rogers 860 guineas as a three-year-old and was later exported to Sweden.

Fred Winter was a regular customer of Tom Costello's at the time. He liked Midnight Court as a four-year-old and when the horse began to show form over hurdles he returned to Ireland to buy him twelve months later.

Costello recalls: "Fred sat on Midnight Court and also saw him schooled. I told him he would not see the best of the horse until he jumped fences. He was a great 'lepper' and a decent horse when he got his ground; but he could not *walk* in the soft."

As soon as he began galloping seriously at his new stable it became clear the Irish import was exceptional and he duly won with impressive ease over hurdles on his debut here at Chepstow in November 1976.

John Francome recollects appreciatively: "He worked like a decent horse from the start and the whole yard had a right touch on him first time."

Midnight Court proved a natural when put to fences, improved immeasurably after a summer's break and by the time of the Gold Cup was unbeaten in six races that season. Other horses, prepared for the biggest test of all at Cheltenham in March, ran, like Midnight Court, elsewhere. Brown Lad returned home to make racing history by becoming the first horse to win the Irish Grand National three times. Aged twelve, carrying 12 st. 2 lb on the soft ground that was by then so crucial to his performance, he beat Sand Pit, in receipt of 30 lb, by three-quarters of a length. Fort Fox was a creditable fourth but Bannow Rambler, a third refugee from the Festival, ran poorly.

The alarmingly free Tied Cottage, second in the 1977 Gold Cup, raced instead at Aintree, led the Grand National field at a suicidal pace before succumbing heavily and spectacularly at the infamous sixth fence, Becher's Brook. Neither he nor Bannow Rambler would be coming back to Cheltenham that season. Others who dropped out on the second occasion included Gay Spartan and Uncle Bing.

When the Gold Cup survivors did reassemble on April 12th the ground was notably faster than it had been a month earlier. The American chaser Fort Devon, in splendid form all season, started favourite at 2–1. Midnight Court, aged seven and running in only his eleventh steeplechase, wore a special bit to prevent his tongue escaping over it. He was a solid second favourite at 5–2. Bachelor's Hall, winner of the Mackeson and Hennessy Gold Cups and the King George VI Chase, and old Brown Lad were the only others seriously backed, though there was a flicker of interest in the 1976 winner Royal Frolic, who had been showing some of his previous sparkle after recovering from a leg injury. Bill Smith, once of Moss Bross and the rider of Fort Devon, was so confident that he declined John Francome's suggestion that the winning jockey should buy the loser a suit.

The going was to prove the decisive factor that day. It was much too quick for Brown Lad, who was soon toiling at the rear as Fort Devon led from Forest King and Fort Fox at a steady pace. Further back Midnight Court had settled well, to his jockey's relief.

John Francome, arguably the most naturally talented jockey ever to ride over fences, recalls: "He was a really good jumper and never gave me a moment's worry. He stayed, quickened up like a dream and you could do what you liked with him."

Fort Fox was dropping back when he shed his jockey at the fifteenth fence and as Brown Lad continued to struggle to stay in touch Royal Frolic was the first to press the leader in the final mile. Midnight Court, too, closed up rapidly, running downhill for the final time, and slipped through into the lead on the inside as Fort Devon, perhaps feeling the ground, hung right-handed away from the rails.

"Midnight Court was running a bit lazily but when I gave him a couple of cracks he zipped up Bill Smith's inner," relates Francome laconically.

Clear over the last two fences Midnight Court maintained his gallop to the winning post where John Francome, in a rare and uncharacteristic display of bitterness, flashed a "V" sign at the Press stand. Royal Frolic was still second between the last two fences when John Burke felt him falter. The final fence was enticingly close. Royal Frolic tried valiantly to pop over it, failed to rise high enough, and crashed to the ground in a grave-digger of a fall. He lay exhausted for several minutes, shaken and winded, before rising unsteadily to his feet. As Fort Devon slowed on the punishing hill Brown Lad, his stamina at last coming into play, thundered past to claim second prize in a tight finish with Master H and Bachelor's Hall.

The racing world shared Fred Winter's delight at winning a Gold Cup as a trainer after so many crushing disappointments down the years. John Francome, too, was visibly pleased for the man who had stood solidly by him in his hour of need.

He asserts: "Our horse improved all year. I think he would have won on the original date of the race."

Had the Banks case been held sooner John Francome would not have ridden Midnight Court in the 1978 Gold Cup but the Jockey Club is not noted for the speed of its inquiries and the date was eventually set for the end of April. The verdict? Francome was banned for the rest of the season, effectively five and a half weeks, and fined £750, for passing information for favours. The sentence imposed on Banks was, by comparison, extreme. Found guilty of surreptitiously obtaining information about a trial, he was banned from racing for three years and fined £2,500.

Like so many precocious Gold Cup winners before

Midnight Court and John Francome win the rescheduled race a month later

and since Midnight Court never again reached the degree of excellence he displayed throughout that season. A niggling problem behind a knee prevented him running the following winter. When he did race again at the end of 1979 he was soundly beaten twice. Later he was fired on both front legs in an attempt to heal a strained tendon. He did win once more, over hurdles, in January 1981, but in subsequent races the spark that once made him such a fine steeplechaser seemed to have been all but extinguished. He fell three times later that season and was the last weary finisher in the 1981 Gold Cup.

It seemed like the end. However, the Jacksons thought it might be worth one last try as a hunter. So late in the autumn of 1981 he was sent to Lionel Enstone's livery yard at Saltby to qualify with the Belvoir pack. It proved an inspired move. In his final season as a racehorse Midnight Court, by then eleven, and ridden by Winter's son-in-law Oliver Sherwood, an outstanding amateur of his day, won all three of his hunter chases with much of his former élan.

Each summer the old horse would return to George and Olive Jackson's home for a long holiday.

Their son Bruce, harbouring ambitions to ride in point-to-points, kept a horse for that purpose with Enstone while still a schoolboy. But his hopes that he might enjoy a spectacular debut as a jockey on his mother's Gold Cup hero between the flags were dashed when the horse fell heavily while schooling. Midnight Court tore muscles and ligaments on his back and hip in that fall. His racing days were over. Nursed back to fitness by Mary Bromily he embarked on a more permanent role as a hunter, first for a season in Dorset, then later for two and a half seasons with the Cotley Harriers, one of the last private packs in the country. Usually he was ridden by Claire Baskett, but such was his adaptability he was sometimes used as a spare horse by the Master and Huntsman of the Cotley, Vivian Eames.

Only when his hip injury began to give trouble again did Midnight Court return to the Jacksons' home at Letcombe Bassett near Wantage into complete retirement. In his final years he was looked after with much devotion by Mike Poole and was put down painlessly in the top paddock nearest to his owner's house in September 1989.

PIPER CHAMPAGNE CHELTENHAM GOLD CUP.   April 12th 1978.   £23,827.50.   *Good.*

1	Midnight Court	7 12 0	J. Francome	5–2
2	Brown Lad	12 12 0	T. Carberry	8–1
3	Master H	9 12 0	R. Crank	18–1
4	Bachelor's Hall	8 12 0	M. O'Halloran	7–1
5	Fort Devon	12 12 0	W. Smith	2–1 Fav
6	Cancello	9 12 0	D. Atkins	45–1

7 lengths, 1.   Owned Mrs O. Jackson.   Trained F. T. Winter.   Bred Airlie Stud.
6m. 57.3 seconds.   Also 11 Royal Frolic (J. Burke) Fell, 20 Fort Fox (T. McGivern) U.R., 50 Otter Way (J. King) P.U., 80 Forest King (J. J. O'Neill) P.U.   10 ran.   Tote win: 42p.

Midnight Court: b.g. 1971 (Twilight Alley–Strumpet)

13

ALVERTON

(1979)

THE ENDURING APPEAL OF JUMP racing is the cosy familiarity you can establish with the hardy performers who race year in year out for our pleasure. The best flat racehorses usually charge across the stage like a meteor and are then invariably rushed off to stud with indecent haste. Like very grand cousins they are seen so seldom it is impossible to know them well or appreciate them fully.

Alverton, so versatile and willing, was one of those horses who demanded admiration. Despite a series of injuries and setbacks he kept coming back each winter to display a resolution and toughness of spirit that proved a shining advertisement for steeplechasing. In another life Alverton might have been a gritty Yorkshire sergeant in the last war, resolute, uncompromising, outstandingly courageous and impervious to pain.

Like so many of canny Peter Easterby's finest jumpers Alverton began racing on the flat. His dam, Alvertona, owned by a Yorkshire farmer, Bill Pratt, won twice as a two-year-old over six furlongs and later a mile in 1965. She was also trained by Easterby. Alverton, by the Cambridgeshire winner Midsummer Night II, was her second foal. Big and backward, he was cut as a two-year-old and then bought from Pratt by Easterby, who later sold him on for £1,500 to one of his established owners Stanhope Joel, with a contingency that if he won a race he would double the purchase price. The deal was done by Paddy Brudenell-Bruce who managed the racing interests of Joel, his elderly father-in-law. Stanhope Joel lived for much of the year on his own idyllic Caribbean retreat, Perot's Island. He had been an owner for many years and his vivid green and pink striped colours had been carried to countless victories, the vast majority on the flat. He also owned the 1962 Whitbread Gold Cup winner Frenchman's Cove.

Alverton ran once as a two-year-old over six furlongs, an experience which is not normally required of future Cheltenham Gold Cup winners. He won three times the following autumn, exhibiting the qualities of honesty, enthusiasm and stamina that would endear him to many racegoers in the years ahead. He also won twice over hurdles that winter, ridden by the ageless Paddy Broderick with the looks and style of a battered policeman. It was old Paddy who felt Alverton go badly lame and pulled him up at Newcastle in February 1974. There had not been any previous hint of leg trouble but the horse had broken down badly on both forelegs. After being fired and rested he did not race again until October 1975. Within a month he was winning again on the flat and over hurdles.

It was a prelude to a year of roistering success in 1976 when he continually defied the handicapper. Alverton won seven races on the flat that year and was second in the Tote Ebor at York, Easterby's local meeting, dividing Sir Montagu, later second in the French St Leger, and Shangamuzo, who subsequently won the Ascot Gold Cup.

When Stanhope Joel died in October 1975, Alverton was left to his widow and three daughters, who collectively became owners of the Snailwell Stud. Since Tilly Jones, the youngest of the three, lived in sun-kissed Bermuda she sold her share to another sister, Dana Brudenell-Bruce, and for the rest of his life Alverton raced in the name and colours, pink and green checks, of the Snailwell Stud.

When Alverton reached an impossibly high position in the handicap over hurdles Easterby switched him to fences at the start of 1978 with spectacular results. He was ridden by the dynamic young Irish jockey Jonjo O'Neill, who set a new record total of 149 winners when he became champion for the first time in 1978.

So to Cheltenham where he won the Arkle Chase in typically dogged fashion. Alverton ended the season unbeaten in four races over fences. The sky now seemed the limit for this attractive horse with such natural jumping ability allied to his frequently demonstrated class on the flat.

"Bye he was a tough hoss and thrived on racing," reflects Easterby admiringly.

Thus Alverton began the winter of 1978 on everyone's list of twelve horses to follow. You could not name a more suitable candidate, yet he started with

four successive defeats. He was beaten by Silver Buck at Wetherby and brought down by a faller next time out. Alverton then felt the full force of the handicapper's scales as he failed, narrowly and honourably, to concede weight at Sandown to Diamond Edge, later to win the Whitbread and Hennessy Gold Cups. Since stamina was clearly not a problem Peter Easterby entered his jaunty chaser in both the Cheltenham Gold Cup and Grand National.

Early in March Alverton recorded his first victory of the season in the Greenall Whitley Breweries Chase at Haydock, a race that Royal Frolic had won

Drama in the snow

on his way to Cheltenham two years earlier. The manner of his very easy defeat of Rambling Artist by twelve lengths in soggy conditions offered compelling evidence that Alverton should be taken very seriously indeed in calculations for the Gold Cup twelve days hence.

Like so many owners Dana Brudenell-Bruce, elegant and extremely knowledgeable, had misgivings about risking her family's horse in the Grand National. She confirms: "After Alverton won the Greenall Whitley he had to go for the Gold Cup. I was so relieved that he would not have to run in the Grand National."

Alverton was not Easterby's sole card in the race that year. Night Nurse, twice winner of the Champion Hurdle, had taken notably well to fences, with five consecutive successes before a rare defeat by Silver Buck in a severely punishing duel at Haydock the day before Alverton's victory. Both Easterby horses were looked after by the same lad, Jack Warrell, who chose, out of loyalty, to lead up Night Nurse at the Festival.

A 20–1 chance a week earlier, Alverton started joint 5–1 favourite with old Brown Lad, by then thir-

Tied Cottage crumples to the ground at the last fence

teen, partly because so many serious contenders dropped out in the final days before the Festival. Gay Spartan, comfortable winner of the King George VI Chase, stood as short as 9–4 but pulled up lame at exercise on the Saturday before Cheltenham. Jack of Trumps, backed by his owner the intrepid J. P. McManus to win an estimated £200,000, was also a late casualty with a muscle strain. The 1977 winner Davy Lad had been retired and leg trouble ruled out Midnight Court. The enigmatic Border Incident was once again missing; he would not appear until April. Yet another likely contender, Diamond Edge, was in-

jured on the eve of the race. A further crucial absentee was the much travelled Grand Canyon, who damaged a leg at Ascot in December soon after winning the Colonial Cup in South Carolina.

Tommy Carberry, significantly, chose to partner Tied Cottage, a 12–1 chance, in preference to Brown Lad. Night Nurse stood at 6–1 with Gaffer, a massive, long-striding horse, who despite his experience was held in the highest regard by his trainer Fulke Walwyn. There was quiet confidence in Royal Mail, bred in New Zealand and the winner of the P. Z. Mower Chase on his previous outing. Royal Frolic,

Alverton gallops on to victory

back again, was on offer at 20–1 after several indifferent displays.

The going was already heavy when the meeting opened on the old course. By Thursday the weather was unspeakable, with the hint of a blizzard adding to the hazards as Tied Cottage dashed off in front as though the hounds of hell were at his heels. It looked a suicidal gallop in the prevailing conditions but Tied Cottage raced best when allowed his head and Tommy Carberry, perched boldly up his neck, knew it would be pointless to attempt restraint.

"The horse was so impatient you just sat on him and hoped he realised that if he did not do something at a fence he was going to have a fierce fall. If only he had relaxed a bit more to preserve something for the finish," he laments.

Tied Cottage had stretched the field to breaking point by half-way. Those who chased him early on were soon displaying signs of distress and as he galloped towards the third last fence still well clear of Royal Mail and Alverton it seemed that he could not be caught.

Jonjo O'Neill recalls: "I was racing flat to the boards from a mile out, yet Tommy still seemed a long way ahead. I doubted if I would get to him."

Tommy Carberry was concerned to find that Alverton was making ground when he stole a quick peep as he came round the elbow, but while he concentrated on preserving his lead the picture behind was changing dramatically. As Royal Mail dropped away Alverton was the only one left to pose a challenge and suddenly he was closing fast on the tired leader. The gap was down to barely three lengths at the second last as Jonjo O'Neill pulled Alverton to the middle of the course to avoid being brought down if Tied Cottage fell.

Between the last two fences Tommy Carberry chanced one last peep over his right shoulder. What he saw must have turned his heart to stone.

"Ten strides off the last Jonjo's arriving beside me and my lad had nothing left in the tank. He felt as though he was clean out of petrol," he relates expressively.

So the protagonists, the hunter and the hunted, came to the fateful last fence. Tied Cottage ran in a little too close. Alverton, in contrast, took off fully a stride further away than his rider anticipated. For a moment the two horses were in the air together in ghostly unison, their shapes merging with the swirling snow that covered Cleeve Hill behind them.

Poor, exhausted Tied Cottage clipped the peak of the birch then capsized in a crumpled, steaming heap. Beside him the lion-hearted Alverton landed steeply but safely and set off up the final, daunting hill in splendid isolation. Few, if any horses had earned a Gold Cup more than Alverton with the thickly calloused front legs and unquenchable will to win.

Jonjo O'Neill, his devoted rider, insists: "To make up all that ground and reach the leader Alverton gave me more than any jockey had a right to expect. Even though he was very tired he stood so far off the last fence I could not believe we would reach the other side."

Who would have won if both horses had stayed on their feet? The betting would surely favour Alverton. If you press Tommy Carberry he does not disagree.

"Tied Cottage was unconscious as he took off. I left him alone and was just hanging on to everything I had. He lay down rather than fell," he explains.

Moments later Royal Mail popped laboriously over the final fence.

Carberry adds "Even then I half thought of re-mounting and trying for third place because they took half an hour to reach me but I did not fancy carrying Tied Cottage up the hill. He was so shaken he lay there whinnying."

Eventually Aldaniti and Bob Champion scrambled past the heaving figure of Tied Cottage to claim third prize. Their day would come gloriously and unforgettably at Aintree two years later. Only four other horses finished in that momentous Gold Cup. Many of us, transfixed by its stunning climax, waited anxiously in the stands until Tied Cottage clambered shakily to his feet.

Fate dealt Alverton the cruellest reward for recovering so readily from his exertions that day. He was, of course, still in the Grand National on an undeniably tempting mark of 10 st. 13 lb. As a Gold Cup winner he would never be so generously handicapped again. Peter Easterby broached the subject with Dana Brudenell-Bruce. Though her instincts dictated otherwise she could not fault her trainer's logic. The horse had a wonderful chance at the weights and was in vibrant form after Cheltenham. He had to run. It was an entirely professional decision and the correct one.

She relates: "Though I was apprehensive about risking such a class horse in the race I could not refuse. Peter was right."

The sporting policy of running the Gold Cup winner sixteen days later in the Grand National looked fully justified as Alverton, going supremely easily among the leaders on the second circuit, approached Becher's Brook, the most infamous fence in the world. Sensibly Jonjo O'Neill took him towards the outside of the fence where the drop is less pronounced.

There was no warning of the horror to come. Alverton, such a safe and secure jumper, simply galloped full-tilt into the solid fence, turned a ghastly somersault and was already dead as he crashed to the ground on the landing side. Eye-witnesses, including Bob Champion, who had fallen at the same fence on the first circuit, believe Alverton suffered a heart attack as he prepared to jump Becher's.

"It is the most likely explanation because the horse never attempted to take off and did not move once he came down," explains Champion.

The hideous misfortune that claimed Alverton's life so prematurely cannot be blamed on the Grand National or its much maligned fences. Though the worst fears of Dana Brudenell-Bruce had been realised she could take bleak consolation from the manner of his passing.

"At least he died doing something he enjoyed," she reflects sombrely.

PIPER CHAMPAGNE CHELTENHAM GOLD CUP. March 15th 1979. £30,293.75. *Heavy.*

1	Alverton	9 12 0	J. J. O'Neill	5–1 J. Fav
2	Royal Mail	9 12 0	P. Blacker	7–1
3	Aldaniti	9 12 0	R. Champion	40–1
4	Casamayor	9 12 0	B. R. Davies	50–1
5	Brown Lad	13 12 0	G. Dowd	5–1 J. Fav
6	Gaffer	7 12 0	W. Smith	6–1
7	Night Nurse	8 12 0	G. Thorner	6–1

25 lengths, 20. Owned the Snailwell Stud. Trained M. H. Easterby. Bred G. W. Pratt. 7m. 1 second. Also 10 Strombolus (J. Francome) P.U., 12 Tied Cottage (T. Carberry) Fell, 20 Royal Frolic (J. Burke) P.U., 50 Bawnogues (C. Smith) P.U., Mighty's Honour (F. Berry) P.U. and Otter Way (D. Goulding) P.U., 100 Bit of Manny (R. Evans) P.U. 14 ran. Tote win: 44p.

Alverton: ch.g. 1970 (Midsummer Night II–Alvertona)

14

MASTER SMUDGE
(1980)

THE RACE FOR THE 1980 Cheltenham Gold Cup produced an unparalleled tale of two winners. Initially the tearaway Tied Cottage deservedly gained his reward for so many sturdy performances at Cheltenham. When the results of the compulsory post-race urine sample were published, however, it was revealed that traces of a prohibited substance had been discovered. The findings of the analytical chemists left those that sit in judgement on the matter with no alternative. In May Tied Cottage was disqualified and the race awarded to Master Smudge, a horse once sold by his breeder to a band of travelling gypsies for some cases of whisky.

It was an unsatisfactory but inevitable conclusion to a contentious case, since everyone present at Cheltenham would testify that they had witnessed overwhelming evidence of the superiority of Tied Cottage on the day.

It was his second memorable feat inside a year, for only two weeks after Alverton's death the spirit of steeplechasing had been movingly demonstrated by the victory of Anthony Stanley Robinson on Tied Cottage, his own horse, in the 1979 Irish Distillers Grand National. Robinson, a Midlands businessman with a consuming passion for jump racing, had been ill with cancer for some time. It was not generally known that the English authorities, in their wisdom, were so concerned about his health after a major operation that they declined to renew his amateur's licence.

Displaying his usual enterprise and vigour Robinson merely changed his tactics, applied for an Irish licence and received it in time to partner Tied Cottage in the Irish Grand National in place of Tommy Carberry, who had broken an ankle.

Carberry, the impish professional, says graciously: "Tied Cottage relaxed better in front for Anthony than anyone. Nobody was more entitled to ride the horse."

At Fairyhouse in mid-April the horse was certainly fitter than his wildly enthusiastic forty-one-year-old rider. Together they led at a roaring gallop for more than three miles until headed at the second last fence by Prince Rock. A formidable battle ensued. Prince Rock still held a slender advantage over the last but was immediately pressed again by Tied Cottage.

"Stylish" is certainly not the first adjective that would leap to mind to describe Anthony Robinson's riding, but years of practice had made him pretty effective in a finish and now, close to exhaustion, he forced Tied Cottage back in front in the nick of time.

As an example of triumph over adversity Anthony Robinson's feat stands unrivalled in the history of jump racing in Ireland. Typically he shunned publicity and insisted that his illness should not be mentioned.

Robinson bought Tied Cottage as a four-year-old at Doncaster sales. Bred by Aynsley Ridley on his farm in Northumberland, Tied Cottage was by the Yorkshire Cup winner Honour Bound out of an unraced mare Cottage Ray, who had cost Ridley £200. Sent to Doncaster for the first time as a rather small, lively three-year-old Tied Cottage was bought for 800 guineas by Hugh Williams, son of Evan Williams who had won the Gold Cup twice as a jockey.

Hugh relates: "He was a lovely, quality horse but a complete header to break ... a total fruit and nut case. He spent his time bucking off his riders."

Word of such wilful behaviour spread quickly around the sales ring when Williams took the horse back to Doncaster a year later. Robinson virtually stole Tied Cottage for only 650 guineas. The vendor made a thumping loss after keeping him for a year.

Anthony Robinson kept his horses in Ireland with Dan Moore, who had guided L'Escargot so astutely. Tied Cottage continued to be a handful with Dan Moore but his owner, who took his business very seriously indeed, would fly over frequently to ride him at exercise whenever possible. Twice in those early years Tied Cottage and his owner disappeared from the wide open spaces of the Curragh at an alarming pace.

Tommy Carberry, his brown eyes twinkling merrily, chuckles: "One morning we were searching for them in a fog for ages. The horse just took off and flew across roads and crossings. Once he got into a gallop the strongest man in the world could not hold him."

Undeterred, Anthony Robinson rode Tied Cottage on his debut over hurdles at Fairyhouse. Since neither brakes nor steering were functioning correctly the combination parted company abruptly at the very first flight. A fortnight later Dan Moore ran four in the same race at Punchestown with Cathal Finnegan given the task of educating the arm-wrenching Tied Cottage. They won, unfancied and unbacked, at 33–1.

Tied Cottage then missed a year with back trouble, but he returned as boisterously hard-pulling as ever. Though Anthony Robinson won over hurdles on him he hoped that fences might cure the horse's impetuous nature. Small, barely 16 hands, strongly built and short in front Tied Cottage attacked his schooling fences with gay abandon. He proved an invigorating ride and won three chases that first season, including the Sun Alliance Chase at the Festival.

The next year he finished second to Davy Lad in the Gold Cup, was second behind Billycan in the Irish Grand National and ended an eventful campaign with an honourable display in the French Grand National.

By the time of the 1980 Cheltenham Gold Cup, sponsored for the first time by the Tote, Tied Cottage was twelve. He had not won a single race during the season but his manner of racing was still as recklessly energetic as ever. The betting at Cheltenham that year favoured Diamond Edge, who had beaten Tied Cottage decisively at Sandown early in February. Jack of Trumps, ridden by Jonjo O'Neill, was again strongly supported in the market by his owner J. P. McManus but another rising Irish star Bright Highway was out of action. The jet-black Border Incident, a thrillingly athletic jumper, came to the race for the

first time aged ten after many injuries, setbacks and disappointments.

Every racehorse yields a story, but none of the runners in 1980 could possibly match the implausible sequence of events that had brought the 14–1 chance Master Smudge to Cheltenham as the main hope of the West Country. His sire Master Stephen was an obscure premium stallion and his dam an untalented mare, Lily Pond II, whose only success came in 1960 at 100–1 in a maiden point-to-point run by the Cattistock Hunt at a course near Yeovil that has long since been closed.

His breeder Henry Radford, who sported a black patch over one eye, ran a smallholding in Somerset. Unimpressed by the small and wiry produce of his mare he sold him to a band of travelling gypsies for a quantity of whisky!

Soon afterwards a local pig farmer John Tarr spotted Master Smudge tethered beside a gypsy camp as he drove one morning along the road between Martock and Crewkerne. He turned back, asked if the lean and hungry chestnut might be for sale, and after some spirited haggling bought the future Gold Cup winner for £75.

In his role as a haulier Arthur Barrow used to take some of John Tarr's pigs to market each week. When he saw Master Smudge cantering across a muddy field at the farm he, too, asked if the horse was for sale. John Tarr wanted £400. Arthur Barrow offered £300. A deal was finally agreed at £312, plus, for luck, the head-collar he was wearing!

"He was not a picture postcard but I bought him as a speculation on the way he moved," relates Barrow by way of explanation of one of the steeplechasing bargains of the century.

Although his father Ken held a permit to train at the family's 30-acre farm in the lee of the Quantock Hills Arthur Barrow was not experienced in the ways of racing. His new purchase tended to walk up the country lanes on his hind legs when he was broken in and was trained on his own for the very good reason that his owner did not possess any other horses at the time. The initial entry Barrow made for Master Smudge was in a selling hurdle. Fate intervened when a hiccup in the registration of the horse's name prevented him running.

Master Smudge raced for the first time instead in a novices' hurdle at Taunton in April 1976, led from half-way and though collared on the flat finished an eye-catching third.

Tied Cottage jumps the final fence safely this time and is well clear of Approaching

Barrow recalls, "I was ashamed of the way he looked in the paddock but it did not affect his performance. If he had run in a seller he must have won and I would have lost him."

In the following years Master Smudge raced frequently and effectively over all types of distances and ground. The leaner he looked the better he performed. Some of his wins from the front were spectacular.

"He had half a dozen eggs and an apple in his feed every day but unless you could count his ribs at twenty paces there was no point in taking him to the races," asserts Barrow who took over the permit when his father died. Briefly the horse was on the market but though several high-flying trainers expressed an interest none came up with a firm offer.

Master Smudge took an uncomfortably long time to adapt to jumping fences. He made frequent mistakes at open ditches and shed his jockey in three of his first four steeplechases, but he usually kept his feet and was always running on at the end of his races. By the end of the season he ranked with the very best after beating Sweet September and Silver Buck in the Sun Alliance Chase and then finishing a close second to Diamond Edge in the Whitbread Gold Cup. He was far from a forlorn outsider when he returned to Prestbury Park for the 1980 Cheltenham Gold Cup, run once more on heavy going.

Tied Cottage, who else, scorched into a lead he would never relinquish. Older and a little wiser, perhaps, he was no longer quite so impossibly headstrong. Even so the pace he set led to considerable carnage as the chasing pack tried to close the gap in the second half of the race. The Vintner fell at the fifteenth fence, Diamond Edge blundered several times and Border Incident, moving sweetly in fourth place, hit the seventeenth fence, the final ditch, so hard that he ejected John Francome like a spent cartridge.

"We were running away at the time. The only question was how far we would win," reported Francome.

Much further back, Master Smudge misjudged the same fence and almost came down. Royal Mail fell in third place at the next fence, bringing down Jack of Trumps and then hampering Approaching.

Turning downhill, Tied Cottage was briefly pressed by Diamond Edge and then by Approaching. At this stage Master Smudge, though staying on as usual, was still far behind in seventh place. A soaring leap at the penultimate fence sealed victory for Tied Cottage. This time he was the one who came up the hill alone with Tommy Carberry sitting motionless in his moment of triumph. Fifteen-year-old Mac Vidi, owned, bred and trained at her guest house on the edge of Dartmoor by Pam Neal, was plodding into second place until Master Smudge, wearing his customary fluffy white noseband, swept past on the hill. Only six finished.

The bombshell exploded a fortnight later. Dan Moore's wife Joan, at Aintree for the Grand National meeting, was informed by the Irish Turf Club that traces of a prohibited substance, theobromine, had been detected in the post-race urine sample of Tied Cottage. Caffeine and theobromine had also been found in the samples of two of Mick O'Toole's runners at Cheltenham, Chinrullah, easy winner of the Queen Mother Champion Chase on the Wednesday and fifth in the Gold Cup the following day, and Kilkilwell, third in the Kim Muir. All faced certain disqualification.

Poor Anthony Robinson's first indication of impending disaster came from a newspaper hoarding as he was departing by train to Liverpool. Arthur Barrow was contacted by a newspaper reporter on the telephone at Chippenham market as he waited to collect some cattle.

It transpired that nothing improper had occurred. Extensive investigations revealed that the source of the prohibited substances was a batch of cocoa shells transported in a cargo ship. On its next journey from Rotterdam to Ireland the boat carried soya beans, which are the protein source of racehorse nuts. Traces of cocoa remained in the cargo hold, with distressing results for the connections of several horses that ran at Cheltenham.

The minute amounts of the illegal particles in all three horses were not sufficient to make a mouse run faster, let alone enhance the performance of a racehorse. The Jockey Club, however, was hidebound by its rules and all three Irish horses were formally disqualified at an inquiry on May 21st, though no blame was attached to any trainer.

So Master Smudge was officially declared the winner of the 1980 Gold Cup. Anthony Robinson, typically, insisted on paying trainer and jockey their full percentage of the prize money that he would have received.

Joan Moore insists, quite rightly: "The disqualification was ridiculous because the amount found in

*The eventual winners of the 1980
Gold Cup, Master Smudge and
Richard Hoare*

Tied Cottage was infinitesimal, but under the rules there was nothing we could do."

As soon as the verdict was known, Anthony Robinson sportingly rang Arthur Barrow to arrange a suitable date to hand over the Gold Cup. At first they considered making the exchange at a motorway service station but eventually the trophy was presented to Arthur Barrow by Dame Elizabeth Ackroyd, a director of the Tote, and Robinson at a brief ceremony at Warwick's final jump meeting on May 26th.

Barrow and his wife Pauline later threw a party in the village hall for the entire population of Over Stowey. With the money from Master Smudge's many victories he built more stables, sold his lorries, became a public trainer and converted some old farm buildings into attractive holiday flats.

He reflects: "We were absolutely delighted to finish second and the last thing I wanted was to win in that way, though I think Master Smudge deserved a bit more credit at the time.

"Anthony Robinson was a gentleman throughout. The biggest regret of my life was to win the Gold Cup and not have the chance to meet the Queen Mother."

The racehorse nuts used by Dan Moore's horses were manufactured by Ranks (Ireland) and supplied by an old family friend, Captain Paddy Stone, the managing director of Pegasus (Ire). Capt. Stone, an honourable man, was deeply upset at the turn of events and began a vigorous campaign for compensation for the owners of Tied Cottage and other horses disqualified at the time in England and Ireland in a spate of similar cases. Eventually Ranks' insurers agreed to pay Anthony Robinson and other racehorse owners a sum equivalent to the prize money they had lost so cruelly.

His son Michael Stone, who now runs the family companies with his brother David, confirms: "We said at once we would guarantee compensation and if all else failed, father would have paid them out regardless from his own money."

The depth of dismay that engulfed Paddy Stone may best be understood by his immediate decision to cease distributing racehorse nuts in Ireland. Though it cost his company dear he could not bear the thought of his friends and clients facing further disqualifications of their horses from feed supplied by him.

Instances of contamination dropped dramatically after representatives of the Irish Turf Club urged manufacturers of racehorse nuts to improve their quality control. Several years later the leading turf authorities including those in England and Ireland introduced threshold levels for four substances including theobromine. If Tied Cottage had won the Gold Cup ten years later he would not have been disqualified.

There was a further tragic postscript to the 1980 Gold Cup. Within months of the race both the trainer and owner of Tied Cottage were dead. Dan Moore was sixty-nine; his health had been failing for some time. Anthony Robinson succumbed to cancer at the age of forty-three after an outstandingly brave fight. Remarkably he rode his beloved Tied Cottage in a race at Cheltenham in April less than four months before his untimely death.

Tied Cottage raced until he was fifteen and remained with Joan Moore for several years until she moved to a smaller property. He then joined Tommy and Pamela Carberry at their home near Ashbourne. The old horse looked in particularly good form when I called to see him in the spring of 1991 but was subsequently put down early in April after developing a heart condition. He was twenty-three.

Master Smudge won over £100,000 before his retirement in 1985, aged thirteen. He was covered in mud and disgustingly fat the day I visited him in the summer of 1991. His story displays the heartbeat of jump racing.

TOTE CHELTENHAM GOLD CUP.   March 13th 1980.   £35,997.50.   *Heavy.*

1 Master Smudge	8 12 0	R. Hoare	14–1
2 Mac Vidi	15 12 0	P. Leach	66–1
3 Approaching	9 12 0	B. R. Davies	11–1
4 The Snipe	10 12 0	A. Webber	66–1

5 lengths, 2½.   Owned and trained A. Barrow.   Bred H. Radford.
7m. 14.2 seconds.   Also 5–2 Fav Diamond Edge (W. Smith) P.U.,
5 Jack of Trumps (J. J. O'Neill) B.D., 6 Border Incident (J. Francome) Fell, 13-2 Tied Cottage (T. Carberry) Disq., 9 Chinrullah (F. Berry) Disq., 33 Royal Mail (P. Blacker) Fell,
50 Kilcoleman (T. McGivern) P.U. and Secret Progress (R. Barry) P.U.,
100 Kas (J. Burke) P.U., Narribini (R. Linley) P.U. and The Vintner (C. Grant) Fell.
15 Ran.   Tote win: Tied Cottage 43p.

Tied Cottage, who won by eight lengths from Master Smudge, and Chinrullah, who finished fifth, were both later disqualified after traces of a prohibited substance were detected in post-race dope tests.

Master Smudge ch.g. 1972 (Master Stephen–Lily Pond II)

The Dikler leads over the last fence in 1972 from the doughty winner Glencaraig Lady

Tim Kilroe and his family admire Forgive 'N Forget after his fine victory in 1985

Willie Robinson (right) and Pat Taaffe watch approvingly as Dawn Run is led out at Leopardstown in December, 1985

A study in excellence. Dawn Run (far side) and Run and Skip soar over the last fence at the end of the first circuit in the 1986 Gold Cup

A bleak midwinter scene as a blizzard envelops Cheltenham shortly before the 1987 Gold Cup

One of the most compelling visions in sport. The field streams over the first fence in the 1987 Gold Cup beneath the snow-capped peaks of Cleeve Hill

Yahoo is still just ahead at the last fence in 1989 as Desert Orchid prepares for his unforgettable late victory charge on the final hill

A fascinating view from a different angle as the 1990 Gold Cup reaches its unexpected climax. Norton's Coin (centre) begins his thunderous winning run

Charter Party is safely over the last fence in the 1988 Gold Cup ahead of Cavvies Clown

The start of the 1991 Gold Cup

Desert Orchid is a picture of elegance after a circuit of the 1991 Gold Cup as Arctic Call blunders perilously beside him. They are followed by the winner Garrison Savannah

Jenny Pitman receives her trophy from The Queen Mother with Garrison Savannah's three proud owners in attendance

15

LITTLE OWL
(1981)

GIFT HORSES ARRIVE in a variety of disguises. Jim and Robin Wilson's came in the enormous, hairy-heeled shape of Little Owl, a legacy from their aunt Bobby Gundry, who died three days after the 1980 Cheltenham Festival. A year later Little Owl won the greatest prize of all in jump racing, the Tote Cheltenham Gold Cup, ridden by Jim Wilson, the finest amateur of his day, wearing the colours of his brother Robin, a Derbyshire farmer.

Bobby Gundry had owned horses on the flat with Rufus Beasley and Pat Rohan and jumpers with Anthony Gillam and Peter Easterby. She lived at Hovingham near Malton, quite close to the stables of the most versatile of Yorkshire trainers Peter Easterby, who bought Little Owl, a light bay, as an unbroken three-year-old for 2,300 guineas at Doncaster sales in 1977.

The big gelding, rather backward and plain, was descended from a useful racemare Spangle, who was rescued by Harry Ferris from a consignment of horses on their way by boat to a slaughterhouse in Dublin. Spangle's daughter, Black Spangle, was unplaced in three races after giving birth to her first foal at the age of three. Black Spangle belonged to Harry's sister-in-law Grahamie Ferris from Poyntz Pass near Newry in Co. Armagh. Mated with the Triumph Hurdle winner Cantab, a prolific sire of jumpers, Black Spangle produced Little Owl.

Sometimes, out hunting, Peter Easterby would suggest Bobby Gundry sent another horse to him. Much to his surprise she chose Little Owl from several prospective jumpers he showed her the day after the Doncaster sale. Tall and rather weak at that stage, Little Owl looked like a late-maturing horse who would appreciate plenty of time to develop; yet he won all four of his races as a four-year-old

hurdler.

How ironic that on his first visit to Cheltenham in 1979 he should be beaten into second place in the Coral Golden Hurdle Final by the perennial Festival hero Willie Wumpkins, ridden by none other than Jim Wilson. When Jim subsequently partnered Little Owl to facile victories over hurdles later in the season at Market Rasen and Wetherby in May he was left in no doubt about the horse's potential.

His progress over fences in the following two seasons was little short of spectacular, but since his campaigns were invariably brief he was by far the most inexperienced chaser in the field for the 1981 Gold Cup. His only defeat as a steeplechaser had been an unlucky one at the 1980 Festival, when he fell after being badly hampered in the Sun Alliance Chase.

Even after his deeply impressive win in the Timeform Chase at Haydock early in March 1981, the brothers Wilson were uncertain about going for the Gold Cup. The horse, they reasoned, was only seven and barely more than a novice, since he had run in only eight steeplechases. Other entries in the Ritz Club Chase and Kim Muir perhaps offered more realistic opportunities for him. Who could blame them for believing Little Owl's best years lay ahead? Peter Easterby did not share the doubts.

Caressing and relighting his favourite pipe with exaggerated care, Jim Wilson recalls: "We very much gave Peter the chance to pull out. But he pointed out that the horse might not be right the next year, that he might not get to Cheltenham. It was his decision to try for the Gold Cup."

More cautious trainers would not have run him in the Gold Cup at that stage and the joint owners would not have disagreed if Easterby had preferred to wait another twelve months.

Good old-fashioned Yorkshire common-sense

won the day. Canny Peter Easterby explains his views thus: "I've always believed if a horse is right you should let him run. Let tomorrow take care of itself."

Easterby had begun the meeting with yet another superb victory in the Waterford Crystal Champion Hurdle, his fourth in six years, with old Sea Pigeon. On the morning of the Gold Cup Jim and Melinda Wilson held their annual pre-race lunch party for forty or so guests at their attractive stables in the village of Ham, on the edge of Cheltenham, where they ran an equine swimming-pool business. Showing iron self-discipline the host restricted himself to one glass of champagne before making his excuses and leaving for the racecourse barely two miles away.

The field for the race looked particularly strong. Silver Buck, the undoubted star of the all-powerful Dickinson team, headed the market at 7–2 despite a slight question mark about his stamina. He had already won the King George VI Chase twice. Everyone's favourite, Night Nurse, twice winner of the Champion Hurdle, was back at Cheltenham, once more bidding at the age of ten to become the first horse to complete the elusive double in the Gold Cup. When he was three he had appeared as lot 447 at Doncaster Sales with a suspicion of a heart murmur and was led out unsold well below his reserve price of 2,000 guineas.

"No one wanted him," recalls Easterby happily. Later his old school friend Reg Spencer, a chartered surveyor, bought Night Nurse for rather less than 2,000 guineas shortly after he had won his first race at Ripon. Spencer's purchase was to prove an outstanding bargain but the horse's reward for years of compelling honesty was, by 1981, a handicap mark that stretched even his courage beyond the limit. This time he was joint second favourite at 6–1 with his stable companion Little Owl.

There was strong support once more for the Irish hope Jack of Trumps owned by the fearless gambler J. P. McManus and some sentimental backing for thirteen-year-old Tied Cottage, the victim of misfortune in two Gold Cups already and now ridden by a new jockey, Liam O'Donnell. The 1978 winner Midnight Court started 14–1 this time and Diamond Edge was an even longer price after banging a tendon a fortnight before the race. Spartan Missile, a truly exceptional hunter who had won The Foxhunters at Cheltenham and Liverpool in 1979, was ridden by his remarkable owner fifty-four-year-old

John Thorne, a man who had fought with the Parachute Regiment in the Second World War. Despite their fine record together Spartan Missile was a 33–1 chance.

Rain overnight increased the doubts about the favourite's stamina. Before racing, a rumour swept the course that he might be withdrawn; but he was one of fifteen starters who sloshed steadily to post in testing going that no doubt had something to do with the success of the 66–1 outsider Baron Blakeney in the opening Daily Express Triumph Hurdle. Despite the conditions, Tied Cottage dashed into the lead with the undiminished enthusiasm of a two-year-old and still held a clear lead when he rushed headlong into the sixth fence, sending Liam O'Donnell catapulting to the ground.

"Once Tied Cottage had gone things were a lot easier," Jim Wilson reflected later. "Little Owl was a thorough stayer who killed off the opposition. I would like to have made more use of him but Peter was worried I might overdo it and told me to give him a chance."

With Tied Cottage running loose, Diamond Edge led briefly before Night Nurse took command at the tenth fence. He remained there, too, for more than a mile, jumping so boldly and eagerly that some of us began to believe that we were about to witness a historic victory. As he ran downhill for the final time Silver Buck and Little Owl were closing stealthily.

Jim Wilson, champion rider at the Festival the previous year, was now in a quandary. All his instincts told him to go for home on Little Owl as though his life depended on it, but Peter Easterby had begged him to wait until the second last fence before making his move.

Sitting and suffering in mounting frustration he then endured the embarrassment of allowing Tommy Carmody to dash Silver Buck through on his inside round the final bend. So the two horses moved up to challenge Night Nurse at the second last fence. It was to prove the decisive point of the race. Little Owl met the fence on a long stride, threw an extravagant leap, and landed in front. Beside him Silver Buck blundered so comprehensively that all chance of winning had gone.

Little Owl came to the last fence increasing his lead, and sealed victory with another spectacular jump; but behind him Night Nurse, his honest, plain head held out low, was staging yet another fine rally on the course that had witnessed many of his most

Little Owl and his owner Jim Wilson thrillingly over the last fence ahead of Silver Buck (centre) and Night Nurse

stirring deeds. As he passed Silver Buck and began to close on Little Owl startling waves of sound came rolling down the hill.

Jim Wilson recalls: "Perhaps it was because Night Nurse was coming. Whatever the reason the sheer volume of noise made my horse falter and prick his ears after the last. It was as if we were running into a funnel of deafening sound."

Little Owl was staying on strongly but for a moment half-way up the hill it seemed that Night Nurse, already winner of thirty-one races over jumps, might snatch his most famous triumph of all. The battle-scarred veteran with bumps on his legs and a heart as big as himself had long been the most popular chaser in training and now he reminded us just why as he reduced the gap dramatically, cheered to the echo by thousands of his admirers.

But it was not to be. Galloping on relentlessly

Happiness is . . . Jim and Robin Wilson receive their trophy from Mrs Woodrow Wyatt

Little Owl held his stable companion's inspired charge by one and a half lengths. Silver Buck, who appeared not to stay in the tiring ground, was ten lengths away third, just ahead of Spartan Missile. Sixteen days later the hardy hunter and his gallant rider would be involved in an unforgettable finish with Aldaniti and Bob Champion in the Grand National.

Peter Easterby, for once, was almost speechless at Cheltenham: "I never expected to see two of my horses coming up the hill like that. I didn't know which one to shout for so I just shut up. I wouldn't have minded a dead heat," he confessed as he greeted his two heroes.

In his moment of triumph Jim Wilson regretted that his aunt had not lived to see Little Owl's finest victory. "I'm certain she was looking down on Cheltenham from a better vantage point," he said with feeling.

"You know I never even touched the horse with the whip. He would always find more and if I had ridden him more positively he would certainly have been more impressive, because he was such a thorough stayer."

For a while Little Owl became quite a celebrity. The landlord of the New Inn in Cheltenham was sufficiently moved to change the name of his pub to the Little Owl. Naturally the horse made the short journey from Jim Wilson's stables to be guest of honour at the reopening ceremony. Another pub, in

Co. Carlow, Eire, also took the horse's name.

On the day of the 1981 Gold Cup Little Owl proved an exceptional chaser. He beat a strong field with authority. The sky seemed the limit in the years ahead; but for whatever reason he never reached the same degree of excellence again. He completed the course only once from four outings the following season and though he did win twice in 1982–83 it proved to be only a temporary recovery. Various physical ailments, including a lengthy bout of the dreaded virus, restricted his appearances. Late in his career, aged eleven, he ran in hunter chases; but the flame that burned so brightly in his younger days seemed to have been extinguished for ever.

Little Owl lives in splendidly comfortable retirement with Jim and Melinda Wilson, no more than a long, steady canter from the scene of his finest triumph. Jim Wilson, with the lean hawk's face and dry sense of humour, was a genuine amateur in the true spirit of the Corinthians. He was the equal of all but the very best professionals but once racing was over for the day he returned to his other pursuits with equal enthusiasm. He gave up race riding, with some reluctance, in 1985 and turned to training racehorses in Ham.

Little Owl spends his days in the paddocks there with other horses that are being rested. Most summers he is invited to open a local fete and in 1990 he enjoyed a day trip to Sandown as one of the guests at Aldaniti's birthday party which raised funds for the Bob Champion Cancer Trust.

TOTE CHELTENHAM GOLD CUP.   March 19th 1981.   £44,258.75.   *Soft.*

1	Little Owl	7 12 0	Mr A. J. Wilson	6–1	
2	Night Nurse	10 12 0	A. Brown	6–1	
3	Silver Buck	9 12 0	T. Carmody	7–2 Fav	
4	Spartan Missile	9 12 0	Mr M. J. Thorne	33–1	
5	Diamond Edge	10 12 0	W. Smith	16–1	
6	Jack of Trumps	8 12 0	N. Madden	7–1	
7	Royal Judgement	8 12 0	R. Rowe	100–1	
8	Approaching	10 12 0	R. Champion	33–1	
9	Midnight Court	10 12 0	J. Francome	14–1	

1½ lengths, 10.   Owned R. J. Wilson.   Trained M. H. Easterby.   Bred Mrs J. Ferris.
7m. 9.9 seconds.   Also 15–2 Tied Cottage (L. O'Donnell) Fell, 10 Royal Bond (T. McGivern) P.U., 33 Chinrullah (P. Scudamore) P.U., 100 Fair View (R. Barry) P.U., Raffi Nelson (S. Smith Eccles) P.U. and So and So (Mr D. Gray) P.U.
15 Ran.   Tote win: 48p.

Little Owl: b.g. 1974 (Cantab–Black Spangle)

16

SILVER BUCK
(1982)

IF SILVER BUCK HAD BEEN a human he could not have survived the tribulations of racing and training without the aid of tranquillisers. Nervous, neurotic, suspicious and spooky: all these symptoms of instability were displayed throughout his eventful life and contributed, ultimately, to his untimely death.

Jack Doyle, veteran bloodstock agent, Irish rugby international and inimitable raconteur, bought Silver Buck twice inside a year at Ballsbridge. Bred north of the border in Co. Antrim by Edith Booth, the horse was sold cheaply to Brian Bamber, who entered him at Goffs as an unnamed three-year-old in November 1975. The future Gold Cup winner, a dark brown, unspectacular gelding, more the shape of a flat horse, was knocked down to Jack's representative Frank Barry for a modest 1,000 guineas in a private deal. He was acting for Jack and Biddy O'Connor, breeders of the champion sprinter Bay Express.

The O'Connors hoped their new purchase might be a suitable horse for their young son to break in and ride at their Rock Abbey Stud at Cashel in Co. Tipperary. Events were to prove that he was entirely unsuitable. Highly strung and suspicious of humans, the lively new arrival proved an impossible handful. So in June 1976, he passed through the ring at Ballsbridge once more and was bought again by Jack Doyle, this time acting for an English trainer, for 2,000 guineas.

Silver Buck's sire Silver Cloud was a distinctly useful stayer with Jack Jarvis. His dam Choice Archlesse, who won a modest hurdle race at Cartmel, shared the same sire Archive as the mighty Arkle.

When his English client failed to pay up Jack Doyle took the horse back to the family's home at Springfield twelve miles south of Dublin. The next day Jack's son Peter saddled him up, then popped out of the stable for a moment to collect his hat.

Peter, now a bloodstock agent, too, recalls: "When I returned the horse had gone berserk, put a hole in the roof, another in his knee and was trying to sit up in the manger."

The injury required fifteen stitches. Tender, loving care, the treatment for the patient's nervous disposition, lasted many patient months, much of it in the soothing hands of Peter's sister-in-law Katie Delahunt. Peter named the neurotic horse Silver Buck.

"We were stuck with him. No one wanted the little beggar," relates Peter Doyle. Eventually he considered the horse sufficiently settled to be used as a temporary galloping companion for a winning point-to-pointer Great Ben. Silver Buck, the unwanted tearaway, won the gallop by almost a furlong! At this stage he joined Peter's brother Paul Doyle, who trained at the Curragh, but the horse's abject behaviour on his intended point-to-point debut at Oldcastle in Co. Meath suggested his mental instability might always prevent him from fulfilling his undoubted potential.

Peter Doyle describes the mayhem that afternoon: "The horse flatly refused to allow Timmy Jones to mount him in the paddock though he did eventually hop on his back out on the course. The next thing Silver Buck threw yer man into a ditch and charged through some wire."

After that unpromising debut Silver Buck won two point-to-points in the spring and later, at Clonmel, swept home imperiously in a bumper race despite depositing his rider Colin Magnier unceremoniously in the paddock.

"We had 7–1 to our money that day. It was some touch. The bookies were blistered with him," relates Peter Doyle appreciatively.

Enter the controversial figure of Barney Curley, a man who trained for five years as a priest before turning irresistibly to gambling and racing. The biggest punter in Ireland at the time, Barney bought Silver Buck for £7,000 within days of his bumper victory.

"I thought he was tough. Pat McCann, who vetted him for me, said the horse had the strongest heart he had ever tested," relates Barney, who soon set in motion Silver Buck's transfer to the all-conquering Dickinson family then based at Gisburn, near Clitheroe, in Lancashire. Tony Dickinson was the trainer at the time but through the years his hard-working wife Monica Dickinson and their son Michael would also hold the licence. All three played a crucial part in their enduring success story. Since theirs was a democratic concern, more often than not in discussions and debates of significance two of the family would outvote the third!

That first season in England Silver Buck ran initially in the colours of Monica Dickinson before becoming the property of the family's solicitor Jack Mewles. He won four hurdle races, usually ridden by lofty Michael Dickinson. However, Thomas Tate, an enthusiastic amateur and Michael's brother-in-law, can proudly claim the honour of being the first man to win on the future Gold Cup hero in England.

The following autumn one of the stable's most loyal owners Christine Feather was looking for a suitable new horse. Wise Tony, a wonderful judge of young stock, offered her the choice of two . . . Silver Buck and Cavity Hunter.

She confesses: "I didn't like the look of Silver Buck one bit. He was very spooky and shot about his box as if he was going off his head."

Christine Feather picked Cavity Hunter, but another of the stable's owners was even more anxious to buy him so she generously agreed to take Silver Buck instead. It was a gesture that would not give her any cause for regret, though she watched in disbelief when her new horse was schooled over fences for the first time.

"He roared up to the fence, stopped dead and his jockey Tommy Carmody flew straight into the wing," she chuckles.

Silver Buck regarded practice fences with contempt throughout his long and prosperous residence with the Dickinsons.

"He would do anything to get out of jumping; stopping, skidding and ballooning over if there was no other way. He was so bad at the job it broke your heart," asserts Michael Dickinson. When Silver Buck did consent to jump fences at home he did so best for his lad Robert Earnshaw, a quiet, self-effacing farmer's boy with calming horseman's hands and the modern habit of wearing an earring. In his box the horse was deeply suspicious of his lad. Nervous and temperamental, he often bit the patient Earnshaw and for several years would not let him touch his ears. The enticement of copious amounts of mints eventually helped calm Silver Buck's fears to some degree.

"He lacked trust and confidence in people and at first I could not get near him. He took ages to accept me. He was cheeky and had a habit of doing silly things, but he was my pride and joy," he reflects.

Serious injury ended Michael Dickinson's role as a jockey. When Silver Buck began jumping fences in the late autumn of 1978 he carried a new jockey, twenty-two-year-old Tommy Carmody, already a star in Ireland. Despite his bruising introduction the eager Carmody soon set up a formidable winning partnership with Silver Buck. They won their first four steeplechases with undoubted authority, though the horse was establishing a pattern of behaviour that would remain constant throughout his life. During a race, jumping fences at speed, his enthusiasm was beyond reproach. Once in front in the closing stages he was alarmingly idle.

So to Haydock and a duel of consuming intensity with the former champion hurdler Night Nurse, who had made an equally bright start over fences. The pair took each other on, head to head, over Haydock's tricky fences in a quite stunning battle for supremacy in the Embassy Premier Chase Final. Night Nurse just led for the first half of the race but Silver Buck was always naggingly at his girths and took charge with eight fences remaining. They slugged it out like two old-fashioned, bare-knuckled boxers fighting to the finish. In the closing stages both horses were out on their feet. It was Silver Buck, younger by a year, who struggled first over the line two and a half lengths ahead of his exhausted rival.

Those of us lucky enough to witness this uplifting encounter stumbled from the stands, drained of all emotion. Both horses reached so deep down into their souls, were so utterly spent that despite appearances to the contrary they could not possibly have recovered in time when the Cheltenham Festival began eleven days later. Silver Buck finished a weary third in the Sun Alliance Chase behind Master Smudge.

Silver Buck and his lad Robert Earnshaw on their way to victory over Bregawn and Graham Bradley. Sunset Christo

Night Nurse dropped out of contention soon after half-way in the Gold Cup two days later.

The ordeal at Haydock did not have a lasting effect on Silver Buck. He proved a prolific winner of steeplechases in the years ahead and took the King George VI Chase twice but it was not until March 1981 that he first contested the Cheltenham Gold Cup aged nine. He started favourite, too, at 7–2, but a wholesale blunder at the second last fence ended any lingering hopes of victory and he finished well beaten in third place behind Little Owl and Night Nurse. After the race, traces of blood emerging from his nostrils suggested that he had broken a blood ves-

sel. By then Silver Buck was trained by Michael Dickinson, who took over from his father as planned in the autumn of 1980 and masterminded the move to a purpose-built yard at Harewood in Yorkshire.

When Tommy Carmody returned to Ireland in the summer of 1981 Michael Dickinson enterprisingly decided to give five promising lads in the yard a chance to prove themselves. Robert Earnshaw was, perhaps, foremost a horseman but he knew and understood Silver Buck better than anyone in the yard and won on him at the first attempt at Wincanton. Next time the new combination fell at Chepstow. John Francome was recruited before Silver

is third

"We were all a bit suspicious at the time," he relates. "You could not have hit the nail in straighter if you had tried."

The Dickinsons' vet was concerned that the nail might have damaged the pedal bone in his foot but X-rays did not detect any further injury. Usually so lively and hyperactive, Silver Buck was now confined to his box for five dreary weeks. His foot was placed in buckets of cold water for days on end. Rest, constant treatment and patience finally ensured his full recovery but time was fast running out if he was to make his date with destiny at Cheltenham.

"There were moments when none of us thought he would get to Cheltenham," confirms Earnshaw.

Far from fully wound up, Silver Buck appeared at Market Rasen on March 6th, ridden by Kevin Whyte, gave two stone or more to his eight rivals, made all the running and won comfortably. It was a highly encouraging comeback. On the same day Robert Earnshaw rode Bregawn, another of the stable's high-flyers, into second place at Haydock. The Dickinson duo were to dominate the Gold Cup twelve days hence.

The field of twenty-two runners for the 1982 Gold Cup was the largest on record. Its size reflected the prevailing belief that the race was wide open, that there were flaws in all the leading contenders. Night Nurse, the most popular jumper in training, was favourite at 11–4 to improve on his narrow second the previous year. Little Owl, his conqueror then, was hopelessly out of form and would not be returning to Cheltenham.

There was infectious confidence in the chief Irish hope Royal Bond, winner of the Leopardstown Chase, carrying twelve stone. The lightly raced Venture to Cognac, ridden by the owner's son Oliver Sherwood, was another serious contender, but widespread doubts about Silver Buck's ability to last three and a quarter miles in the most testing conditions imaginable ensured that he was freely available at 8–1. His stable companion Bregawn was an 18–1 chance. Patient and skilful handling by Robert Earnshaw had helped transform the doughty little chestnut into a rapidly improving handicapper but this time he was ridden by Graham Bradley. Earnshaw, to his surprise and delight, was on Silver Buck.

Other top-class contenders included fourteen-year-old Tied Cottage, running in his fifth Gold Cup, Grittar, the Grand National favourite, Diamond Edge, dashing winner of the Whitbread and Hen-

Buck's impressive victory in the Edward Hanmer Memorial Chase late in November and was booked again for his annual Christmas outing to Kempton for the King George VI Chase as Robert Earnshaw was required for Wayward Lad in the same race.

Snow and frost wiped out the Boxing Day programme that year but Bucket, as he was known in the yard, could not have attempted his hat-trick anyway. When Robert Earnshaw walked into his box on the morning of Boxing Day the horse was so painfully lame on his off hind-foot he could not bear to put it on the ground. The anxious stable lad discovered a nail driven deep into the sole of the horse's foot.

Silver Buck returns in triumph

nessy Gold Cups, and the previous year's Sun Alliance winner Lesley Ann, trained by the very astute David Elsworth.

The years truly rolled back as sprightly Tied Cottage, jumping and galloping with the zest of a horse half his age, set his customary blistering pace. Many of the runners were unable to keep up, and soon after half-way horses began to drop out one by one as their jockeys accepted that further pursuit was pointless. After a circuit the chasing pack was headed by three Northern challengers Sugarally, Sunset Christo and Bregawn with Night Nurse and Silver Buck in midfield.

"The pace was so good I was able to settle Silver Buck better than I dared hope," relates Earnshaw.

Night Nurse was already beaten as Silver Buck began to close on the leaders approaching the final mile, and an uncharacteristic mistake when he pecked badly on landing over the fourth last barely checked his progress. Remarkably, old Tied Cottage regained the lead here from Sunset Christo, Bregawn and Diamond Edge with Silver Buck patently travelling best of all.

Robert Earnshaw admits: "We were going so well we hit the front much too soon on the run to the second last. If only I had waited longer he would have been far more impressive."

Tactics did not matter now. However he was ridden Silver Buck would have won that day. He cleared the second last fence imperiously, brushed safely through the top of the final jump and though idling in front as usual readily held the renewed challenge of his stable companion Bregawn by two lengths.

Way behind in third place, fully twelve lengths

adrift, came Sunset Christo, bred to be a hunter and later successful in the show ring before he began winning point-to-points. He was one of two horses owned by young Carol Hawkey and trained by her father Ray under permit at their home in the heart of the Cleveland countryside. Diamond Edge claimed fourth prize with Grittar, running a superb Aintree trial, in sixth place. As the Dickinson duo cantered upsides in triumph the two jockeys embraced each other in a sporting display of camaraderie.

Graham Bradley explains: "Neither of us could speak. We just hugged each other until we pulled up. It was one of the best feelings of my life."

By training the first and second in the Gold Cup in his second season Michael Dickinson, only thirty-two, served notice of his boundless ambition and earnest, single-minded approach to the business of training racehorses to the exclusion of all else.

Poor Silver Buck, neat, athletic and utterly willing, did not live to enjoy the retirement his supreme endeavours demanded. He came back to Chelten-ham, of course, twelve months later, to play his part in the historic domination of the Gold Cup by his stable's runners. By the summer of 1984 he had won a total of two point-to-points, one bumper race, four hurdles and thirty steeplechases. At the time his total of prize money, £177,185.15, was a record.

When it began raining one September morning at Harewood in 1984 Graham Bradley, on Silver Buck, and Ronnie Beggan on another horse trotted back to the yard to collect their waterproof clothing. Beggan held Silver Buck as his rider remounted. Perhaps the horse was feeling fresh. Possibly he was startled by the crackling of waterproofs. Whatever the reason, Silver Buck's lifelong nervous disposition now proved fatal. With his jockey perched precariously half-way over his back he rushed full-tilt across the yard and ran head-first into the far wall in a sickening collision. Though he survived the impact Silver Buck died later that morning. It was a cruel and violent end for a noble racehorse.

TOTE CHELTENHAM GOLD CUP.   March 18th 1982.   £48,386.25.   *Heavy.*

1	Silver Buck	10 12 0	R. Earnshaw	8–1
2	Bregawn	8 12 0	G. Bradley	18–1
3	Sunset Christo	8 12 0	C. Grant	100–1
4	Diamond Edge	11 12 0	W. Smith	11–1
5	Captain John	8 12 0	P. Scudamore	40–1
6	Grittar	9 12 0	Mr C. Saunders	16–1
7	Venture to Cognac	9 12 0	Mr O. Sherwood	6–1
8	Royal Bond	9 12 0	T. Carberry	4–1
9	Tied Cottage	14 12 0	G. Newman	25–1
10	Two Swallows	9 12 0	A. Webber	100–1
11	Lesley Ann	8 12 0	C. Brown	10–1
12	Sugarally	9 12 0	C. Tinkler	100–1
13	Peaty Sandy	8 12 0	T. G. Dun	40–1

2 lengths, 12.   Owned Mrs C. Feather.   Trained M. Dickinson.   Bred Mrs S. Booth. 7m. 11.2 seconds.   Also 11–4 Fav Night Nurse (J. J. O'Neill) P.U., 25 Henry Bishop (R. Rowe) P.U., 33 Border Incident (J. Francome) P.U., 50 Earthstopper (Mr G. Sloan) Fell and Master Smudge (S. Smith Eccles) P.U., 100 Snow Flyer (R. Champion) P.U., Straight Jocelyn (H. Davies) P.U., 150 Drumroan (C. Dugast) P.U., 300 Wansford Boy (R. Dickin) P.U. 22 Ran.   Tote win:95p.

Silver Buck: b.g. 1972 (Silver Cloud–Choice Archlesse)

17

BREGAWN
(1983)

MICHAEL DICKINSON CHANGED THE FACE of the Cheltenham Gold Cup irreversibly. Tall, pale and increasingly intense, a trainer for barely three years, he displayed the anxiety of someone close to a nervous breakdown in the weeks before the 1983 Festival, then watched in dazed disbelief as his runners filled the first five places in the Gold Cup. By the sheer weight of his effort, the depth of his commitment to succeeding in the race that matters above all others, he had ensured a record that would stand untouched forever. It was, quite simply, a magnificent achievement; and those who carped churlishly that some of the placed horses might have won elsewhere at Cheltenham missed the point that the owners of the quintet fully supported their trainer's audacious, single-minded assault on the Gold Cup.

An important part of the foundation of his relentless pursuit of success was established during two summers working as an unpaid assistant for Vincent O'Brien, a man who had left his own indelible mark on the Gold Cup before devoting his attention to flat racing. Twice while he was a leading jump jockey Dickinson wrote to O'Brien asking for a temporary role as a pupil in the summer. Twice he was turned down. Finally he drove almost three hundred miles to Epsom to confront the great man.

He admits: "Once I spotted him there I started to approach him but twice ran out of courage. I then followed him from the grandstand and spoke to him in the car park. He said he would find out about me and later agreed to take me."

On his second day at O'Brien's stables near Cashel the eager young pupil bought a large notebook to record every single detail of the training operation. After two summers the book was full.

"I thought he was the best trainer in the world and wanted to discover how it worked. I learned that he paid so much attention to detail and his methods have influenced me enormously. In my own modest way I tried to imitate just about everything he did."

At home Michael Dickinson enjoyed a wonderful education in the art of training horses from his parents. From modest beginnings in a hunting yard both Tony and Monica rode with immense success in point-to-points before developing a formidable training partnership in the North of England. Tony, known affectionately as "The Boss", had an unrivalled eye for buying likely young prospects and the knack of bringing them on. Monica excelled at feeding horses and running the yard.

Thus Michael Dickinson inherited a finely tuned, well-organised racing machine when he took over the licence from his father in the autumn of 1980. Within months he increased the tempo appreciably. By the force of his character he speedily developed Harewood into the most formidable training operation in National Hunt racing. Soon records were tumbling to the fleet-footed Dickinson jumpers. His percentage of winners to runners was startlingly high at around 50 per cent; the pace of his training regime was unrelenting.

Michael Dickinson, at times obsessive to the point of fanaticism, became champion trainer in his second season. At Christmas 1982 he set another record with twelve winners on Boxing Day. Exactly a week before the 1983 Cheltenham Festival he reached the fastest century of winners ever achieved over jumps.

In 1983 Dickinson, who was thirty-three a month before the Festival meeting, supplied five of the eleven runners in the race that has deservedly turned into legend. Silver Buck and Bregawn, first and second the previous year, were back again. They were joined by the brilliantly promising Wayward Lad, winner of the King George VI Chase at Christmas, Captain John, a dour stayer who had finished fifth in the 1982 Gold Cup, and Ashley House, a very decent handicapper owned by Joe McLoughlin from Newbridge just a short canter from the Curragh in Kildare.

Of all the chasers that Michael Dickinson trained Bregawn was a most improbable champion. Small, independent, stubborn, a horse with a free will and a mind very much of his own, he liked to make the running and seemed to resent company in a race. He was not ideally built for jumping and at first fell frequently over fences. Later, when he developed a satisfactory method of negotiating the obstacles, he became fully proficient in the highest class.

Bred by James Fitzgerald, a bachelor farmer from Glenmore near Waterford, Bregawn was by Saint Denys, second in the Irish 2,000 Guineas, out of the unraced mare Miss Society who came from a sound jumping family. The product of this mating was so unimpressive as a young horse that he was led out of the sales ring at Ballsbridge without a bid and taken back to Co. Waterford.

Joseph Crowley, a permit holder from Piltown, in Co. Kilkenny, was the only man to show an interest in Bregawn that day. He subsequently made the short journey to Glenmore and bought the future Gold Cup winner as an unbroken three-year-old for £1,000.

"The little horse was half a size too small. That probably put most people off," he recalls. Breaking in Bregawn proved a thoroughly invigorating experience. The horse had boundless spirit. The problem was channelling it in the right direction. Once the intrepid Crowley was flung like a rag doll on to the roof of a shed. His perseverance was rewarded with a bumper victory by the lively chestnut at Punchestown in January 1979.

Alerted to the horse's burgeoning reputation, Martin Kennelly travelled to Piltown with the express purpose of buying Bregawn. Large tumblers of whisky were produced by Joseph Crowley and sunk by both parties. Kennelly, a burly building contractor with a bluff, open manner, bid £12,000. Crowley asked for £20,000. After several hours of boisterous drinking and dealing the pair agreed to split the difference. Bregawn became the property of Kennelly for £16,000, won a race over hurdles trained by Christy Kinane and was then sent to Yorkshire to join Tony Dickinson. When Michael Dickinson took over from his father in the summer of 1980 Bre-

gawn's attention was turned to fences.

At first his jumping was alarmingly erratic. That first season he fell three times and unseated his rider on another occasion. The most costly error of all came on his first visit to the Cheltenham Festival when he came down three fences out holding a clear lead in the Ritz National Hunt Chase. He also won six steeplechases. Several jockeys, amateur and professional, rode the jaunty little chestnut in that first eventful campaign over fences. Graham Bradley, a supreme stylist, eventually became his regular partner.

He reveals: "At home the horse was an absolute nutcase. So quirky. He would root himself at the bottom of hedges. Just plant himself at any time. You could not move him with a tractor and chain and you could not bully him. That would only make him worse. You had to wait patiently for him to change his mind. When he got going he worked like a brilliant horse."

In his second season over fences Bregawn progressed impressively, with four successes in handicaps before finishing second to Silver Buck in the 1982 Gold Cup. But during the run-up to the following year's Gold Cup that Michael Dickinson would dominate as no trainer had done before, Bregawn's intransigence was a constant concern, particularly at the start of his races. Though he won the Hennessy Cognac Gold Cup from Ashley House with a typically tenacious display he gave away many lengths in his final two races before the Festival by obstinately refusing to set off until the others had gained a substantial advantage. Even so, he was in front by half-way at Wincanton and failed by only half a length to hold Combs Ditch, a high-class horse who sometimes needed a supply of oxygen after his races.

Graham Bradley insists: "That race won me the Gold Cup. He had enjoyed a long rest after Christmas and blew so much afterwards he was almost gurgling. I felt he would improve twenty lengths by Cheltenham."

Bradley's confidence was tempered by a repeat of Bregawn's mulish behaviour at Hereford only twelve days before the Gold Cup. "This time he gave away twenty lengths at the start. He walked round like a lamb with the others, then as soon as they lined up stood rooted to the spot. I was petrified it might happen in the Gold Cup," he relates.

After generously allowing the others at Hereford

an unhealthy lead Bregawn, so talented but increasingly unpredictable, caught them, remarkably, by the seventh fence and won with insolent ease by the length of the nearby High Street.

Silver Buck was not in quite the same commanding form that season. Bidding for an elusive third success in the King George VI Chase he had finished only third to his stable companion Wayward Lad. When a throat infection was diagnosed shortly afterwards he was taken for treatment to the equine centre at Bristol University. Silver Buck did not race again until winning a minor event at Market Rasen shortly before Cheltenham. Though stable confidence was waning Robert Earnshaw, his lad and jockey, declined the chance to switch to another of Michael Dickinson's contenders.

"I could have ridden almost any one of the five but Mrs Feather had been very good to me. I suppose my allegiance to Silver Buck cost me the chance of getting back on Bregawn," he explains.

Dickinson's all-conquering team of horses was in rampaging form all winter. When it emerged that he would field five runners in the Gold Cup, bookmakers offered odds of 5–1 on that he would provide the winner. Others bet 100–1 that his runners would fill the first five places, a price that was eagerly snapped up by those close to the yard.

A hock injury hampered Wayward Lad's Gold Cup preparation. At one stage it seemed he might not be ready in time. Until the last moment it was touch and go; but run he did, ridden by Jonjo O'Neill since John Francome was required by Fred Winter for Brown Chamberlin. Dermot Browne, the stable's amateur, rode Ashley House with "Gipsy" Dave Goulding, who flaunted an earring, on Captain John, a horse that had recently recovered from strained muscles in his shoulder and back.

Though Bregawn still belonged to Martin Kennelly he was now running in the colours of his brother Jim, a genial farmer from Timahoe near Portlaoise. An exchange of ownership was conducted for diplomatic reasons. Bregawn, temporarily, became the property of Jim Kennelly for the token sum of £1. Jim travelled from Ireland to see the race. Martin remained at home at the Mylerstown Stud near Naas to entertain an aunt from Canada he had not seen since he was a boy. He would watch the momentous race on television.

Only Combs Ditch was seriously backed to prevent a Dickinson monopoly of the 1983 Gold Cup.

His trainer David Elsworth was exceptionally bullish about the horse's chance. The public took note. The price of Combs Ditch, ridden by bustling Colin Brown, dropped from 6–1 to 9–2. Despite continued anxiety about Bregawn's intractable behaviour at the start he was the best backed of Dickinson's quintet and started favourite at 100–30. Silver Buck drifted markedly from 3s to 5–1, while Wayward Lad was steady at 6–1.

Down at the start Dickinson's reliable travelling head lad Graham Rennison jogged round and round beside Bregawn with a tight grip on the reins. This time the horse was almost cantering when the tapes rose. Whiggie Geo, a 500-1 outsider, led over the first four fences at a sedate pace until Graham Bradley grabbed the race by the throat on the hardy Bregawn.

"We were not going fast enough. People thought I was mad to take up the running so soon but I knew I had to force the pace or Wayward Lad and Silver Buck would beat me for speed at the finish," he explains.

The rest of the historic Gold Cup involved an en-

A historic finish. Bregawn (second right) jumps upsides

tirely private battle of attrition between the Dickinson cohorts. Jumping with a telling blend of precision and boldness Bregawn led at a pounding gallop, tested first by Ashley House, then more searchingly by Silver Buck, Captain John and Wayward Lad. The expected threat of Combs Ditch did not materialise. Once more he would need the assistance of oxygen after the race. The fierce pace was also too much for Fred Winter's duo. Fifty Dollars More was pulled up soon after half-way and Brown Chamberlin was weakening when he fell at the seventeeth fence.

Bregawn had stolen a useful lead at the top of the hill, but Captain John was beginning to narrow the gap and looked the biggest threat of all to the leader until he blundered horribly at the third last fence, the twentieth, and pitched onto his nose. Two fences out it was the turn of Bregawn to make a mistake. It was not a serious one, but the manner in which he nudged the fence with his knees cost him a vital two lengths at a time when his stable companions were closing like a pack of marauding vultures.

Wayward Lad, Silver Buck and Captain John were all in thunderous pursuit now, and as Bregawn rose at the final fence his jockey sensed rather than saw another horse jumping level with him on the stands side.

"I thought it was Combs Ditch but knew afterwards it was Captain John," relates Graham Bradley. What he had not seen was the handsome Wayward Lad make stealthy progress tight on the far rail. Once on the flat, Bregawn was immediately under attack on both sides. Whatever his peccadillos in the past no one could possibly question his courage and integrity now. Just when it seemed he might be engulfed, Bregawn fought back with the utmost valour as he strained every muscle and sinew in his desire to fend off those who sought to pass him.

"When you are at the foot of the hill the winning post seems a long, long way away. I thought we would never reach it. My horse was very tired and I was frantic that we might be caught," recalls Bradley.

Out in the centre of the course Captain John, by

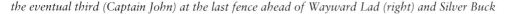

the eventual third (Captain John) at the last fence ahead of Wayward Lad (right) and Silver Buck

Michael Dickinson, trainer of the first five in the 1983 Gold Cup

now exhausted, hung first right-handed and then left-handed. Over on the far rail Wayward Lad, just short of peak fitness, was unable to sustain a final, telling challenge. Half-way up the hill Bregawn began to draw clear again. This time he would not be denied. At the line he had won a famous victory by five lengths from Captain John with Wayward Lad one and a half lengths away third. As the doughty winner slowed to a trot his jockey turned round in the saddle, noted the identities of the second and third, then watched with a mixture of pride and disbelief as Silver Buck and finally Ashley House were next to cross the finishing line.

Michael Dickinson, the dynamic architect of this matchless feat, watched the drama unfold on a television beside the weighing-room before rushing out to greet his famous five, who all squeezed into the cherished winner's arena. Once he had spoken to the owners of each horse he agreed to an impromptu television interview with me for the BBC. He seemed relieved more than elated in those first heady moments before the enormity of his achievement had sunk in. Drained emotionally and physically, he revealed that he had lost a stone through worry since Christmas and, I suspect, a few pounds more from

his coathanger frame in the final days before the Gold Cup.

Hours after the last race the rustic figure of Jim Kennelly, complete with flat cap, bulging raincoat and solid farmer's lace-up boots, was to be seen in the Mandarin bar leading the singing in a noisy rendition of "The Boys of Kilmichael". That evening the Dickinson family, their jockeys and friends enjoyed a lively celebration at the Flying Pizza restaurant in Leeds. As Graham Bradley rose to leave on the wrong side of midnight, Monica Dickinson revealed a glimpse of the discipline and dedication behind the record-breaking success of the stable.

"Don't be late in the morning," she advised the victorious jockey. "6.55 in the yard as usual."

The game continued at Harewood for a few more years but the main player did not remain much longer. In November Michael Dickinson announced that he would be switching to the flat as private trainer for Robert Sangster. Bregawn ran once more in the Gold Cup for him in 1984, almost pulled himself up in the middle of the race, lost an impossible amount of ground then rallied to such purpose that he failed to claim fourth place by less than a length.

Graham Bradley reflects: "He was never the same after winning the Gold Cup. He tried his heart out that day and was pushed to the limit. Perhaps it got to the bottom of him."

When Michael Dickinson moved to Wiltshire to begin his unhappy liaison with Robert Sangster at Manton his mother Monica took over the licence at Harewood. Bregawn's infuriating behaviour demanded fresh sanctions. Martin Kennelly brought him home in an attempt to freshen him up with some hunting, ridden by the local blacksmith Colm Gainey. Early in March 1985, trained by Paddy Mullins and ridden by his son Willie without a whip, Bregawn did win a handicap hurdle at Limerick. He ran in the Gold Cup for the final time a week later, resolutely declined to exert himself and eventually refused at the final fence. It was an ignominious conclusion to the Festival career of one of the bravest winners in the history of the Gold Cup.

Back in Ireland Bregawn still had one more trick to play. Late in September, aged eleven, he ran in a two-mile bumper race on the flat at Listowel against horses half his age. Once more he made his customarily tardy start. This time, without any obstacles to jump, he made up the lost ground with ease, led early in the straight and won with contemptuous ease. The

Old friends. Bregawn in retirement in Ireland with his owner Martin Kennelly

old soldier had been swinging the lead. He ran a few more times before retiring to a life of comfort at Martin Kennelly's Mylerstown Stud close to Punchestown racecourse where he first displayed his exceptional ability.

When I called to see him in the summer of 1991 Bregawn, aged seventeen, was in typically lively form. Sharply alert with a quizzical gaze, sound limbs and distinctive black patches on both flanks, he looked altogether too small to have been such a brilliant chaser. When Martin Kennelly watches him outpacing much younger stock in the paddocks he wonders at the inflexible character of the hardy little chestnut with a mind of his own.

"The speed of him still, it's unbelievable. He flies across the fields," he sighs admiringly.

TOTE CHELTENHAM GOLD CUP.   March 17th 1983.   £45,260.   *Good to Soft.*

1	Bregawn	9 12 0	G. Bradley	100–30 Fav
2	Captain John	9 12 0	D. Goulding	11–1
3	Wayward Lad	8 12 0	J. J. O'Neill	6–1
4	Silver Buck	11 12 0	R. Earnshaw	5–1
5	Ashley House	9 12 0	Mr D. Browne	12–1
6	Richdee	7 12 0	C. Hawkins	40–1
7	Midnight Love	8 12 0	C. Grant	66–1
8	Combs Ditch	7 12 0	C. Brown	9–2

5 lengths, 1½.   Owned J. Kennelly.   Trained M. Dickinson.   Bred J. Fitzgerald.
6m. 57.6 seconds.   Also 8 Fifty Dollars More (R. Linley) P.U., 10 Brown Chamberlin (J. Francome) Fell and 500–1 Whiggie Geo (Mr N. Tutty) P.U.   11 Ran.   Tote win: £5.

Bregawn: ch.g. 1974 (Saint Denys–Miss Society)

18

BURROUGH HILL LAD
(1984)

THE IMPLAUSIBLE TALE of the strapping, jet-black Burrough Hill Lad, imposing winner of the 1984 Gold Cup, has one chilling similarity with that of the shining white charger Desert Orchid. Both so nearly ended their days in harrowing falls at the last flight of hurdles at Kempton Park. Burrough Hill Lad's moment of destiny came in January 1980 in a novice race won by Corbiere, who would later become his stable companion and fellow standard-bearer for forthright Jenny Pitman, the outstanding female trainer of her generation. The two horses jumped the final flight together. Burrough Hill Lad crashed painfully to the ground and lay prone for so long that those at the scene feared the worst.

Happily he did eventually clamber awkwardly to his feet and a lengthy session with Ronnie Longford, the equine osteopath, later enabled him to make a full recovery from displaced vertebrae in his back and neck. Throughout his frequently interrupted life as a racehorse Burrough Hill Lad was a hardy survivor. Two bouts of leg trouble had kept him on the sidelines before he joined Jenny Pitman, and further problems would prevent his fully displaying his crushing superiority in the mid-eighties. When he was fit and sound Burrough Hill Lad was a formidable powerhouse, a thick-bodied, heavy horse, built like a sprinter behind the saddle yet possessing the most devouring, long stride.

He was bred by his owner Stan Riley out of Green Monkey, an untalented mare he bought at Leicester Sales for 650 guineas.

"She was skin and bone when I chose her but I knew a lot about her background," he relates mysteriously. Three of Green Monkey's foals won over sprint distances. Burrough Hill Lad, who possessed limitless stamina, was the product of a mating with the unfashionable Richboy at a covering fee of £450.

"I bred him for the flat but he was much too backward to make a two-year-old," recalls Riley, a tall, bearded restaurateur from Leicestershire, who named the future Gold Cup winner after the hills above his old farm. Burrough Hill Lad was on the market for £2,000 as a young horse.

"Oh yes, I wanted to sell him but I was not going to give him away. He had such a flowing action galloping across the field behind my restaurant," he explains. The huge, undeveloped black horse raced over hurdles as a three-year-old, an experience not shared by too many Gold Cup winners. Stan Riley, who liked to reduce his training costs to the bare minimum, would shed almost a stone each autumn so that he could ride his young horse in preparatory road work. Once, hacking perilously along a railway embankment, they were lucky to avoid a bruising encounter with a passing train! Phil Tuck rode Burrough Hill Lad in his first race and to his first victory, an early association that would be gloriously revived at the 1984 Festival.

Jimmy Harris, cruelly crippled in a race fall, trained Burrough Hill Lad to win twice over hurdles as a novice. The next season the horse joined Harry Wharton. Two more victories by the big horse with the impressive stride offered rich promise before he broke down. After a year's absence he was moved by Stan Riley once more and sent to Jenny Pitman in Lambourn. The horse's sheer size and strength suggested he was wasting his time over hurdles, but his initial clumsy attempts over fences on windswept Mandown high above Lambourn proved a searching test of endurance for both the obstacles and his riders.

Jenny observes: "If he met his fences wrong he left a bloody great hole in them. Being a long-striding horse he found it difficult to shorten. He would leave a pile of birch and pieces of wood on the other side and not even check his stride. He crunched the life out of them."

Despite numerous practice sessions the big horse tended to guess when he was wrong. Once, on the schooling grounds, he buried poor Colin Brown, who was also ejected like a spent cartridge by calamitous blunders in races at Haydock and Cheltenham. The trainer persevered. When Burrough Hill Lad did manage a clear round, victory was a formality at Newton Abbot, twice, and Aintree.

Jenny Pitman reveals: "Even then I thought potentially he was the best I had trained. If he had ever jumped like Corbiere he would never have been beaten." After two impressive triumphs the following autumn Burrough Hill Lad was pitched against the mighty Silver Buck at Haydock. Was it too early to be taking on the best?

"Nonsense," scoffed Jenny at the time. "For twelve months I've said I would not build mountains for this horse to climb. Now he is ready for the peak. I gather Silver Buck's trainer Michael Dickinson is not too worried about my horse but is more frightened of the trainer."

It was the sort of lively propaganda you would expect from the challenger's manager at the weigh-in before a title fight. Silver Buck, conceding 21 lb, emerged the winner of this bout, but there was a valid excuse for his vanquished opponent. Burrough Hill Lad strained a check ligament during the race. The injury was treated with the traditional but now illegal method of line firing. He would again be out of action for a year.

Burrough Hill Lad came back over hurdles in December 1983, finished a highly encouraging third and was then sent to Chepstow to take advantage of some unusually generous handicapping in the Coral Welsh National at Chepstow.

Jenny Pitman relates: "I nearly fell out of my chair when I saw he had been given little more than ten stone. I've never been so confident before a race and told all my owners to help themselves."

A sustained ante-post gamble ensued from 20–1 to 100–30 on the day. You could hear the cries of anguish from scorched bookies echoing across the Severn Bridge as Burrough Hill Lad won just as easily as his trainer had anticipated, ridden for the first time by the mop-haired champion John Francome. In the next two months the horse's startling rate of progress

took him irresistibly to the head of the market for the Gold Cup. Successive facile victories at Sandown were followed by a virtual match against the reigning champion Bregawn at Wincanton. When Bregawn tried to refuse, Burrough Hill Lad was left to win at his leisure.

The gifted champion jockey, however, was required by Fred Winter to ride the much improved Hennessy winner Brown Chamberlin in the Gold Cup. He would not be released from his contract. The view of most observers that John Francome would have ridden Burrough Hill Lad, given a free choice, is not supported by the jockey.

"I don't think I would have deserted Brown Chamberlin," he reflected while working on his new stables early in 1991. "You see loyalty works both ways. Fred Winter had always been very good to me. So had Brown Chamberlin's owner Mrs Samuel. But I did think Burrough Hill Lad would win."

No sooner had the admirable Phil Tuck been called up to replace Francome than he was kicked brutally in the face in a fall at Sedgefield. His nose was badly broken, not for the first time, and his breathing impaired. When he next arrived at the races shortly before Cheltenham he looked like a man who had endured twelve punishing rounds with Mike Tyson, but despite his battered appearance he assured Jenny Pitman that he would be fit to ride Burrough Hill Lad.

The final week before the 1984 Gold Cup was notable for a series of persuasive rumours suggesting that all was not well with Burrough Hill Lad. Specifically the big, black horse was said to be breaking blood vessels at home. Wherever Jenny Pitman turned she was assailed by constant, nagging inquiries. Affronted at such uninformed reports she insisted in typically robust manner that the horse was in the very best of health. Bookmakers are cunningly well-informed in speculation of this type. If the ante-post favourite for the Derby coughs at midday you can be sure the phones at Ladbrokes and Hills will be ringing within minutes. The more Jenny Pitman protested, the further Burrough Hill Lad's odds were extended. Within days he had drifted from 7–4 to 4–1.

Seventy-two hours before the Gold Cup the harassed trainer was devastated to discover unsightly large lumps all over Burrough Hill Lad's body. In despair she rang her vet Barry Park, who dashed to the stables, took a blood test and forcefully reassured the trainer.

Jenny recalls: "Barry told me that these massive lumps can appear briefly when a horse is spot-on. He was not concerned. In fact he told me to mortgage the stables and put the lot on the horse for the Gold Cup. Thank goodness the lumps had gone the next morning."

Phil Tuck travelled to Lambourn to watch countless video films of the Gold Cup with Jenny Pitman. They decided to adopt waiting tactics until leading in the final stages, where they expected Brown Chamberlin to veer sharply right-handed in the finishing straight as he had done in the past. Wayward Lad, who had gained a splendid second success in the King George VI Chase, and soundly beaten Brown Chamberlin in the process, was a warm favourite in the face of sustained opposition to Burrough Hill Lad in the ring. Bregawn, by then hopelessly intractable, was a 10–1 chance to retain his crown but his three stable companions, Captain John, Silver Buck and Ashley House, were missing this time from the scene of their trainer's record-breaking triumph twelve months earlier. Linda Sheedy, a mother of twins, created a little bit of history by becoming the first woman to ride in the Gold Cup – on the plodding 500–1 shot Foxbury, who was eventually pulled up.

Bregawn, for once, started with the rest of the field but two of Fred Winter's trio, Brown Chamberlin and Fifty Dollars More, shared the pacemaking over the first half-dozen fences. Brown Chamberlin, despite tending to jump to the right, then took a clear lead. Wayward Lad was in trouble more than a mile from home, blundered out of contention at the nineteenth fence, gurgled uncomfortably and was pulled up. Subsequent blood tests failed to reveal any clues to his uncharacteristic display. What a difference twelve months can make. Michael Dickinson, who dominated the race so completely in 1983, was further dismayed to see Bregawn throw away his chance by twice downing tools during the race quicker than a militant picket.

In the final mile Burrough Hill Lad and the 1983 Whitbread Gold Cup victor Drumlargan were the only two horses able to stay with Brown Chamberlin. But while Drumlargan merely kept on grimly, Burrough Hill Lad, racing near the rail as planned, closed on the leader approaching the final bend. Both here and after the last fence, Brown Chamberlin veered violently right-handed, giving away precious ground. In truth it would not have mattered if he had

run as straight as a gun barrel.

John Francome, never guilty of wasting his time on self-praise, reflects quite seriously: "That was the best ride I ever gave a horse. He never put a foot wrong but Cheltenham was always going to be the wrong way round for him. He lost a lot of ground going right-handed but you are better off letting them go that way."

Jenny Pitman was close to fainting as she watched the drama unfold from the roof of the stands. "It was going so perfectly it was just like unfolding the pages of a script that had already been completed," she relates.

Timing his victory charge with the precision he had planned so meticulously with the trainer, Phil Tuck brought Burrough Hill Lad to lead at the final fence. Brown Chamberlin, leaning acutely right-handed, rallied bravely once he reached the running rail in front of the stands. He might as well have attempted to catch the wind as Burrough Hill Lad bounded joyously clear on the flat like a giant war-horse. At the line victory was his by three lengths with Drumlargan eight lengths away third. Further behind, wily Bregawn finished to such purpose he would have claimed fourth place from Scot Lane in a few more strides.

Eleven months earlier Jenny Pitman had become the first woman to train a Grand National winner, with Corbiere. Now she had added jump racing's most prestigious race. It was a quite outstanding feat by the volatile Jenny, who only a few years before had been training a handful of point-to-pointers. Her stout-hearted defence of Burrough Hill Lad in the week before the race had been gloriously vindicated but she was far too ill to celebrate. Trembling uncontrollably, feeling violently sick, she was on the verge of collapse. Somehow she made her way down endless flights of stairs to greet the winner she had trained with such exemplary patience.

To this day she shakes her head in disbelief at the improbable cocktail of events that led to Burrough Hill Lad's Gold Cup triumph.

"When you think of his breeding at the very grass roots, his bad legs, his dodgy jumping, all those awful stories. It was unbelievable. I felt his Gold Cup victory had put a point over. It proved that my winning the Grand National with Corbiere was not a fluke," she explains proudly.

Burrough Hill Lad's mighty success earned the grateful Stan Riley a handsome first prize of

£47,375. Riley surely set an unusual precedent by becoming the first man to own a Gold Cup winner while drawing the dole. At the time, having sold his restaurant, he was collecting, quite legitimately, £27 a week unemployment benefit from the State at his local employment office in Leicester.

When the rugged Burrough Hill Lad won the Hennessy Cognac Gold Cup with quite memorable authority the following autumn and then added the King George VI Chase he threatened to dominate jump racing as no horse had done since Arkle. But training and owning jumpers would test the patience of a saint and in the years to come frequent injury would prevent Jenny Pitman and Stan Riley ever running him in the Gold Cup again. He was withdrawn

shortly before the Gold Cup in both 1985 and 1986 and made one last attempt at a comeback at Wincanton in February 1988, but was not entirely sound afterwards.

Every now and then Stan Riley would hint that the horse was for sale. Jenny Pitman could not face the thought of the great chaser going elsewhere, perhaps running in point-to-points in his old age against horses who would not have touched him in his prime. Eventually she agreed a deal with Riley which ensured that she could control the destiny of Burrough Hill Lad for the rest of his days.

Who can possibly doubt Jenny Pitman's devotion to her horses as she reveals: "At the time things were very hard for us. Money was tight and I could not

A superb action shot by George Selwyn. Burrough Hill Lad (centre) pursues Fifty Dollars More

Jenny Pitman salutes Burrough Hill Lad watched by the horse's bearded owner-breeder Stan Riley

really afford the horse. But other requirements had to wait. When I went out and stroked him afterwards I had a feeling inside that money cannot buy.''

Since the boxes at Weathercock House are invariably full, Burrough Hill Lad enjoys a healthy and active retirement with one of Jenny's owners Kay Birchenhough near Weymouth in Dorset. In his teens the old horse has proved a surprisingly sensible hunter with the South Dorset. History relates that only the cruellest misfortune prevented him joining the select band of horses who have won more than one Cheltenham Gold Cup.

TOTE CHELTENHAM GOLD CUP.			March 15th 1984.	£47,375.	*Good.*
1 Burrough Hill Lad	8	12 0	P. Tuck	100–30	
2 Brown Chamberlin	9	12 0	J. Francome	5–1	
3 Drumlargan	10	12 0	Mr F. Codd	16–1	
4 Scot Lane	11	12 0	C. Smith	100–1	
5 Fifty Dollars More	9	12 0	R. Linley	28–1	
6 Bregawn	10	12 0	G. Bradley	10–1	
7 Canny Danny	8	12 0	N. Madden	40–1	
8 Royal Bond	11	12 0	F. Berry	33–1	
9 Observe	8	12 0	B. de Haan	16–1	

3 lengths, 8.   Owned and bred R. S. Riley.   Trained Mrs J. Pitman.
6m. 41.4 seconds   Also 6–4 Fav Wayward Lad (R. Earnshaw) P.U., 33 Everett (S. Shilston) P.U., 500 Foxbury (Mrs L. Sheedy) P.U.   12 Ran.   Tote win: £4.10.

Burrough Hill Lad: br.g. 1976 (Richboy–Green Monkey)

19

FORGIVE 'N FORGET
(1985)

THE CONSTANT GRIM WASTAGE of steeplechasers through injury, leg trouble and death in action remains the unacceptable face of jump racing. At times even the most hardened enthusiast must feel uneasy at the recurring image of a big-hearted chaser, horribly damaged in a fall, waiting forlornly for the merciful release offered by a vet's humane killer. Yet horses are born to run and jump. They do so willingly and joyously, often immediately after a fall, unencumbered by the presence of a rider on their backs. Jumping truly is the name of the game and the very real risks ever present for both jockey and horse are part of the enduring appeal of the sport.

Improvements in the construction of fences, wings and running rails have all helped to reduce the dangers, but steeplechasing remains by its very nature a hazardous business. Those of us who make the annual pilgrimage to Cheltenham each March would not do so if every race was run on the flat or over small, flimsy, insubstantial obstacles that did not pose a challenge.

The good-looking, high-spirited chestnut Forgive 'N Forget was bought by canny Jimmy Fitzgerald as a replacement for Tim Kilroe's two ill-fated chasers Fairy King, who broke his back in a race fall, and Brave Fellow, who died from a heart attack on the gallops. Some substitute; Forgive 'N Forget, invariably sporting a fluffy white noseband, ran at the Festival six years in succession, always honourably, sometimes superbly.

He won the 1985 Gold Cup with a dazzling charge up the final hill and was the victim of hideous misfortune when he broke a hind pastern, sickeningly, in the closing stages of the 1988 Gold Cup. The fact that he looked very much like winning the race at the time offered bleak consolation to those closest to him. The months ahead would be a little emptier for

Jimmy Fitzgerald, Tim Kilroe, his jockey Mark Dwyer and lad "Strappy" Scott who had led him so proudly in the parade.

Dwyer, the dashing champion apprentice of Ireland, and the headstrong Forgive 'N Forget, heavily backed winner of a bumper race at Leopardstown as a five-year-old, arrived within days of each other at Fitzgerald's windswept farm, on the edge of Malton in North Yorkshire, in the late autumn of 1982.

The young jockey's healthy birth had been a triumph over the worst anxieties of the medical profession. It was feared that an attack of German measles during his mother's pregnancy might have caused irreparable damage to the unborn child.

Bright and ruggedly energetic, one of eight children, he left school illegally, aged fourteen, to pursue his ambition in racing. Increasing weight turned his attention to jumping after a meteoric career on the flat had yielded sixty-six winners. Tall, with slim legs and a prize fighter's torso, Mark Dwyer possesses an excellent racing brain and quickly became a leading jump jockey until he dislocated his right shoulder painfully and repeatedly in a series of falls which caused him to miss the 1984 Festival. Radical surgery the following autumn finally solved the problem that threatened his career.

Forgive 'N Forget was the product of a breeding of extremes. He was out of the prolific and speedy mare Tackienne, who produced nine winners from her first ten foals. Her sole success on the racecourse came over five furlongs as a two-year-old. Later, when she appeared in the Goffs sales ring on November 22nd 1976, Tackienne was already in foal to the grey Precipice Wood, a thorough stayer whose victories included the Ascot Gold Cup. The mare, bred for sprinting, attracted little interest and was knocked down to a bid of 600 guineas from Tommy

Walsh, who liked to keep the odd mare at his farm at Poulakerry in Co. Tipperary.

Thirteen months later Tackienne's vivacious chestnut foal was bought by Bill Byrne of the Barrackstown Stud as a speculative investment for 1,700 guineas.

"He was as good a lunatic as you ever came across, as mad as a hatter," reports Byrne colourfully. "I entered him in several sales but he always broke himself up before he got there. One day he was in bits in his box. He was a hardy beggar all right."

The future Gold Cup winner missed so many subsequent appointments in the sales ring through self-inflicted injuries and accidents that Tattersalls (Ire) generously waived his entry fee when he was finally sold by Byrne at Ballsbridge in November 1980 for 4,300 guineas. The unbroken and unnamed chestnut, still an ill-mannered handful, kicked two bystanders as he was led round before entering the ring. His purchaser, the genial agent Frank Barry, quickly passed him on to the legendary punter Barney Curley, who named him Forgive 'N Forget, and put him into training with Liam Brennan at the Curragh. The horse ran in the name of the trainer's wife Valerie.

When Forgive 'N Forget landed a gamble in his bumper at Leopardstown after four successive defeats the local stewards were not in the mood to forgive and forget. Both Brennan and his rider Anthony Powell were summarily suspended.

Soon the horse was bought by ruddy-cheeked Jimmy Fitzgerald in a private deal for Tim Kilroe, a lifelong racing enthusiast who was brought up in the small village of Curragh in Co. Roscommon and had made his fortune in the construction business in England. This time the horse changed hands for 35,000 guineas.

Jimmy Fitzgerald, born in the romantically named one-pub Tipperary village of Horse and Jockey, had begun as an apprentice with John Oxx on the Curragh but moved to England at the age of sixteen and achieved his first win over jumps on Robert's Choice at Southwell in 1956. A typically cheerful and hardy jockey in the North of England, Jimmy Fitzgerald won the Scottish Grand National on Brasher at long defunct Bogside, claimed a single Festival success on Harvest Gold in the 1966 George Duller and was extremely proud to have ridden in the 1960 Gold Cup.

A ghastly fall at Doncaster in November 1966 left him with a fractured skull and permanent deafness in his left ear. His life as a jockey was over. He bought

Norton Grange, a 120-acre farm near Malton, erected four boxes and embarked with only two horses on the rocky path that would see him become one of the most versatile trainers in the sport.

Forgive 'N Forget's early skirmishes at Malton served notice of an outrageous talent. He wanted to rush everywhere, pulled impulsively, possessed rare speed for a staying horse and was a nightmare in traffic. The very sight of a moving lorry would send him scurrying urgently up banks and into ditches. He could also whip round wickedly on a sixpence. From the very start the wily Fitzgerald tried to harness his restless energy at home and in his races, tactics that would eventually ensure the greatest dividend of all. Forgive 'N Forget began his first season in England as a raw novice over hurdles, ridden by Mark Dwyer, and ended it by giving his incurably Irish trainer the victory he had craved at the Cheltenham Festival since his first visit in 1954.

The most obvious target for the rapidly improving chestnut would have been one of the novice hurdles at Cheltenham. The robust manner of his triumph in a qualifier for the Coral Golden Hurdle in knee-deep mud at Ayr dictated otherwise. While the rest of the runners struggled in the appalling conditions Forgive 'N Forget and Mark Dwyer splashed home with eye-catching ease. Less than two months later they took the Final at the Festival with impressive authority.

The next year Forgive 'N Forget returned to Cheltenham as firm favourite for the Sun Alliance Chase after his decisive victory in the Timeform Chase. This time he was ridden by John Francome in place of Mark Dwyer, out of action with a dislocated shoulder. It was a booking that Jimmy Fitzgerald would bitterly regret. Francome, usually such a sound judge of pace, switched off Forgive 'N Forget at the rear, and at one stage was at least ten lengths adrift of his field. In the second half of the race the favourite made up an enormous amount of ground but by the time he began his challenge in earnest the winner A Kinsman had flown.

Jimmy Fitzgerald turned scarlet in anger at what he considered to be grossly exaggerated waiting tactics. Francome pointed out that a mistake at the second last fence had cost his mount dear. The trainer was inconsolable. He believed Forgive 'N Forget was the best horse he had ever trained and immediately backed him at 33–1 to win the following year's Gold Cup.

Reunited with Mark Dwyer the next season Forgive 'N Forget continued to progress. Strongly built, with plenty of bone, he was not the most natural jumper but was always safe. He won the Rowland Meyrick Chase easily at Wetherby on Boxing Day, failed narrowly to add the Whitbread Trial at Ascot and prepared for Cheltenham by outsprinting By The Way at the finish of the Timeform Chase. It was Burrough Hill Lad who dominated the ante-post market in the weeks before the 1985 Cheltenham Festival. Carrying the crushing burden of twelve stone he was quite magnificent in winning the Hennessy Cognac Gold Cup and gained a thrilling victory over Combs Ditch in the King George VI Chase at Kempton.

When he completed the formality of a walk-over in the Gainsborough Chase early in February he was recording his fifth consecutive success. Frost and snow then prevented him running in several suitable Cheltenham trials. He travelled to Haydock early in March for the Greenall Whitley Chase and finished fourth under the punishing weight of 12 st. 7 lb. It was, in the circumstances, an entirely satisfactory display; but an injury the week before the Festival put his appearance in doubt and he was withdrawn on the eve of the Gold Cup.

A nagging cut under the knee on his near foreleg prevented him running. The wound was caused by his teeth raking along the side of the leg as he galloped with his head held unusually low. A variety of protective boots had been tried on his lower limbs but it proved extremely difficult to cover the point of the injury at the back of his knee. If the Gold Cup had been ten days later Jenny Pitman believes he would have recovered. She simply ran out of time.

"You always had your back to the wall with this horse. He stood so straight on his front legs he was a nightmare to train," she observes.

Brown Chamberlin, the runner-up the previous year, missed the entire season. Others who were ruled out by injury included Observe, Lettoch and the mercurial mare, the reigning Champion hurdler Dawn Run, who strained a ligament in a foreleg shortly after a highly encouraging debut over fences at Navan in November.

Forgive 'N Forget so nearly joined the casualty list when heat was discovered in his off forefoot three days before the Gold Cup. A corn was suspected but a thorough veterinary examination failed to locate

Half Free and the blinkered Drumadowney just lead Forgive 'N Forget at the penultimate fence

A victory touched with elegance. Forgive 'N Forget reserves his best jump for the last fence

the cause of the problem and the next morning the heat was gone. Even so it was decided not to risk aggravating the problem further by fitting the customary light aluminium racing plate to the offending foot. Thus Forgive 'N Forget ran in the Gold Cup with the undoubted disadvantage of wearing one heavier, steel exercise shoe and three racing plates.

In the regrettable absence of Burrough Hill Lad, Combs Ditch, who had run him so close at Kempton, was installed as favourite for the Gold Cup. He had experienced a novel preparation over hurdles at Ascot. There was quiet confidence in the consistent former hunter Earls Brig, owned and trained under permit by his breeder Billy Hamilton on the Scottish borders at Hawick. Forgive 'N Forget was marginally preferred as third favourite at 7–1 ahead of Righthand Man and Wayward Lad, both trained by

Monica Dickinson.

The infuriating Drumadowney, a rogue reformed, was an intriguing first Gold Cup runner for Tim Forster, a hugely successful yet permanently pessimistic trainer. Drumadowney had pulled himself up in three of his first four races in this country. Forced early retirement beckoned until, adorned with blinkers, he earned a reprieve with a brilliant all-the-way victory at Cheltenham in November. His subsequent behaviour had been faultless, with three more facile successes from the front.

Drumadowney it was, who set out to make all the running as freezing rain and sleet assailed the Gold Cup field, and he was still in front when Earls Brig, in close attendance, charged recklessly through the last ditch at the top of the hill. It was a mistake that cost him any chance of victory. Drumadowney, still technically a novice, lost a little ground with an error at the next fence and was immediately pressed by Half Free, owned by jump racing's first Arab owner Sheikh Ali Abu Khamsin. Swooping downhill for the final time both Forgive 'N Forget and Combs Ditch were poised just behind the leading pair and as Half Free ran a little wide on the final bend Mark Dwyer took the opportunity to ease Forgive 'N Forget towards the far rail.

Half Free, whose stamina was slightly suspect, still led approaching the final fence but a brilliantly athletic leap here took Forgive 'N Forget thrillingly into a lead of fully two lengths. It was an advantage he would not relinquish. Quickening away instantly from a chasing pack of half a dozen challengers, his handsome nose-banded head thrust out defiantly, Forgive 'N Forget drifted a little right-handed as he neared the winning post. It was a victory touched with elegance.

On the flat Half Free, patently tired, was unable to resist the combined late rush of Righthand Man and Earls Brig. Drumadowney rallied bravely to take fourth prize. No one could possibly question his resolution. Many horses prematurely labelled ungenuine are subsequently found to have a physical problem. That summer poor Drumadowney, only seven, was found dead while turned out in a field in Dorset. He had suffered a massive haemorrhage.

Wayward Lad, running in his third Gold Cup, was again a severe disappointment. His former stable companion, the 1983 winner Bregawn, was far behind when he refused at the last fence. Forgive 'N Forget would return to Cheltenham three more times to contest the Cheltenham Gold Cup. He was superb in defeat against Dawn Run in 1986, ran unaccountably badly in the snow in 1987 and was offering every hope of an unexpected second triumph when his off hind pastern shattered as the 1988 race was reaching its climax. He was stalking Cavvies Clown and Charter Party, the pair who dominated the finish, when the limb gave way in the very act of crossing the fourth last fence. Somehow Forgive 'N Forget kept on his feet on landing but tragically the injury was so severe there could be only one course of action.

Within minutes his life was over. Steeplechasing had claimed another notable victim. Forgive 'N Forget, a splendid ambassador for the sport, won sixteen races. His ashes, together with the racecards of his four Gold Cups, now lie behind a distinctive plaque in a wall at Cheltenham near the Royal Box. It is a suitably permanent memorial to an admirable racehorse.

TOTE CHELTENHAM GOLD CUP.   March 14th 1985.   £52,560.   *Good.*

1	Forgive 'N Forget	8 12 0	M. Dwyer	7–1	
2	Righthand Man	8 12 0	G. Bradley	15–2	
3	Earls Brig	10 12 0	P. Tuck	13–2	
4	Drumadowney	7 12 0	H. Davies	9–1	
5	Half Free	9 12 0	R. Linley	9–1	
6	Boreen Prince	8 12 0	N. Madden	20–1	
7	Combs Ditch	9 12 0	C. Brown	4–1 Fav	
8	Wayward Lad	10 12 0	R. Earnshaw	8–1	
9	Homeson	8 12 0	J. J. O'Neill	100–1	
10	Door Latch	7 12 0	J. Francome	25–1	
11	Ballinacurra Lad	10 12 0	P. Leech	33–1	
12	Sointulla Boy	10 12 0	Mr T. Houlbrooke	100–1	

1½ lengths, 2½.   Owned T. Kilroe & Sons Ltd.   Trained J. Fitzgerald.
Bred Thomas Walsh.   6m. 48.3 seconds.   Also 22 Rainbow Warrior (K. Morgan) P.U. and Bregawn (Mr W. P. Mullins) Ref and 40 Greenwood Lad (R. Rowe) P.U.
15 Ran.   Tote win: £7.70.

Forgive 'N Forget: ch.g. 1977 (Precipice Wood–Tackienne)

20

DAWN RUN
(1986)

THE VERY NAME DAWN RUN conjures a web of nostalgia that contains a thousand glorious images. We remember her unrivalled splendour, that shining toughness of spirit, the intensity of purpose, her fearlessly aggressive jumping and the bleak shock of her grim death on a field of battle in a foreign land. Yet for all her wonderfully inspiring deeds in public I treasure the memory of a cold morning in Co. Kilkenny when Dawn Run's name was but a whisper on the wind and thoughts of a unique, record-breaking double at Cheltenham were no more than elusive, impossible dreams.

I can picture the scene as if it was yesterday. The big, headstrong, raw-boned almost masculine mare, charging almost imperiously with a tiny, all too frail elderly grandmother of nine perched precariously on her back. Somehow they are still together after completing five energetic and surprisingly tight circuits at the head of Paddy Mullins' string of horses.

At the time her rider and owner, the redoubtable Mrs Charmian Hill, was fighting a losing battle with the racing authorities in Ireland. Displaying an unfortunate sense of timing the Irish stewards informed Mrs Hill they would not renew her licence the very day before she won on Dawn Run at Tralee in June 1982.

"I fought it like mad, of course. It was maddening because I had won two more races after coming back from a fall that nearly killed me," she explained shortly afterwards.

Now you might suppose that the licensing stewards had Charmian Hill's best interests at heart in this decision but pointing this out to her was a course fraught with danger.

"Don't you dare say I have retired," she once commanded me. "They are forcing me out. I'm surprised they have done it because I've shown I can win races.

Besides, I'm so peculiar I'm a draw at the races."

Charmian Hill, in short, was every bit as stubborn, determined and at times obstinate as the superb mare who carried her colours with sustained distinction. Their fateful first meeting came at the Ballsbridge Sales on November 2nd 1981. Looking for a suitable mare to ride in bumper races Charmian Hill had compiled a short list of ten to inspect. The first she saw was a big, unfurnished three-year-old filly, broken and barely backed, by the prolific stallion Deep Run out of Twilight Slave, an unraced mare who had cost John Riordan from Rathcormack, Co. Cork, 300 guineas as a yearling at Goffs in November 1963.

"The moment she walked out of the box I was mad keen to buy her," Charmian Hill recalled two years later over dinner in Waterford. "My maximum was 6,000 Irish guineas but she had such a marvellous pedigree on the dam's side I thought she would make at least 10,000. How the English buyers missed her I don't know."

She bought the unnamed three-year-old for 5,800 Irish guineas and took her straight to the family home Belmont, at Ballinakill on the edge of Waterford, with 30 acres of grounds running down to the river Suir. There she lived with her husband Dr Eddie Hill, a highly entertaining character who frequently displayed a natty line in conjuring tricks. At that time the Hills' daughter Penny would rise at dawn each morning to train for a marathon. The new acquisition was quickly named Dawn Run. Usually Mrs Hill owned horses on her own. This time her son Oliver, a Dublin property man, took a share in Dawn Run. Soon Charmian Hill was riding her filly every day. An old schooling fence stood idly in a field beside the house. The temptation was too much.

"We hopped over it every day but she did not need

any lessons on jumping. She was the easiest horse I have ever started off," observed the proud owner. In the spring of 1982 Dawn Run was put into training with wise Paddy Mullins, a naturally shy, almost reticent man with a countryman's understanding of horses, a voice as soft as an Irish mist and an enduring record of success with jumpers stretching over four decades. He had also taken the prestigious Champion Stakes at Newmarket with the mare Hurry Harriet in 1973.

Soon Dawn Run was entered in bumper races. Naturally her intrepid owner intended to ride her. She had come very late to race riding at the age of forty, starting in point-to-points and later winning races on the flat over hurdles, hunter chases and even the most perilous of all jump races, a novices' chase. Even so, she was lucky to survive a horrific fall at Thurles in November 1980.

"The horse broke his neck and I almost broke mine," she once assured me calmly, as if describing a stumble in the garden of her home. Charmian Hill weighed only six-and-a-half stone when she left hospital after four months' treatment for neck, back, rib and internal injuries; but retirement was the last thing on her mind. After two introductory races Dawn Run and her ageless owner gained a famous victory in the curiously named Devils Bit flat race for amateur riders at Tralee on June 6th 1982. The legend had begun.

A letter to the Irish Turf Club signed by several leading jockeys including the frequent amateur champion Ted Walsh failed to gain a reprieve for Charmian Hill. At sixty-three her life as a jockey was over. Paddy Mullins' son Tom, an amateur, won two more bumper races on Dawn Run that autumn. When the mare began racing over hurdles she was ridden by Tom's amiable brother Tony, a promising young professional, who invariably made the running on her. They won impressively at Navan, Leopardstown and Punchestown but when Dawn Run came to England for the Sun Alliance Novices' Hurdle at Cheltenham Charmian Hill insisted, to Paddy Mullins' dismay, on using a more experienced jockey, who must be Irish. Her choice was Ron Barry. Displaying enormous talent on her first visit to the Festival Dawn Run just failed to concede 13 lb to the high-class future chaser Sabin du Loir.

Back in England three weeks later and reunited with Tony Mullins, the hardy mare with the almost tangible will to win took a handicap hurdle at Liverpool on Friday with distinctive ease then gave the Champion hurdler Gaye Brief the fright of his life in the Templegate Hurdle less than twenty-four hours later. Receiving only 6 lb the brilliant novice ran the Champion to a length.

Though Charmian Hill was prevented from riding in races she continued to drive the 35 miles from Waterford to Goresbridge once a week to partner her powerful mare at early morning exercise. They led the string as of right though, she explained one day, "If Dawn Run was behind others she would pull me to the front anyway. After several laps she has usually caught the tail-enders."

Already Charmian Hill harboured boldly ambitious plans for the mare who featured in ante-post betting for the 1984 Champion Hurdle. Her faith in the horse was wholly contagious.

"The Champion does not excite me at all," she would say. "Dawn Run will make a far better chaser. Even if she wins the Champion by twenty lengths she will go chasing next season. I believe she will become the first horse to win both the Champion Hurdle and the Cheltenham Gold Cup."

Her dream strengthened as a series of forceful victories saw Dawn Run's price shorten for the first of those two high-flying objectives. Early that winter Charmian Hill had upset her trainer yet again by insisting on a further change of jockey. Tony Mullins, later champion of Ireland twice, was displaced after winning on the mare at Down Royal in November 1983. When she beat Amarach at Ascot later that month she was ridden by the dynamic former champion Jonjo O'Neill. Dawn Run and her new rider then beat the title-holder Gaye Brief in a stirring duel at Kempton before taking the Wessel Cable Champion Hurdle with complete authority. So to Cheltenham, where the big, brave mare, starting an odds-on favourite and in receipt of 5 lb sex allowance, duly became Champion after a spirited tussle with the unconsidered outsider Cima.

Further glittering triumphs followed that spring and early summer at Liverpool, then superbly at Auteuil, first in the Prix la Barka and finally the French Champion Hurdle. Now all of Ireland shared Charmian Hill's faith in her noble mare, who returned home safely for a welcome break at grass at Belmont.

"There is a very male side to her," Charmian Hill reflected. "At one time I said she was a hermaphrodite. She is tough and very bossy and can be very

All in a day's work. Jonjo O'Neill and Tony Mullins with Dawn Run, the mare who epitomised the spirit of steeplechasing

moody if she does not have her own way. When she is out with other horses in the summer she acts as master of the herd.''

Tony Mullins adds: ''Everyone imagines she was a dear old Irish mare but she would run you out of her box as soon as look at you.''

It was Tony who rode Dawn Run in an exciting debut over fences at Navan in November 1984 that offered untold promise for the future. Truly her potential seemed limitless; but within weeks leg trouble, the bane of steeplechasing, interrupted her training programme. A strained ligament was diagnosed. A less patient trainer might have pressed on regardless. Paddy Mullins calmly heeded the warning. The mare would not run again that season. Rest

would prove the best cure of all.

The following summer, shortly before she was due to rejoin Paddy Mullins, Dawn Run, the most valuable mare in National Hunt racing, was lost for twelve hours in Waterford City. On her return from a day's racing, Charmian Hill was informed that three of her horses were roaming on a housing estate two miles away. Dusk was falling as the anxious owner set out in search of them. ''That evening was a nightmare,'' she related later. ''Someone had left a gate open and the three had gone out straight across the main road between Waterford and Dunmore. When we spotted Dawn Run I tried to catch her with some women and children. I told them to be brave and wave their arms to corner her.''

The strong-willed mare, however, was enjoying her new-found freedom. She rushed at her owner with bared teeth, then swung round and kicked her painfully on the thigh. Charmian Hill and her weary posse eventually drove the horses back across the main road but then lost them as they clattered off in the gathering gloom. Further pursuit was impossible.

The next morning Charmian Hill, noticeably lame, found all three horses in a nearby field. Dawn Run was unhurt. Later that year she returned to action at Punchestown in mid-December, beat some of the best chasers in Ireland with dismissive ease and was immediately promoted as a leading contender for the Gold Cup. Paddy Mullins' whispered reservations about her inexperience were swept away in the euphoria of the moment. After a second facile success at Leopardstown at the end of the year it was agreed that Dawn Run must be given a taste of English fences before attempting the elusive double

at the Festival. The reconnaissance mission at Cheltenham on January 25th proved to be a disaster, particularly for Tony Mullins.

Setting off with her customary vigour in the Holsten Distributors Chase the big mare jumped with a pleasing mixture of boldness and accuracy for the first two miles. Her spring-heeled leaps at the second last and last fences on the first circuit brought gasps of admiration from the crowd. Clearly Tony Mullins was gaining in confidence. As the great mare galloped on gaily towards the sixteenth fence, the final open ditch, her jockey asked her to stand off the fence rather than go in close and pop over.

Dawn Run started to come up, changed her mind in a moment of uncertainty, put in an extra stride, somehow scrambled safely over but ejected her hapless jockey as she twisted left-handed on landing. Showing remarkable agility Tony Mullins ran alongside Dawn Run until he had brought her to a halt.

Dawn Run (no. 14) is only third over the final fence behind Forgive 'N Forget and Wayward Lad (far side)

Unfortunately he was on the off side, or wrong side, and by the time he had clambered nimbly on to her back again the remaining runners had gone beyond recall. Though the cause was lost, Dawn Run completed the race without mishap in last place.

"We came here for a school round but it has been a very expensive lesson," reflected the principal owner. Dawn Run's prohibitive Gold Cup odds of 5–2 remained unchanged, but in the following days speculation was rife that Tony Mullins would be replaced. Paddy Mullins, a fiercely loyal family man, fought hard to retain his son but Charmian Hill was adamant. Jonjo O'Neill would again ride Dawn Run at Cheltenham. The best-laid plans in jumping are often thwarted by the weather. Frost prevented the new partnership attempting a full-scale rehearsal in the Diners Club Chase at Punchestown. Instead Dawn Run, badly in need of practice over fences, was ridden by Jonjo O'Neill in two very public schooling sessions at Gowran Park and Punchestown.

When she arrived at Cheltenham, Dawn Run had raced in only four steeplechases. Seldom, if ever, has a horse been less prepared for the supreme test. Yet what she lacked in experience the rugged mare, with a heart of oak, more than made up with a compelling degree of resolution. The task was undeniably formidable, but not impossible. In 1952 Mont Tremblant, a six-year-old, had claimed the Gold Cup in his fifth race over fences. So, too, had Roman Hackle in 1940. Captain Christy, also, had been a novice in 1974.

A lucrative sponsorship deal rested on Dawn Run's performance in the Gold Cup. She had already been signed up by Dawn Dairies; success at the Festival would ensure a major advertising campaign. The absence of Burrough Hill Lad unquestionably improved her chance. He had succumbed once more to leg problems soon after winning the Gainsborough Chase with much of his old flamboyance. Forgive 'N Forget was set to defend his title after an indifferent season. In a rare jumping lapse he had unseated his rider at Wetherby and was then only fourth to Combs Ditch in the Peter Marsh Chase at Haydock. Mark Dwyer's instructions from Jimmy Fitzgerald could not have been more precise. Whatever else happened he was not to track Dawn Run.

Righthand Man and Earls Brig, second and third the previous year, were back, too. So was old Wayward Lad, having gained a memorable record third success in the King George VI Chase on Boxing Day.

Arctic temperatures had prevented his usual warm-up race before the Festival but a review of his form at Cheltenham suggested that the finishing climb was a hill too far for him. Run and Skip, a habitual front-runner, had earned his chance with a comfortable victory in the Coral Welsh National.

The bare, scorched turf and barren countryside surrounding Cheltenham bore vivid testimony in mid-March to a prolonged spell of bitterly cold weather that had halted racing for almost a month. On going that was officially good, Dawn Run was a solidly backed favourite at 15–8 to defy the lessons of history. She it was, who took the field along from the start at a searching gallop. Little Run and Skip, by the same sire Deep Run, but massively dwarfed by the mare, was the only one to go with her. For more than a circuit her jumping was impressively fluent but her hind-legs splashed awkwardly into the water, and she then blundered alarmingly at the eighteenth fence on the far side of the course under Cleeve Hill.

Jonjo O'Neill, tenacious as ever, sat admirably tight. He had wanted to give the mare a well-earned breather but now the chance had gone for ever. The mistake cost Dawn Run priceless ground and her advantageous position close to the rails. As Run and Skip showed in front for the first time his jockey Steve Smith Eccles thought: "That's the end of her."

Imagine his surprise a few moments later when Dawn Run came sweeping through on the inside to reclaim the lead with a confident jump at the difficult third last fence. Just behind the leading pair both Wayward Lad and Forgive 'N Forget were making significant progress. The race clearly lay between the quartet.

Round the final bend, surging towards the penultimate fence, the four were almost in line. Desperate measures were required now. Jonjo O'Neill, displaying a flagrant disregard for his own safety, drove the mare into the fence like a man inspired and gained the mighty leap his courage demanded. Dawn Run landed in front again but was then swallowed up once more as Wayward Lad and Forgive 'N Forget swept imperiously past in a matter of strides. They landed over the last fence upsides, victory beckoning, with the mare apparently struggling to hold on to third place from Run and Skip.

Wayward Lad, under the strongest possible pressure from Graham Bradley, leaned sharply left-handed towards the far rail as he won his battle for supremacy with Forgive 'N Forget. Half-way up the

Emotion overflows as Charmian Hill and Jonjo O'Neill are carried shoulder high above the cheering crowds

hill he had pulled two, almost three lengths clear. Just as his success seemed assured the Irish mare began as glorious and determined a finishing charge as you will ever see on the punishing Cheltenham hill.

Though the cause seemed lost she would not give in. Displaying indomitable spirit, driven with strength and purpose by the most dynamic jockey of the day, Dawn Run began to close. Gradually, agonisingly, inexorably, she was narrowing the gap but would the post come too soon? Towards the end poor Wayward Lad looked like a frail boat bobbing up and down on the same spot as if held back by an invisible anchor. Suddenly, wonderfully, with 25 yards to run, the incomparable mare was level. Now there could only be one result. On the line Jonjo O'Neill punched the air in jubilation as the roars and the cheers of the massed crowd echoed like endless waves of gunfire across the famous landscape.

Remarkably Dawn Run, an inexperienced novice over fences, set a new record time for the race of 6 minutes 35.3 seconds as she became the first horse to complete the elusive double in the Gold Cup. All of us lucky enough to see her make history that day were touched forever by the moment. Utter mayhem broke out as we stampeded to salute her. Solid yeomen with rustic faces and hands like shovels wept unashamed tears of joy. The wildly spontaneous celebrations continued for fully ten minutes while the triumphant heroine and her valiant jockey fought their way back through the chaotic scene. This was their finest hour. Emotion overflowed as they returned to the greatest Irish roar ever heard at the Festival. Thousands of English admirers joined in the boisterous applause. We knew we had witnessed one of the supreme achievements in sport.

Dawn Run was unable to enter the winner's circle until Paddy Mullins, normally the most mild-mannered of people, came in like a tiger, forcing back the cheering mob. Charmian Hill found herself hugged and kissed by complete strangers, and was then tossed unceremoniously into the air. How typical that Jonjo O'Neill carried Tony Mullins on his shoulders on to the victory rostrum.

Later Jonjo would reflect: "The mare was very determined once she was motivated to do it. But you would not want to boss her very much." Then he added graciously, "She always used to run a lot sweeter for Tony than me."

Wayward Lad's trainer and supporters have consistently claimed that the 5 lb mare's allowance enjoyed by Dawn Run ultimately decided the result of the 1986 Gold Cup. It would be churlish to dismiss their argument, yet cold calculations about pounds and lengths seem strangely inappropriate after such a momentous race. Dawn Run's unforgettable late thrust for glory was more to do with soaring spirit, the stubborn, aggressive, single-minded refusal to accept defeat. Like an exhausted, brawling pugilist she had risen from the canvas at the count of nine and delivered a knock-out blow in the final round. As an example of triumph against overwhelming odds her victory stands alone in the history of the Cheltenham Gold Cup.

How ironic that Dawn Run should fall at the first fence at Liverpool on her next visit to England. A month later, reunited once more with Tony Mullins, she beat Buck House at level weights in a rare and thrilling sponsored match over two miles at Punchestown. Afterwards Paddy Mullins said on television that the mare would be retired for the season. Char-

mian Hill dictated otherwise. She insisted that Dawn Run should remain in training for a second attempt at the French Champion Hurdle in June.

Her belief in her horse's invincibility was now absolute. An unexpected defeat by the French-trained Le Rheusois in her preparatory race followed. Tony Mullins, always a realist, advised Mrs Hill that Dawn Run would not beat Le Rheusois next time. Still she would not listen.

Tony recalls: "I pointed out that the other horse ran away from us. Mrs Hill was dumbstruck when I told her my opinion. Her face was full of disbelief."

The faithful, long-suffering Mullins was replaced yet again when Dawn Run returned to France at the end of June for the French Champion Hurdle at Auteuil. This time she was ridden by the immensely experienced French jockey Michel Chirol. Dawn Run was disputing the lead with Le Rheusois, the eventual winner, when she failed to take off at the fifth last flight, plunged through it and died instantly as she crashed to the ground. The greatest chase jumping mare of all time had broken her neck. It was a tragically bleak end to the life of the horse who had brightened our lives immeasurably.

Visitors to Cheltenham can now gaze at a splendid half-size bronze of Dawn Run in her rightful position beside the arena that witnessed such unprecedented scenes of joy when she returned in triumph in 1986. She will never be forgotten.

TOTE CHELTENHAM GOLD CUP.   March 13th 1986.   £54,900.   *Good.*

1	Dawn Run	8 11 9	J. J. O'Neill	15–8 Fav
2	Wayward Lad	11 12 0	G. Bradley	8–1
3	Forgive 'N Forget	9 12 0	M. Dwyer	7–2
4	Run and Skip	8 12 0	S. Smith Eccles	15–2
5	Righthand Man	9 12 0	R. Earnshaw	25–1
6	Observe	10 12 0	J. Duggan	50–1

1 length, 2½.   Owned Mrs C. Hill.   Trained P. Mullins.   Bred J. Riordan.
6m. 35.3 seconds. Race record.   Also 9–2 Combs Ditch (C. Brown) Carried out,
20 Cybrandian (A. Brown) P.U., 25 Earls Brig (P. Tuck) Fell, Von Trappe (R. Dunwoody) Fell
and 500 Castle Andrea (G. Mernagh) P.U.   11 Ran.   Tote win: £2.50.

Dawn Run: b.m. 1978 (Deep Run–Twilight Slave)

21

THE THINKER
(1987)

A SUDDEN, UNWELCOME BLIZZARD sweeping down from the frozen peak of Cleeve Hill severely disrupted the 1987 Gold Cup. The snowstorm arrived without warning during the race before the Gold Cup, and became heavier during the parade for the big race. Almost an inch of snow fell inside an hour. Runners and riders faded into vague, blurred images as they cantered gingerly to the start. Their very presence there was a token display of optimism over reality. A steward was already at the scene accompanied by the Jockey Club's Inspector of Courses Neill Wyatt. After anxious discussions with the jockeys the inevitable conclusion was reached that conditions were unsafe for racing. Horses and riders filed back to the paddock area as the snow continued to fall relentlessly. Abandonment seemed inevitable.

Philip Arkwright, the briskly efficient clerk of the course, now exhibited an iron nerve. The show would go on.

He explains: "The ground was fairly warm and the amount of snow falling was not yet critical. I was determined to play for time."

A ghostly gathering of horses, jockeys, lads, trainers and owners was becalmed, some anxiously, some cheerfully, others with growing irritation as Cheltenham was enveloped in a massive white blanket. Down in the packed enclosures and in the stands the massed crowd waited for news with good-natured patience. In the busy tented village guests sheltered from the bleak conditions, anaesthetised against the weather by unlimited supplies of alcoholic refreshment.

An anonymous phone call from nearby Tewkesbury offered a glimmer of hope. "Hold on," said the caller. "The sun is shining again here." Professional forecasters could not have been more accurate.

Soon there was a break in the clouds to the west. Within minutes the snow stopped falling and a rapid thaw began. Would it be enough to ensure racing before darkness fell? Time was pressing now. The feature race was already an hour late.

Suddenly the paddock was a flurry of activity. Horses, heavily rugged, jig-jogged past; huddled jockeys, a few eager, most in disbelief, emerged from beneath large, colourful umbrellas. Trainers rushed to tighten girths and issue last-minute instructions.

Snow still lay thickly on the ground but the order had gone out to remount. Philip Arkwright, a dapper military figure, hurried to the start to fend off a possible revolt from any jockeys who might voice disagreement with the decision to race. He was accompanied by the senior steward Capt. Johnny Macdonald-Buchanan, M.C. The starting area positively bristled with authority. After a brief inspection the captain declared the racing would commence.

Philip Arkwright recalls: "In my view it was perfectly safe to race. There was no question of snow balling up under the horses' feet. The crowd had been staggeringly patient but we could not reasonably have sent horses back again and asked them to come out a third time.

"The tension at the start had reached fever pitch and the jockeys were beyond making their own decision. They needed to be told."

The drama was not over. Fifteen seconds after the announcement was made the starter warned the harried clerk of the course that the jockeys were unhappy at the decision.

Arkwright relates: "I told him to press on as ordered." Military might had won the day.

The betting for the race was dominated by Forgive 'N Forget, who had come right back to his best form in winning the Vincent O'Brien Irish Gold Cup at Leopardstown in mid-February. It was a welcome revival, for after his valiant show behind Dawn Run a year earlier he had returned to Yorkshire shin-sore and dehydrated.

"Even so I felt that was the best race he had ever run," reflects his jockey Mark Dwyer. "This time he felt terrific going down to post the first time but after the long delay in the snow I was not at all happy with him at the start. I knew we were not going to win."

Old Wayward Lad, by then twelve, and without a win all season, was back for his fifth attempt at the Gold Cup. We wondered if his sterling effort in defeat twelve months earlier had left a permanent scar. There was light support for Bolands Cross, an erratic jumper, and a late gamble from 10–1 to 13–2 on the progressive Northern hope The Thinker as punters realised that melting snow would increase the premium on stamina. A year earlier at the Festival he had finished in the rear on unsuitably fast

going, carrying a modest 10 st. 12 lb in the Kim Muir Chase. Subsequently he had won the Midlands Grand National run over four and a half miles on heavy ground by no less than fifteen lengths. Now he was second favourite for the Gold Cup on the strength of recent sparkling performances at Wetherby and Haydock.

The Thinker's jockey Ridley Lamb was one of a handful of riders who was keen for the Gold Cup to go ahead despite the effect of the swirling snowstorm.

He explains: "I realised the weather was playing into my hands as the ground was becoming softer by the minute but we had almost too much snow! At one point the fences were so white they blended into the background. I desperately wanted to race but I did not think we would."

Burrough Hill Lad was missing once more. He did not appear at all during the season. His trainer Jenny Pitman endured a second reverse when the imposing

A sudden blizzard delays the start of the 1987 Gold Cup. Forgive 'N Forget returns from the start

Stearsby, ante-post second favourite at the time, was found to be lame on the morning of the race. He had suffered a minor cut in a schooling accident at the start of the week. West Tip, winner of the 1986 Grand National, was ignored in the betting at 50–1. Chris Grant, the indestructible jockey whose forceful style of riding had earned him the enduring nickname of "Rambo", replaced Lorcan Wyer, injured earlier in the day, on Cybrandian. So the 1987 Gold Cup began eighty-one minutes behind schedule at 4.51 on going that resembled a white carpet with distinctive green patches.

Cybrandian led in the early stages from Door Latch, Mr Moonraker, Earls Brig and Charter Party who came down at the fifth fence. Earls Brig was pulled up soon after half-way and Bolands Cross unseated Peter Scudamore with a wholesale blunder at the third open ditch. Crucial mistakes slowed Forgive 'N Forget, too. A mile from home it was clear that he would not be winning.

Turning downhill towards the third last fence, so often a fateful point in the Gold Cup, The Thinker had just moved into second place behind Cybrandian when he dived dangerously through the top of the fence, landed flat-footed and lost his momentum.

"That mistake seemed to knock all the stuffing out of him," reported Ridley Lamb later.

Round the elbow into the straight, old Wayward Lad led the chasing group but the bold-jumping Cybrandian, ridden with customary vigour by Chris Grant, was still in front at the last fence. On the flat Wayward Lad fought briefly for the lead on the far side. Then he was gone as if held back once more by an invisible hand as he met the rising ground. The steep climb up that final daunting hill at Cheltenham had been the scene of so many dynamic finishes in the Gold Cup. Now it was to provide one more.

Hanging violently right-handed in the closing stages through sheer exhaustion Cybrandian was suddenly challenged on the stands side by The Thinker. The battle for supremacy was short, sharp and decisive. Poor Cybrandian had given his all. In the shadow of the post The Thinker bounded forward to claim the glory. Door Latch, staying on dourly, just held third place from West Tip. Wayward Lad, so often the bridesmaid at Cheltenham but a champion elsewhere, was only fifth.

Racing was united in its delight for the triumphant trainer Arthur Stephenson who, true to his dictum that little fish are sweet, had chosen instead to supervise seven runners at his local meeting Hexham. Now he had landed the biggest catch of all.

No one has been more successful in the history of jump racing than canny Arthur Stephenson, widely known as W.A., who was almost forty before he became a public trainer. At the time of the 1987 Gold Cup he had prepared over 2,200 jumping winners and well over three hundred more on the flat at his windswept farm in the village of Leasingthorne, once a mining stronghold in County Durham.

Arthur Stephenson began in racing by riding and training his own horses, most of them hunters. His first treasured success as an owner and trainer came with T.O.D., a horse he rode to victory in the Whitsuntide Open Hunters' Chase at Hexham on June 8th 1946, a race that offered a prize of £100. A dozen years later a close friend Alan Elliott persuaded him to become a public trainer. Soon the records began to tumble. In 1969 he became the first man to train a hundred winners over jumps in a season. Seven more centuries have followed.

The wily Stephenson, rarely seen in public without his flat cap, suffered intermittently from ill health in the spring of 1987. He watched the Gold Cup on television at Hexham and was thankful to avoid the subsequent interrogation by the media at Cheltenham.

Conducting a conversation with W.A. can be rather like wrestling with jelly. He will bounce the question back at you with a politician's practised skill, all the while smiling at your discomfort.

"Those fellows in your business always seem to want something sensational," he once chided me. "They are not horsemen or practical men; they ask such stupid questions!"

He will tease and joust without revealing a thing to the most expert interviewer. Yet back at the farm, where corn and potatoes grow in fields beside the gallops, you soon discover the good-natured countryman behind the bluff, protective shield. Arthur Stephenson has a superb eye for a horse and an even better one for a bargain. Above all he is a dealer. For more than thirty years he has imported batches of young horses from Ireland, turned them out on his farm to mature, then brought them on patiently to race.

"I'm always a seller," he declares. "Any horse I have is on the market and I always try to match the right horse with the right owner. I have to sell to keep my head above water. If I can't sell them then I raffle them!"

One of Arthur Stephenson's most faithful Irish contacts down the years has been Tom Costello, the man who sold Midnight Court to Fred Winter. Astute Tom masterminds a veritable equine empire from his home near Newmarket-on-Fergus in Co. Clare. Such is their trusting relationship he will sometimes send the trainer a lorry-load of horses unseen.

"W.A. has been coming to see us for years," confirms Costello. "That's why he gets preference on a lot of good horses for sale. I sold him The Thinker in the spring of 1985."

The chunky chestnut foal who would win the 1987 Gold Cup was bred on a small farm at Drumsurn near Londonderry in Northern Ireland by Victor Semple. His dam, the unraced mare Maine Pet, had cost the princely sum of £100 as a five-year-old. Maine Pet was bought partly to run with children's ponies on the farm. Put to Little Owl's sire Cantab she produced The Thinker, who was bought as a foal at Ballsbridge by Michael White, a dealer and farmer from Ballygran in Co. Limerick, as an afterthought.

White had already left the sales arena after a long session when his son John called him back to inspect the final lot of the evening, padding quietly round the ring. Small, light-framed but athletic, Maine Pet's foal was unremarkable at that stage. Most buyers had already departed; the bidding was light. Michael White thought the foal was cheap enough and bought him with a bid of 1,350 punts. When the horse developed and strengthened White passed him on for 3,800 punts to a friend, Paddy McCormack, a neighbour of Tom Costello.

The Costello family inspects hundreds of young horses each year throughout the length of Ireland. Tom liked The Thinker and bought him as a four-year-old from Paddy McCormack.

"He was small enough and I paid handy money for him," he relates.

The Thinker won point-to-points and two chases for Tom Costello. At Limerick Junction, backed from 20–1 to 7–2, he landed a notable gamble before he was acquired by Arthur Stephenson acting for Tom McDonagh, a civil engineer originally from Co. Mayo. Winning the Gold Cup tends to ruin a horse's handicap rating for the rest of his racing career. Inevitably opportunities are restricted unless that horse improves. The Thinker, who displayed an attractive white blaze on his face, continued to race with a

Snow still covers Cleeve Hill as Cybrandian (centre) leads at the last fence from the winner The Thinker (left) and Wayward Lad (right)

pleasing willingness and came tantalisingly close to winning the 1989 Seagram Grand National under top weight.

Two years later he broke his near hind leg above the hock while exercising at home as he prepared for a final assault on the 1991 Seagram Grand National. It was a tragic end to a particularly tough and durable horse who was a resolute stayer in the mud.

Despite continuing ill-health his trainer eschews retirement.

"Retire," he scoffs. "I don't put a date on my place in the workhouse just yet. I enjoy bringing on young horses and leave the gallivanting to others."

TOTE CHELTENHAM GOLD CUP.   March 19th 1987.   £55,500.   *Good to soft.*

1	The Thinker	9 12 0	R. Lamb	13–2	
2	Cybrandian	9 12 0	C. Grant	25–1	
3	Door Latch	9 12 0	R. Rowe	9–1	
4	West Tip	10 12 0	P. Hobbs	50–1	
5	Wayward Lad	12 12 0	G. Bradley	11–1	
6	Golden Friend	9 12 0	D. Browne	16–1	
7	Forgive 'N Forget	10 12 0	M. Dwyer	5–4 Fav	
8	Mr Moonraker	10 12 0	B. Powell	50–1	

1½ lengths, 2½.   Owned T. P. McDonagh Ltd.   Trained W. A. Stephenson.
Bred V. Semple.   6m. 56.1 seconds.   Also 8 Bolands Cross (P. Scudamore) U.R.,
9 Combs Ditch (C. Brown) P.U., 25 Earls Brig (P. Tuck) P.U. and Charter Party
(R. Dunwoody) Fell.   12 Ran.   Tote win: £5.50.

The Thinker: ch.g. 1978 (Cantab–Maine Pet)

22

CHARTER PARTY
(1988)

OBSESSIONS DEVELOP FROM the earliest stirring of ambition. David Nicholson's concerned the Cheltenham Gold Cup. It began two days after his third birthday when his father Frenchie rode to victory in the 1942 Gold Cup on Lord Sefton's Medoc II. His son's pride in that achievement is undiminished half a century later. For the first twenty-two years of his life David Nicholson lived in a house whose grounds ran down to the racecourse at Prestbury Park. As a small boy he remembers watching entranced by the sight of the peerless Martin Molony on Silver Fame winning the 1951 Gold Cup narrowly from Glen Kelly on Greenogue.

"I was standing on the line and the judge got it wrong. He should have given the verdict to Greenogue," he insists in typically forthright tones.

Later David Nicholson, known universally in racing as "The Duke", also rode in the Gold Cup. He was third on Snaigow in 1966 and was harbouring thoughts of victory on Mill House the following year until the big horse omitted to take off at the last open ditch. When he turned inevitably to training, in the remote Cotswold hamlet of Condicote, he waited seventeen barren, frustrating, maddening years before his first success at the Festival with Solar Cloud in the Daily Express Triumph Hurdle in 1986. Fate plays curious tricks. The same afternoon Charter Party gave him a second victory in the Ritz National Hunt Chase.

It was the brave, erratic-jumping and increasingly unsound Charter Party who achieved David Nicholson's compelling lifetime ambition two years later. During a chance visit to the stables one Saturday morning Raymond Mould, a wealthy property man, instructed the trainer to find him two suitable young horses. Seldom has an order been filled so swiftly or skilfully. By Monday night Raymond Mould and his wife Jennifer owned their first two racehorses: Connaught River, who quickly ran up a sequence of victories over hurdles, and Charter Party. The Moulds then sold a half-share in Charter Party to their friends Colin and Claire Smith.

David Nicholson bought Charter Party, a fine, upstanding but rather plain horse as a four-year-old at Doncaster Sales in May 1982 for 8,000 guineas. Since the sire, the anonymous Document, failed to win a race of any description and the family of the dam Ahoy There was rather short of essential black type the price could not be considered cheap.

Nicholson concedes: "He was a big, grand-looking type; a good mover with no pedigree. I took a chance that he would be a racehorse."

The business of breeding racehorses, is, by its very nature, an inexact science. Many breeders, following traditional guidelines, have spent a lifetime trying, without success, to produce a top-class steeplechaser. The eccentric mating arrangements that spawned Charter Party possess all the intangible ingredients of an Irish mist.

Ahoy There, a small filly bred by the Riddell Martins from Co. Meath, proved disappointing at stud after winning a bumper race at four.

"Eventually we decided she was useless," declares Avia Riddell Martin. She had also bought Document cheaply for 750 guineas. Though he was very well bred, being a half-brother to the Queen's top-class horses Above Suspicion and Doutelle, Document had a crooked leg and later appeared to suffer from a wind infirmity. He failed to win a single race.

"We thought he was useless, too," admits Avia with refreshing candour. Document, a big, powerful horse out of the Cesarewitch winner Above Board, was given to a friend Billy Filgate as a stallion. In 1977 he covered Ahoy There free of charge.

"The result," says Avia Riddell Martin, "was Charter Party, the biggest, ugliest camel you have ever seen!" Sent to Goffs as a two-year-old in November 1980, Charter Party was bought for 2,500 punts, then swiftly returned by Bobby Barry, a noted judge of bloodstock, who claimed the horse was a weaver.

The Riddell Martins furiously disagreed with this assessment but gained a useful bonus when they sent Charter Party to the same sales ring a year later. This time he made 5,000 punts to the bid of Willie Browne from the Mocklers Hill Stud. He in turn took a tidy profit at Doncaster seven months later.

Though he did win a minor race in his first season Charter Party's early form suggested that two miles over hurdles was woefully inadequate, but his last run offered immense promise for the years to come. Carrying 11 st. 12 lb in the final of the Haig Whisky Novices' series at Newcastle, Charter Party was well clear at the last flight when he decanted Peter Scudamore with the sort of clumsy mistake that recurred throughout his racing career. The lop-eared youngster took time to learn his trade over fences, yet still won three times as a novice. Given a clear round and a distance of ground he looked distinctly useful but his jumping could still be perilously erratic. He fell on his first visit to the Cheltenham Festival as a seven-year-old in 1985 and threw away a winning chance with another blunder of earthquake proportions at the course a month later. Yet another heavy fall cost him a live chance in the 1985 Hennessy Cognac Gold Cup. Still David Nicholson persevered.

"I knew there was a big race in him if only he would jump. He was a tough devil. He had to be, to retain the desire to win after all the mistakes he had made," reflects the trainer. His patience was rewarded with victory by Charter Party in the Ritz Club Chase. Even so at the end of his races the horse invariably used to gurgle. A wind infirmity was diagnosed. A hobday operation was carried out, and another on his soft palate at the same time. His breathing improved immeasurably, but he failed to win a single race the next season and fell abruptly at the fifth fence in the 1987 Gold Cup.

Intermittent lameness hampered Charter Party's training programme in the months before the 1988 Gold Cup. He ran only four times that season and was lame once more after a sparkling victory over David Elsworth's duo Rhyme 'N' Reason and Desert Orchid in the Gainsborough Chase early in

Good friends Willie Carson and David Nicholson study the runners cantering to the start

February.

Nicholson confesses: "We knew something was hurting him somewhere but could not find out what it was. It showed in his slower paces but once he warmed up he would shake it off. We employed a magnetopulse, osteopaths, vets; you name it, we tried it.

"I did not want to X-ray his feet because I feared it might be the end of the line."

Whatever the problem it did not affect Charter Party's appetite or enthusiasm. On a visit to Henry Candy's picturesque gallops at Kingston Warren high above Lambourn eight days before the Festival he ran away from the speed specialists Very Promising and Long Engagement over a mile and a quarter. Even so, the doubts lingered. As the Gold Cup runners circled at the start the forthright Nicholson was on hand nearby to explain the situation if over-zealous officials wanted to withdraw the horse at the last moment through lameness.

"I was there just in case," he explains.

The spring-heeled grey Desert Orchid, already the most popular horse in training, was an intended runner in the 1988 Gold Cup until heavy rain altered the ground significantly. He raced instead in the Queen Mother Champion Chase over two miles. His trainer David Elsworth was still double-handed in the Gold Cup with the bonny little free-running Cavvies Clown and the improving Rhyme 'N' Reason, who would claim a remarkable victory in the Grand National early the following month. Simon Sherwood replaced the injured Ross Arnott on Cavvies Clown.

The 1984 hero Burrough Hill Lad was retired shortly before Cheltenham. After more comebacks than Frank Sinatra, he appeared for the final time at Wincanton in February, ran with a degree of promise behind Kildimo and Desert Orchid but was sore after a subsequent racecourse trial. The Thinker was absent, too. He did not appear all season.

The betting was dominated by three outstanding recruits to chasing the previous season. Tough, dependable Playschool, the flagship of David Barons' ever-expanding team of imports from New Zealand and recent winner of the Vincent O'Brien Irish Gold Cup, started favourite at 100–30. Kildimo, who had beaten Playschool so decisively in the Sun Alliance Chase twelve months earlier, stood at 6–1 with Cavvies Clown. The French hope Nupsala, an 8–1 chance, had been undeniably impressive in winning the King George VI Chase at Kempton. This would pose a much sterner test. Forgive 'N Forget, without a win all season, had fallen heavily as he challenged Nupsala at the last fence at Kempton and had subsequently been soundly beaten by Playschool in Ireland.

The race for the 1988 Tote Cheltenham Gold Cup offered an unprecedented mix of emotions. Drama, controversy, scandal and above all tragedy unfolded in the time it takes for horses to cover three and a quarter miles over fences at racing pace. Playschool was one of the first casualties. He arrived at the start panting like a rabid dog, ran a lifeless race, and was eventually pulled up by his jockey Paul Nicholls. Dark rumours circulated that the favourite had been nobbled.

Beau Ranger and then Golden Friend made the running until Cavvies Clown took up the gauntlet going out into the country for the final time with Run and Skip, Charter Party, Forgive 'N Forget and Beau Ranger in close attendance. Running to the top of the hill Cavvies Clown, Charter Party and Forgive 'N Forget had escaped from the bunch though Rhyme 'N' Reason was closing steadily when he tumbled at the nineteenth fence, four from home. A moment earlier the 1985 winner had approached the same fence apparently going best of the leading trio.

One second Forgive 'N Forget was moving with a powerful rhythm; the next he was hobbling grotesquely on three legs as he came away from that fateful fence, his shattered hind-leg swinging uselessly. Mark Dwyer, bleakly aware of a dreadful injury, scrambled hastily from his back. Within minutes the Festival's perennial adventurer had been put out of his misery.

"It was a sad, sad day," reflects the jockey whose career in England had flourished so swiftly in unison with the flowing hoofbeats of Forgive 'N Forget.

"I always try not to become too attached or involved, because in jumping you know something like that can always happen; but for so many reasons I was very close to him."

Forgive 'N Forget's tragic departure left the race between Cavvies Clown and Charter Party. Cavvies Clown's slender advantage was blown away at the second last fence by a monumental blunder that sent Simon Sherwood into orbit without reins. A parachute might have offered a more suitable option but when the hapless jockey finally came down he was relieved to find himself once more on the narrow back of Cavvies Clown. It was an athletic recovery but the mistake unquestionably handed the prize to Charter Party, ridden with clinical patience by Richard Dunwoody.

Galloping on relentlessly, he cleared the last in fine style and drew away on the run-in to claim the triumph his trainer had craved for almost half a century. Cavvies Clown, beaten six lengths, held on for second place from Beau Ranger with Nupsala an honourable fourth.

Cheltenham is David Nicholson's local course. After evening stables the entire staff repaired to the village pub with suitably large funds. Raymond Mould held an impromptu party that night nearby at Guiting Grange. Princess Anne, an enthusiastic jockey and one of Nicholson's owners, was among the guests. She was one of the last to leave the cele-

Charter Party pounds up the steep finishing climb ahead of Cavvies Clown

brations and the earliest to arrive at the Nicholson stables the next morning at 6.50 in readiness for first lot after a drive from her home that takes at least half an hour.

Exhaustive tests by the Jockey Club forensic team failed to confirm widespread concern that Play-school, the favourite, had been doped. Yet the suspicion remained that he was the latest victim of a doping gang that had already interfered with several horses in Ireland. Symptoms shown by Playschool before the race matched those of several horses, most of them favourites, that had run abysmally there in the months before the Gold Cup.

David Barons confirms: "I have never been more confident before a race or more certain about a horse's well-being. It was the most sickening business. I don't doubt that my horse was got at."

A new wave of doping on the flat with a com-monplace tranquilliser in the autumn of 1990 bears further comparison with Playschool. Though the case remains open David Barons fears the culprits will never be caught.

A test of a different kind exercised David Nichol-son's mind over Easter. Under Jockey Club rules, if a horse fails a post-race dope test or the result of that test has not been completed in a certain time the trainer has to be informed. On Good Friday, April 1st, David Nicholson was dismayed to receive a formal notice from the Jockey Club that Charter Party was not yet in the clear.

The letter began "We have to inform you there is a possibility . . . . "

It proved an anxiously long holiday weekend for the Nicholson stable. Lads were cross-questioned, supplies of feed checked, doubts were voiced. On the following Tuesday the Jockey Club rang to confirm that all tests were satisfactory. Charter Party would keep the prize.

After the Gold Cup David Nicholson arranged for a series of X-rays to be taken on Charter Party's feet. These disclosed that he was suffering from navicular disease, a condition caused by thrombosis in his front feet. The stout-hearted Charter Party had exhibited rare courage by continuing to gallop and jump on feet that were a constant source of pain. Vets recommended a course of treatment with powders to improve the peripheral circulation but for a time it seemed that the doughty Charter Party had run his last race.

Nicholson reflected with understandable feeling: "Jumping is such a hard game. This horse still had the courage to come back from all his problems and beat the best. He does not deserve this problem."

Happily the ailment did not worsen. When Charter Party returned into training the next autumn he was kept in a stable with a rubber cover on the floor. Pads to absorb the concussion caused by his feet striking the ground were fitted to his shoes but, in accordance with suppliers' guidelines, the drugs that helped ease the discomfort of navicular disease were halted at least ten days before each of his races. The old horse did not win again but ran with notable distinction in taking third prize behind Desert Orchid in the 1989 Gold Cup. He raced for the last time in November 1989, damaged a tendon, and lives in retirement with the Moulds at Guiting Power only a few miles from Condicote.

Occasionally Charter Party receives invitations to attend functions. He was a welcome guest at Richard Dunwoody's wedding, travelled to Sandown for Aldaniti's twenty-first birthday party, has been a major draw at church fetes and opened an Abbeyfield retirement home at Prestbury in the summer of 1990.

Sometimes on a quiet day David Nicholson and his wife Dinah will dust off the video recording of the 1988 Gold Cup and enjoy the sight of Charter Party winning again.

"It still gives me a buzz," confesses the trainer. "I was on a terrific high after the race but felt great sadness that my father had not lived to see it. He had fired my ambition to win the Gold Cup and gave me every encouragement. When I bought Charter Party he was one of the few people who said he would win races."

TOTE CHELTENHAM GOLD CUP.   March 17th 1988.   £61,960.   *Soft.*

1	Charter Party	10 12 0	R. Dunwoody	10–1
2	Cavvies Clown	8 12 0	S. Sherwood	6–1
3	Beau Ranger	10 12 0	P. Scudamore	33–1
4	Nupsala	9 12 0	A. Pommier	8–1
5	Yahoo	7 12 0	T. Morgan	12–1
6	West Tip	11 12 0	M. Hammond	80–1
7	Kildimo	8 12 0	G. Bradley	6–1
8	Golden Friend	10 12 0	D. Browne	40–1
9	Run and Skip	10 12 0	P. Hobbs	50–1

6 lengths, 10.   Owned Mrs Claire Smith.   Trained D. Nicholson.   Bred A. Riddell Martin.   6m. 58.9 seconds.   Also 100–30 Fav Playschool (P. Nicholls) P.U., 8 Forgive 'N Forget (M. Dwyer) P.U., 11 Rhyme 'N' Reason (B. Powell) Fell, 40 Cybrandian (C. Grant) P.U., 50 Foyle Fisherman (R. Rowe) P.U., 100 Stearsby (G. McCourt) Fell. 15 Ran.   Tote win: £9.70.

Charter Party: b.g. 1978 (Document–Ahoy There)

23

DESERT ORCHID
(1989)

HORSE RACING'S ENDURING PUBLIC IMAGE as an amusing triviality without significance was gloriously exposed by events at Cheltenham shortly before dusk on a bleak spring day in 1989. A grey, almost white horse won a long-distance steeplechase in the snow-capped Cotswolds and the nation overflowed with emotion. It was a race that stopped the clock and sent the blood racing through the veins of every one among the massed ranks of frozen racegoers at the course and the millions watching on television.

Desert Orchid's entrancing story moved firmly into legend that day. Hours earlier, as the snow and sleet continued to fall on Prestbury Park and emergency pumps were employed to remove water lying on parts of the course, it seemed inevitable that his name would feature among the last-minute withdrawals that afternoon. The grey's owners were deeply and understandably concerned at asking him to race in such awful conditions and many of the horse's admirers, too, voiced their anxieties.

One man alone stood firm. David Elsworth, the countryman touched with a rare understanding of horses, argued vehemently that Desert Orchid should run. Yes, the conditions were unspeakable but the grey was outstandingly the best horse in the race and might never have the chance again. The doubts lingered until the last moment, but happily Elsworth's eloquence gained the day. Another enthralling chapter was about to unfold in the history of the Cheltenham Gold Cup.

Desert Orchid, a dark, iron grey, arrived at Elsworth's stables at Whitsbury in Hampshire as a raw, backward three-year-old late in 1982. Showing an appealingly stubborn streak that would be displayed at the finish of so many of his races, the new inmate declined to leave his horsebox. After an interesting battle of wills the trainer turned him round and guided him backwards down the ramp. There was a further brief exhibition of his fiercely independent spirit when he refused to enter the box that had been allotted to him. Once more the trainer turned him round and eased him backwards through the door.

At the time David Elsworth, once a jockey, was establishing himself as one of the most versatile trainers in the country. He it was, as a hard-working, intuitive assistant, who orchestrated the startling run of success enjoyed by Col Ricky Vallance. When the Jockey Club objected to the sharply improved form of a Vallance winner at Devon & Exeter the trainer was suspended and his ambitious assistant banished from racing with the advice to withdraw his application for his own licence.

"That decision cost me four years," he says with undisguised feeling. "At the time I had a yard, finance and horses. Naturally people could not wait on the off-chance that I might be granted a licence eventually. The horses were dispersed and I lost the yard. It was the worst period of my life, barren, frustrating and empty."

David Elsworth survived, just, by selling cloth and fabric at West Country markets and later running a livery yard. After a long period of exile from the sport he loves he again applied for a licence to train in his own name in the autumn of 1978, encouraged by a loyal friend, the dashing amateur rider Lt-Col Piers Bengough, since knighted and appointed the Queen's representative at Ascot. This time he was successful.

A dozen years afterwards I asked David Elsworth to name his finest moment in racing. His reply was instantaneous and strangely moving.

"Returning home on the train from London with a trainer's licence," he answered quietly.

He began with a handful of equine rejects in a small farm-yard on Salisbury Plain, progressed to bigger stables at Box, near Bath, before moving to the splendour of Whitsbury. Desert Orchid's colourful journey through life has taken many unexpected turns. One of the most fortunate twists of all was that Richard Burridge and his father James chose David Elsworth to train their eager young grey.

James Burridge, searching for a suitable hunter, had found Desert Orchid's granddam Grey Orchid, already winner of a point-to-point as a five-year-old, in a remote field near Newark. Burridge bought her for £175. She proved to be a resolutely headstrong hunter but Burridge persevered and, to his eternal credit, won a point-to-point on her. Later, mated with an obscure Hunters' Improvement Society stallion called Brother at a modest fee of £20, the flighty mare produced Desert Orchid's mother Flower Child. She, too, proved an impossible handful in the hunting field, was pulled up in four successive point-to-points and was then put into training with Charlie James near Lambourn in Berkshire.

Though Flower Child won two minor chases she is remembered by James as a bold, at times spectacular jumper with boundless spirit, a priceless gift passed on to her son when she was mated at a cost of £350 with the top-class miler Grey Mirage. Richard Burridge bought a half-share in Desert Orchid from his father, and a friend Simon Bullimore took a quarter-share.

The grey's first race in January 1983 so nearly proved to be his last. After running much too eagerly, to the point of exhaustion, he crashed perilously at the final flight of hurdles at Kempton. Those of us there that day remember the incident with chilling clarity.

Desert Orchid lay prone for several minutes. James Burridge was warned that screens might have to be erected if the horse was seriously injured. For one ghastly moment it seemed like the end. At the time Desert Orchid was an anonymous grey. Any horse lying injured is a subject of concern for jumping enthusiasts and the applause that greeted the sight of the grey clambering to his feet reflected the relief of the crowd that fateful day. After that first race David Elsworth offered a perceptive insight into the character of the horse he had known for only a few weeks.

"The problem with most horses is to get 95 per cent of their potential from them. The trouble with this one is preventing him from giving you 105 per cent," he assured James Burridge.

Desert Orchid ran three more times that spring, was beaten in a photo finish at Sandown and ended the season, as he had begun it, a maiden.

Late the following autumn, notably more mature and crucially stronger, he began a sequence of stirring triumphs that demanded his presence in the field for the Champion Hurdle in March. It proved a race too far for a novice. Desert Orchid would return to Cheltenham many times without success before he achieved his most famous victory of all. Already the trainer was anticipating the moment when the bold-jumping grey would begin an exciting new phase of his life over fences. It came after he had fallen for the third time in his life in a warm-up race over hurdles at Kempton in October 1985.

Watching him in those early, carefree skirmishes over fences, ridden by the energetic Colin Brown, was a spine-tingling experience. Setting off like a sprinter who had been locked away for a week Desert Orchid jumped with the joyous abandon of a spring-heeled gazelle darting across the Veldt. Eager, fearless and extraordinarily accurate for a novice, he would launch himself thrillingly from his hocks like a grey projectile. The presence of a challenger beside him merely spurred him to even more extravagant leaps and a naturally athletic ability to improvise at the last moment helped him survive the odd alarming occasion when he did misjudge a fence.

A run of four successive victories caught the public imagination. He was, in short, cleverer at jumping than the most nimble cat. His style of racing suggested he would always be at his best over two miles, yet he was soundly beaten over that distance in the Arkle Chase at the Festival after losing valuable ground by tending to lean right-handed. It was a habit that would be repeated frequently on left-handed courses.

Impressed by the free-running grey's performances over two and a half miles the following autumn David Elsworth, convinced he would stay even further, entered him in the King George VI Chase to the surprise, not to mention disbelief, of everyone else connected with the horse. Once more the trainer was on his own. Once more events confirmed his judgement. Starting at 16–1 and ridden by Simon Sherwood since Colin Brown stayed loyal to Combs Ditch, the lion-hearted Desert Orchid made every yard of the running in the Boxing Day spectacular.

A splendid study of Desert Orchid and Simon Sherwood as they begin a heartstopping victory charge

Elsworth, not a man to crow, admitted afterwards: "I thought I must be losing my touch when everyone dismissed his chance without a second glance."

In the following years Desert Orchid dominated steeplechasing as no horse had done since Arkle. Distance, ground, weight – none of these factors thwarted his unrelenting march through the pages of racing history. He even overcame his much publicised aversion to left-handed courses by winning a race at Liverpool. Unquestionably the finest chaser in the country at two and three miles, he added the traditional end-of-season long-distance marathon, the Whitbread Gold Cup, in April 1988 to his long list of important triumphs.

Spend a morning with Desert Orchid and the happy band of humans closest to him and you are inexorably drawn in by the legend that surrounds him. Yet the reality is that he has been frequently beaten in his long and stirring life as a racehorse. Above all he has been vulnerable at Cheltenham, where he had failed to win in five successive years at the Festival. In 1988 a tilt at the Gold Cup had been called off when persistent rain changed the ground significantly. He ran instead in the Queen Mother Champion Chase and finished second to Pearlyman. A year later David Elsworth was determined to allay the owner's fears and go for Gold.

Walking across the Whitsbury gallops later that summer the trainer confided: "You know I never thought he would win the Gold Cup because Cheltenham is not his course; but often in racing you only get one throw of the dice and I felt we had to take our chance. If the Gold Cup was run at Sandown or Kempton he would have won it year after year. He was the best chaser in training so we had to have a go."

In the months leading up to the 1989 Gold Cup Desert Orchid was unbeaten. He took the King George VI Chase for the second time, successfully gave lumps of weight to two-mile specialists at Sandown and Ascot and rallied bravely to catch Pegwell Bay in the last few strides in the Gainsborough Chase in February.

The generous comments of Pegwell Bay's trainer Tim Forster reflected the widespread affection for Desert Orchid. "You don't mind losing to him quite so badly," he observed.

Richard Burridge, however, was concerned about the ordeal ahead. "The Gold Cup is an ugly race. It is so very tough and exhausts horses. Recent winners have not done very well afterwards and Desert Orchid's welfare is our first priority," he said gravely.

As the snow and rain fell relentlessly on Cheltenham on Gold Cup day the anxious Burridge family finally agreed to a compromise with their trainer. Desert Orchid would run, but if it was clear he hated the conditions Simon Sherwood would pull him up after two fences. Despite the foul conditions the grey was a solid favourite at 5–2. Two previous winners were in the field: The Thinker, who had not run since Christmas, and Charter Party, who had fallen once more at Leopardstown in February in the race won by Ireland's rising star Carvill's Hill, trained by Jim Dreaper.

A big, long-striding horse, Carvill's Hill appeared to possess boundless potential, but a niggling back problem had limited his experience of steeplechasing to only four races. More seriously, he had yet to learn the vital art of adapting if he did not meet a fence on a perfect stride. When in doubt he could not, or would not, shorten his stride and tended to barge through a fence, a habit not recommended for survival at Cheltenham.

The robust Ten Plus, a splendidly old-fashioned chaser and most resolute galloper, was widely fancied to give Fulke Walwyn his fifth Gold Cup win though he, too, was not always fluent at the business of crossing fences at speed. Stamina was his strongest weapon.

With several dour stayers in the race it was rather a surprise to see the handsome white head of Desert Orchid showing in front as they squelched towards the first fence. Simon Sherwood's contingency plan was swiftly forgotten. The pace was by no means testing, but Carvill's Hill was an early casualty at the seventh fence, a ditch, trapped by his own inexperience. Golden Freeze had gone at the previous fence and The Thinker was another faller before half-way. Cavvies Clown moved up briefly to join his stable companion in the lead but then dropped swiftly out of contention.

Racing into the country again towards the foot of Cleeve Hill Kevin Mooney, on Ten Plus, decided the time had come to test Desert Orchid's endurance. Riding vigorously, he sent Ten Plus past the leader at the fourteenth fence and set sail for home. Soon they had established an advantage of two, perhaps three lengths and a buzz of anticipation swept through the packed crowd as Mooney and his willing mount pressed on forcefully towards the notorious third last fence.

Ten Plus, at full stretch, failed to rise quite high enough, clipped the crown of the fence and pitched heavily to the ground. It was a fall that cost him his life. When he rose a moment later he was unable to put his near hind-leg to the ground. The limb was shattered beyond repair.

The tragic fall of Ten Plus left Desert Orchid briefly in front again but soon he was joined and passed on the inside by the unconsidered, mud-loving Yahoo who, to the eyes of the grey's adoring supporters, appeared to be moving with ominous ease. Yahoo swept round the final bend full of running and jumped the second last fence like a fresh horse. For all the world Desert Orchid looked beaten. Surely, we thought, there could be only one possible result now.

The drama that ensued in the next few moments will live for ever in the memories of those at Cheltenham that day. It began with the merest suspicion that Desert Orchid did not accept the defeat that seemed inevitable to everyone present and grew with a gradual realisation that he would not be conquered. Slowly, wonderfully, impossibly, he was reclaiming the lost ground until he was almost level with Yahoo again at the last fence and though he met it on an awkward stride an agile, last-minute adjustment of his step ensured that he crossed it safely.

Yahoo, splashing through the mud with a surprisingly steady rhythm, still held a narrow advantage on

The nation's favourite racehorse is greeted by Janice Coyle and Richard Burridge

the flat but just behind him the grey with the un-quenchable will to win was in full, majestic flight. The tension, by now, was quite unbearable. Half-way up the hill the two combatants were side by side. A second later the muddy white figure of Desert Orchid edged ahead. As he took command, his ears flat back, he moved aggressively left-handed towards Yahoo as if intent on barging him off the course. It was a very public display of Desert Orchid's resolute refusal to submit. Stubborn, intractable, obstinate, he was all these things and more as he continued to intimidate the hapless Yahoo. In the nick of time Simon Sherwood put down his whip and pulled the grey away from his opponent.

At the line Desert Orchid had gained a quite stun-ning victory by one and a half lengths. Charter Party was an honourable third. Prize money in 1989 ex-tended to the first six horses but only five finished. For the second time in three years bedlam broke out on the course. Emotion overflowed just as it had done in the wake of Dawn Run's unforgettable triumph. Glowing tributes were paid to Desert Orchid's toughness of spirit.

"I've never known a horse so brave. He hated every step of the way in the ground and dug as deep as he could possibly go," reported Simon Sherwood.

David Elsworth commented: "I'm such a proud man, I don't know where this is all going to stop."

Desert Orchid's blazing victory in the Gold Cup was his twenty-seventh success and took his earnings way past £400,000, easily a record for a jumper. In the following two years he would add an Irish Grand National, an unprecedented fourth King George VI Chase and several other triumphs to his ever in-creasing accomplishments.

His heart-stopping triumph in the 1989 Gold Cup, however, proved to be the only time he won at Chel-tenham from eight attempts. In two subsequent Gold Cups, in 1990 and 1991, he would finish third. No matter. Long before then he had become the first jumper in training to have his own fan club.

Over almost a decade Desert Orchid proved a wonderfully attractive advertisement for all that is best about jump racing. In the eighties and early nineties he was part of our lives for so long that, un-wisely, we took him for granted like a favourite rela-tive.

When he retires, probably towards the end of 1991, we will remember the big, bold head, the quiz-zical eye, the instantly appealing colour and above all his uninhibited, soaring jumping that offered one of the most compelling visions in sport.

TOTE CHELTENHAM GOLD CUP.   March 16th 1989.   £68,371.25.   *Heavy.*

1 Desert Orchid	10	12 0	S. Sherwood	5–2 Fav
2 Yahoo	8	12 0	T. Morgan	25–1
3 Charter Party	11	12 0	R. Dunwoody	14–1
4 Bonanza Boy	8	12 0	P. Scudamore	15–2
5 West Tip	12	12 0	P. Hobbs	66–1

1½ lengths, 8.   Owned R. Burridge.   Trained D. Elsworth.   Bred J. Burridge.   7m. 17.6 seconds.   Also 5 Carvill's Hill (K. Morgan) Fell, 11–2 Ten Plus (K. Mooney) Fell, 15–2 The Thinker (C. Grant) Fell, 8 Cavvies Clown (R. Arnott) Ref, 16 Golden Freeze (B. Sheridan) Fell, 25 Pegwell Bay (C. Llewellyn) P.U., 33 Slalom (J. White) Fell and 50 Ballyhane (R. Rowe) B.D.   13 Ran.   Tote win: £3.80.

Desert Orchid: gr.g. 1979 (Grey Mirage–Flower Child)

24

NORTON'S COIN
(1990)

WE RETURNED TO CHELTENHAM in greater numbers than ever in 1990 to pay an act of homage to Desert Orchid, but found ourselves witnessing an enthralling triumph at 100–1 by an obscure, wiry chestnut from west Wales whose background was far too implausible to have been scripted by any self-respecting novelist. As the tales emerged of the fastest milk horse in Dyfed and the genial family that attends him in the one-pub village of Nantgaredig we found ourselves drawn inexorably into fantasy. How else do you explain the complex and improbable ingredients of this most unexpected of all Gold Cup results?

The next day we journeyed west from Cheltenham across the river Severn along the M4 for almost two hours before turning into a sheltered valley beside the river Towy near Carmarthen. There at Rwyth Farm, resting wearily in his box, a converted cow barn surrounded by flags, bunting and television cameras, stood Norton's Coin, the most unlikely hero of this or any other Gold Cup.

Briefly the horse was led out at lunchtime to a rapturous reception at the Railway Hotel in Nantgaredig, where long into the previous night toasts were toasted and eulogies sung as only the Welsh can. No wonder. A coachload of supporters had left the village for Cheltenham soon after the horse. They were on Norton's Coin to a man at 100–1; some managed to obtain even longer odds. Bookmakers in Carmarthen and the surrounding villages felt the pain for months. One Corals shop alone, in Carmarthen, lost over £100,000. So many optimists backed the local horse that only a handful could be paid out on the day. Most had to wait for fresh bundles of notes to be ferried to the beleaguered betting shops with empty cash tills.

Sirrell Griffiths, the owner, trainer, lad, work rider, box driver and affable spokesman for Norton's Coin, can reasonably claim to have bred him, too, as he owned both sire and dam at the time of conception in 1980. A burly, cheerful man, with a ready smile and an open house, he sat in his crowded kitchen nursing his tenth cup of coffee the morning after the Gold Cup and patiently unravelled the wonderfully rich maelstrom of events that led to the presence of Norton's Coin at Cheltenham.

Dairy farmer, cattle dealer and long-time permit holder, Griffiths sold a lorry early in 1980 to a neighbouring farmer, Bill Morgan. While delivering the lorry he spotted an unraced three-year-old filly, Grove Chance, in a field. She did not, in all conscience, possess an ideal pedigree for a jumping broodmare, being out of the speedy Spotty Bebe who had won twice over five furlongs. However Spotty Bebe's sire Credo was a thorough stayer, as was Grove Chance's sire, the locally based St Columbus, later responsible for the Grand National winner Maori Venture. Griffiths persuaded Morgan to part with Grove Chance for £425. It was, remarkably, the only time he ever visited the farm.

Earlier he had paid 700 guineas to stand an anonymous stallion Mount Cassino, winner of two races on the flat, at his farm in the heart of Nantgaredig. Mount Cassino had been brought to Wales by another local man, Keith Lewis, and his favours were largely confined to hunter mares, ponies and cobs. Grove Chance was one of only a handful of thoroughbred mares he ever covered. Theirs was not a meticulously planned mating on the best breeding lines – it was simply a marriage of convenience.

Dealing is a way of life for many stockmen, so when a friend, Percy Thomas, was looking for a mare in foal Griffiths sold him Grove Chance. Since the Thomas farm is but a short canter away on the far side of the River Towy, Griffiths was present at the birth of Norton's Coin and later helped break him in, but by then both sire and dam were dead. Mount Cassino was put down in 1983 suffering from laminitis and poor Grove Chance damaged herself so badly giving birth to Norton's Coin that she too was put down later.

Sirrell Griffiths saw Norton's Coin probably once a month for the first six years of his life. When the horse had won four point-to-points and a hunter chase he bought him back.

"I did not think Percy would sell and was not sure I could afford the horse," recalls Griffiths. "He asked me if Norton's Coin was worth £5,000. I suggested he was worth much more, but he let me have him for that price and then gave me back £200 luck money," he added.

When Norton's Coin moved to Rwyth Farm as a six-year-old he was unpleasantly aggressive in his box; at times he could be thoroughly nasty. He particularly resented anyone touching his rugs. His canny new owner eased the problem by leaving a clutch of bantams in the horse's stable. They would scratch around his feet and perch on his back. Later the farm cats took up residence in the box, too. Sometimes the horse would be ridden on the roads by a neighbour, David Shattock, later to become Chief Constable of Avon and Somerset police. On the course Norton's Coin delighted the Griffiths family by finishing a close second in the Cathcart Chase at the 1989 Festival. Nick Gaselee, a Lambourn trainer who had been showing a keen interest in Norton's Coin, met Sirrell Griffiths before the horse's next run at Cheltenham in April.

"Shall we talk business before or after the race?" inquired Gaselee.

"Afterwards," replied the Welshman with an uncharacteristic display of confidence.

The rampant triumph of Norton's Coin an hour later ended all chance of a deal. The horse would be staying in Nantgaredig. It was that victory which first set Griffiths wondering about making an entry in the following year's Gold Cup.

"When Jenny Pitman spoke glowingly on television of Golden Freeze, who we beat easily, I thought maybe I would not be completely mad to enter him in the Gold Cup," he explains.

On the day of Desert Orchid's rousing third success in the King George VI Chase at Christmas 1989, Norton's Coin finished far, far behind, fully thirty-

The greatest upset in the Gold Cup's history – Norton's

nine lengths adrift though he had run with rich promise until tiring on the final bend. Few observers noticed his presence as they rushed headlong to acclaim Desert Orchid. It would be a different story at Cheltenham in March. Norton's Coin returned to form with a narrow defeat by the well-handicapped Willsford at Cheltenham on January 27th. After that encouraging performance Sirrell Griffiths determined to enter his pride and joy in the Gold Cup, "Just in case".

When the farm was waterlogged by the January storms Norton's Coin was taken away to exercise on a nearby mountain or on Llanstephan beach just around the headland from Dylan Thomas' home at

Coin (centre) comes to challenge Toby Tobias at the last fence. Desert Orchid is third

the boathouse in Laugharne. Then the horse coughed after finishing a distant, disappointing third at Newbury.

"I did not think much of it at the time. We all cough, don't we," relates Griffiths with the sound logic of a man who had dealt with farm animals all his life. "I knew we had to forget the Gold Cup."

Griffiths wanted to enter Norton's Coin in the Cathcart Chase again but discovered he was ineligible because he had won a hunter chase in 1988. He tried to enter him instead in the Mildmay of Flete Handicap but found, to his dismay, that the closing date for entries to the race had been February 14th.

"It was my mistake. I should have known better

about the entries," he reflects. "If I could have run him in another race at the Festival he would not have been in the Gold Cup."

So, by default, the Gold Cup was Norton Coin's sole engagement at the Festival. Has there ever been a more eccentric entry into racing history? When the horse developed a painfully septic throat in February after Newbury, his presence among the runners for the Gold Cup seemed increasingly unlikely. Griffiths' vet Bertie Ellis prescribed a course of antibiotics over eighteen days to cure the blisters in his throat and advised that the horse could be led out at a walk but should not sweat. Cheltenham seemed a distant, impossible dream.

When Norton's Coin recovered at the end of February the trainer considered giving him a last chance in a racecourse gallop at Newbury. Graham McCourt suggested taking him instead to Peter Cundell's superb gallops at Compton in Berkshire. On March 6th, nine days before the Gold Cup, Norton's Coin ran away from Cundell's best hurdler Celtic Ryde and two others over one and a half miles.

"Graham could not believe it and neither could I," recalls Griffiths. "I was so proud of my horse. Peter Cundell was a changed man from the one who came up in the car. His face was drained."

Later Cundell was heard to ask Graham McCourt incredulously: "What is this bloody thing from Wales?" Many more would be posing the same question the following week.

The night before the Gold Cup a bookmaker friend called to see Griffiths and asked if he wanted £200 each way on his horse at 100–1. Griffiths declined the offer on the understandable grounds that he had never backed Norton's Coin and did not wish to set a precedent.

On Gold Cup morning Sirrell Griffiths rose even earlier than usual to milk his cows, and set off for Cheltenham soon after nine at the wheel of his horse-box accompanied by his wife Joyce and two friends. The two Griffiths boys Martyn and Linley, who both help their father with the horses, travelled by car. On this momentous day one would lead up a Gold Cup winner, the other act as travelling head lad. Those lucky punters still spending their winnings on Norton's Coin months later were unaware of the anxiety felt by his owner on the long journey to Cheltenham.

"I prayed the ground would not be too firm. This horse always comes first and I was ready to pull him out. When I walked the course it was firm enough but there was a lovely covering of grass," he says. The field for the Gold Cup had cut up badly in the final weeks before the race. Charter Party, successful two years earlier, had retired. Playschool and Golden Freeze were both injured and the 1987 winner, The Thinker, was absent, too. He would not be risked on the firm ground. The enigmatic Carvill's Hill stayed in Ireland for the same reason and the dashing novice Celtic Shot ran instead in the Arkle. Bonanza Boy, winner of two Coral Welsh Nationals in the mud, was a challenger, but he was another who would not appreciate going fast. Jenny Pitman's bright young prospect Toby Tobias, still relatively immature, was a late addition to the field despite unseating his rider at Newbury shortly before Cheltenham.

Desert Orchid had been a 4–1 chance in mid-winter but the loss of several leading contenders in the run-up to the race contributed to his prohibitive starting price of 10–11, the first odds-on favourite for sixteen years.

The form guide in the official racecard at Cheltenham declared unkindly: "Norton's Coin looks more of a candidate for last place than first!"

The free-running Ten of Spades took on Desert Orchid from the start, tactics which ultimately ensured that neither horse could win. Behind them the little lop-eared Cavvies Clown, second in 1988, forfeited his chance by declining to set off until the others had gone a hundred yards. Running downhill for the final time both leaders were already very tired when Toby Tobias moved sweetly past them looking very much like the winner. Bonanza Boy was outpaced on the unseasonably firm ground, Pegwell Bay was dropping back and Norton's Coin was moving surprisingly well in fourth. As they turned left-handed round the final bend towards the remaining two fences Desert Orchid was pushed wide by Ten of Spades, who promptly fell at the second last.

It was already clear that Desert Orchid would not be winning this time, and as Toby Tobias surged towards the final fence it was Norton's Coin who came through thrillingly to challenge. Toby Tobias still led half-way up the hill but Norton's Coin, driven with a forceful blend of power and purpose by Graham McCourt, was edging closer with every stride. Fifty yards from the line they were level, but it was the bonny little chestnut from west Wales who bounded forward to claim the most extraordinary victory in the history of the Gold Cup by three-quarters of a length in a record time of 6 minutes 30.9 seconds.

Mark Pitman, riding in his first Gold Cup, experienced the crushing disappointment of having victory snatched from him at the last moment on Toby Tobias in much the same cruel manner as his father Richard had endured on Pendil in 1973.

Desert Orchid, hanging wearily first right-handed and then left, was four lengths further back in third place with Cavvies Clown fourth, beaten by far less than the distance he gave away at the start.

As Norton's Coin returned in triumph Graham McCourt seized Sirrell Griffiths' cap and hurled it high above the heaving crowds who greeted the unexpected winner. After the polite applause on Tues-

Sirrell and Joyce Griffiths with the fastest milk horse in Wales

day for the Champion hurdler Kribensis, bearing the colours of the world's most powerful flat-race owner Sheikh Mohammed, the Welsh roar was, in truth, the happiest sound of all at Cheltenham that remarkable week. Things might be entirely different on the flat but the splendidly rustic figure of Sirrell Griffiths and his romantically bred chaser had produced irrefutable testimony that you do not need to be indecently wealthy to breed and own a top-class steeplechaser. Long may that be so.

Graham McCourt's finest hour was dampened by a three-day suspension for wielding his whip with unreasonable force. The stewards' decision was taken after they viewed photographic evidence of weal marks on the winner's flanks, though the jockey pointed out, quite reasonably, that he would not have won without the use of a whip.

Late that evening Norton's Coin and the Griffiths family returned to a wildly enthusiastic reception in Nantgaredig. There would be precious little time for sleep. The next morning the amiable Griffiths offered a statement that must have struck fear into the heart of every bookmaker still afloat in west Wales.

"The horse is not right, you know. He is better than his form in the Gold Cup suggests," he observed.

Seeing my look of disbelief he added hastily: "I'm serious. It's the same problem he had five weeks ago. If you had seen the mucus discharged from his nose into his water bucket an hour after the Gold Cup you would not credit that he could even have finished the race."

A fortnight later victory became even more implausible when X-rays revealed that Norton's Coin had suffered a hairline fracture of the cannon bone on his off foreleg either from a kick at the start or during the race. The horse was sore for weeks afterwards, though Griffiths confesses disarmingly: "I was too frightened to trot him. I did not want to see him lame."

Norton's Coin was given every chance to recover before going out to grass much later than usual on July 22nd. He was elevated to the status of national celebrity in Wales and his summer's break was interrupted by a series of personal appearances. He opened betting shops and proved more in demand in west Wales than Neil Kinnock. At Easter Sirrell Griffiths filled his treasured Gold Cup with Easter eggs and handed them round in the children's ward of a local hospital.

In July Norton's Coin was given the Freedom of the City of Carmarthen. Crowds thronged the ancient town centre on a hectic Saturday afternoon as the unexpected hero of the Gold Cup was paraded through the streets to the Guildhall, where his owner was presented with an inscribed ashtray by the mayor, Peter Hughes Griffiths. The horse who had emptied bookies' satchels throughout the region was impressively relaxed during the proceedings on a scorching hot day, though he did appear briefly concerned when the Town Crier gave full voice beside him.

By the time Norton's Coin returned into training a little later than usual in the autumn, no less than twenty-six owners had asked Sirrell Griffiths to take their horses, too. Since he is principally a dairy farmer and cattle dealer and his permit allows him to train solely for his own family he had to turn down every request.

"If I lived the other side of the Severn Bridge perhaps I would have thought about it; but we are too far away here. Anyway training for all those people would have given me a permanent headache. We have no gallops as such. I just hack about on roads, tracks, through the woods and on the local mountain."

Most days, after milking the cows, Griffiths can be seen riding as many as nine or ten miles on the unlikely Gold Cup winner.

"I don't know if he needs as much work as I give him but it seems to have worked so far, so I am going to carry on," he says almost apologetically.

Fate did not treat Norton's Coin kindly in the following season. He fell on his reappearance at Haydock, was injured by another horse's flying hooves on a sporting venture to Ireland and fell again a mile from home in the 1991 Gold Cup. Once, memorably, Sirrell Griffiths declined to take him on a long overnight journey in pursuit of a tempting prize on a distant Northern racecourse on the perfectly understandable grounds that he had to stay at home to do the milking. Success, happily, has not changed his priorities.

TOTE CHELTENHAM GOLD CUP.   March 15th 1990.   £67,003.40.   *Good to firm.*

1 Norton's Coin	9 12 0	G. McCourt	100–1	
2 Toby Tobias	8 12 0	M. Pitman	8–1	
3 Desert Orchid	11 12 0	R. Dunwoody	10–11 Fav	
4 Cavvies Clown	10 12 0	G. Bradley	10–1	
5 Pegwell Bay	9 12 0	B. Powell	20–1	
6 Maid of Money	8 11 9	A. Powell	25–1	
7 Yahoo	9 12 0	T. Morgan	40–1	
8 Bonanza Boy	9 12 0	P. Scudamore	15–2	

¾ length, 4.   Owned and trained S. Griffiths.   Bred G. P. Thomas.
6m. 30.9 seconds. Race record.   Also 10 Nick The Brief (M. Lynch) P.U., 20 Ten of Spades (K. Mooney) Fell, 50 Kildimo (J. Frost) Fell, 200 The Bakewell Boy (S. Smith Eccles) P.U.   12 Ran.   Tote win: £114.50.

Norton's Coin: ch.g. 1981 (Mount Cassino–Grove Chance)

25

GARRISON SAVANNAH
(1991)

SECOND THOUGHTS PROVED BEST for Jenny Pitman at Ballsbridge in 1986 when she failed to
buy an attractive jumping prospect whose make and
shape reminded her irresistibly of her 1983 Grand
National winner Corbiere. Jenny's shopping
bonanza was the talk of the Derby sale that week. By
the time she left for Dublin Airport she had bought
nine of the choicest lots for a variety of owners including Strong Gold for 45,000 guineas, Esha Ness
and Royal Athlete. It was the one she left behind that
exercised her mind in the following twenty-four
hours.

"There was something about the horse. He looked
the spitting image of Corbiere with a different
coloured coat. I was so annoyed with myself for failing to buy him, for being so mean with the people
who were trying to sell him, that I swore on the
journey home and all the next day," she recounts
candidly.

In such a mood Jenny Pitman can be less than con-
vivial company. David Stait, who shares her life, suggested the obvious solution. Since she was so upset
why not, he advised gently, contact the sales company to re-open negotiations with the vendor? Soon
a deal was completed over the telephone that
brought the unnamed three-year-old safely under the
control of Jenny Pitman. He proved to be easily the
cheapest of her many purchases that eventful week
and ultimately the best.

Five years later, named Garrison Savannah, he
gained an improbable victory in the Cheltenham
Gold Cup after regular acupuncture treatment for a
damaged shoulder, then came tantalisingly close to
matching Golden Miller's unique feat of adding the
Grand National in the same season.

Garrison Savannah was bred by John McDowell,
a Dublin jeweller, from Merry Coin, a mare given to

him by his cousin Peter McDowell in 1979. Stamina
is not immediately obvious in the pedigree or racing
performance of Merry Coin. Speed was the overwhelming influence in her family though her half-
brother Zongalero, by David Jack, was a high-class
chaser and finished a close second in the 1979 Grand
National.

Merry Coin, by the useful sprint handicapper Cur-
rent Coin, won a maiden race over six furlongs at
Naas in 1972. Though she was initially mated with
sprinters, too, her first foals proved to be big, backward and unquestionably slow. They also possessed
an unexpected degree of stamina. When she was
given to John McDowell, who runs his own Asigh
Stud near Navan in Co. Meath, her mating arrangements were changed significantly. He sent his new
mare four years in succession to Random Shot, who
was awarded the 1971 Ascot Gold Cup on the disqualification of Rock Roi. Once she was barren.
From the other three matings with Random Shot she
produced three lively colt foals. One later died;
another was sold into obscurity and has never been
named.

The lone survivor, later to be called Garrison
Savannah, was sold by John McDowell at Tattersalls
(Ireland) as a foal in November 1983, for 2,700
guineas.

"It has always been my policy to sell foals. The
nomination cost only £300 and I thought I got good
money for him," reflects McDowell, whose uncle
Jack McDowell owned the 1947 Grand National
winner Caughoo, a 100–1 outsider trained by
another uncle, Herbert McDowell.

Ivor Dulohery, from Ballyclough near Mallow in
Co. Cork, was the man who bought Garrison Savannah as a foal. Dairy farming provides his main in-
come but like so many Irishmen he deals in young

horses as a profitable sideline.

"I thought this horse had a nice NH pedigree and stood on four sound legs. I was particularly impressed by his good, solid feet. He proved to have plenty of character as he developed and refused to let our vet put a tube down his throat when we tried to worm him."

Almost three years later, when Garrison Savannah had matured and strengthened, Dulohery sent him back to the Tattersalls sales ring for the annual Derby sale that attracts so many English buyers. Several, including Jenny Pitman, asked to see him trotted up but bidding was light when he appeared in the ring. Eventually the horse who would win a Gold Cup was led out unsold below the reserve price of 5,200 guineas. Within minutes outside the ring Jenny Pitman offered the disappointed vendor 4,500 guineas, then 5,000 guineas. It was not quite enough to tempt Dulohery. Later that evening he took Garrison Savannah back to Co. Cork.

"Well," he explains. "I thought I would sell him easily for handy money and I was not going to give him away."

Jenny Pitman returned to England bitterly regretting the purchase that had slipped from her grasp. Pressed by David Stait she asked Willie O'Rourke, the knowledgeable managing director of Tattersalls (Ireland), to resume negotiations with Ivor Dulohery. When O'Rourke was unable to contact the Dulohery family on the telephone he drove over to see them on Sunday morning. At first Ivor Dulohery held out for 6,000 guineas. Patiently O'Rourke explained that Jenny Pitman was not prepared to pay a penny more than the original reserve price of 5,200 guineas. So the deal was concluded at that price. Soon the horse was on his way to Lambourn.

Jenny Pitman admits, "I did not have a bean at the time nor a suitable order from any owners so I bought him on spec for myself."

Within weeks three racing-mad engineers from Cheltenham, Roger Voysey, John Davies and Malcolm Burdock, visited the trainer on a reconnaissance mission. All three were members at their local racecourse. Now they were considering taking the first plunge into ownership and wanted to seek her advice. Jenny Pitman had just one horse left for sale after her shopping trip in Dublin – the unnamed gelding by Random Shot. Another owner, she explained, had first refusal until the following Wednesday. If not, the three partners could have the horse for a figure close to £7,000.

When the first owner failed to take up his option the future Gold Cup winner became the property of the partners in the name of their own company, Autofour Engineering, which manufactures components for aerospace and defence systems. One of them, Roger Voysey, had just returned from a holiday in Barbados whose racecourse is called Garrison Savannah. Hence the name they chose for their new horse.

Eight months later Garrison Savannah won on his debut in a bumper race at Kempton in February 1987, ridden by John Smith at 25–1. He came from an apparently impossible position to catch his better fancied stable companion Saddler's Night. Garrison Savannah won on his debut over hurdles, too, in November at Worcester. A year later he dominated a staying handicap hurdle at Cheltenham with eye-catching ease but was then out of action for almost twelve months with a stress fracture to his cannon-bone.

When he did race again, it was over fences at Haydock in December 1989. He ran with a degree of promise that day but was very disappointing next time at Kempton and was equipped with blinkers when he was beaten again at Towcester. So to Wincanton where his form was a revelation. He won, unchallenged, by twenty-five lengths. At Cheltenham Jenny Pitman ran two horses in the Sun Alliance Novices' Chase. Mark Pitman chose to ride the stable's outstanding prospect Royal Athlete, a 5–4 chance who fell heavily. Garrison Savannah, partnered by Corbiere's Grand National jockey Ben de Haan, a fine horseman, won decisively with a resolute late run. It was a wonderful victory for his three owners who all live close to Prestbury Park.

Jenny Pitman began the following season with a formidable team of top-class chasers. Toby Tobias and Royal Athlete were some way above Garrison Savannah in the pecking order but he was the only one fit enough to run in the 1991 Tote Cheltenham Gold Cup though his participation, too, was in doubt until the morning of the race. The problem began when Garrison Savannah returned home apparently lame in his shoulder after a highly encouraging reappearance in December at Haydock where he beat all but Celtic Shot.

At first the trainer was hopeful that he would recover in time for the Coral Welsh National on the Saturday before Christmas but extensive veterinary

A bold jump by Garrison Savannah at the final fence

treatment failed to cure the injury.

She recalls colourfully, "The horse was like a rusty train – all creaking and stiff. Trying to get him right for Cheltenham has given me far too many grey hairs."

Early in January, aware that time was slipping away, the anxious trainer called in Chris Day, a vet who specialises in acupuncture and homeopathy.

He recounts, "The horse was very lame, apparently from an injured muscle. The muscle was not functioning and the nerve may have been damaged as well but he seemed to respond from the first treatment, which is not always the case."

Horses, being trusting creatures, do not normally object to the insertion of long needles into their bodies, at least when it is conducted by a specialist. Garrison Savannah, however, resisted violently. At the sight of Chris Day approaching he would stamp his feet in anger and back off into a corner of his box.

Day concedes, "He did not think it was quite the thing for him and made various attempts to make sure we could not do it. I put in about ten needles to start off with but he was rather a resistant patient so we could not use all those needles each time."

Despite the horse's understandable reservations he began to respond to the treatment that Chris Day administered twice, sometimes three times, a week. Alternative medicine successfully stimulated the healing processes in his body. Chris Day chose acupuncture as the first line and supported it with homeopathy. Soon Jenny Pitman felt justified in allowing the horse to resume light exercise. Swimming became a regular part of his training programme. Still there were days when his prospects of running at Cheltenham were as bleak as the weather in mid-February. Certainly there was insufficient time for a preparatory race.

Though Garrison Savannah's name appeared among the declared runners for the Gold Cup, Jenny Pitman did not decide to send him to Cheltenham until he had cantered on the morning of the race and returned sound to his box at her Weathercock Stables in Upper Lambourn. Though she had been able to keep him on the move in the final weeks before the race she could not be certain of his fitness.

Malcolm Burdock recalls, "We had not given up hope of running but in that last week we were living on a knife edge. Although we knew Jenny was doing everything possible it was a very tense time."

Desert Orchid, by then twelve years old, headed the ante-post market for the 1991 Tote Cheltenham Gold Cup for several weeks, though cold logic dictated that he could not win. One unforgettable win on the course from seven attempts told its own story. Yet time and again the old grey marvel had blown away such pessimistic calculations with wonderfully defiant displays of spirit.

David Elsworth set the mood as he reflected realistically, "We know Dessie is going to lose his high performance level. I think it is already on the wane; past the point of equilibrium. Perhaps the enthusiasm is going a bit. It takes him time to be motivated. At Sandown recently he had to dig deeper than ever."

On the day a sustained gamble on Celtic Shot displaced Desert Orchid as favourite. Celtic Shot's odds shortened sharply to 5–2 despite lingering doubts about his stamina and his lack of consistency. Desert Orchid drifted out to 4–1. The mud-loving Cool Ground, arguably the most improved handicapper of the season and sweeping winner of the Coral Welsh National, was steady at 7–1 though the prevailing good going appeared to be against him. Nick The Brief, named after the barrister Nicholas Wilson QC, who once represented his owner–trainer John Upson successfully in a matter of litigation, was a 12–1 chance.

Norton's Coin, the unlikeliest hero in the history of the race a year earlier, stood at 16–1 after a disappointing season. He had completed the course only once from four attempts. Garrison Savannah also started at 16–1. Jenny Pitman decided that her son Mark should adopt a bold, attacking policy on him.

"Oh yes, I told the owners we would commit this horse from the start. We knew he jumped and stayed very well so we had to ride him positively," she confirms.

Unusually, French stables supplied two of the runners, The Fellow and the rank outsider Martin D'Or. The Fellow, a talented six-year-old trained by astute François Doumen, was widely ignored in the betting at 28–1 despite his laudable run into third place behind Desert Orchid in the King George VI Chase. In 1987 Doumen had taken that race with the 25–1 shot Nupsala. Once again he was quietly confident of a major victory in England.

On a warm, spring day the Hennessy winner Arctic Call made the running until blundering haphazardly at the eleventh fence in front of the stands. This left Desert Orchid ahead for five fences until Celtic Shot was rushed forcefully into the lead by Peter Scudamore. The champion jockey had switched the favourite abruptly round the field after a circuit and now attempted to make the best of his way home. Close behind him The Fellow dived alarmingly low through the fifteenth fence, a ditch. His Polish-born jockey Adam Kondrat sat admirably tight but the mistake cost him valuable ground just as the tempo of the race was quickening.

Garrison Savannah, jumping exuberantly, looked anything but an invalid as he tracked the leaders approaching the final mile. Norton's Coin, too, was in contention when he tumbled to the ground after misjudging the final ditch. Turning downhill Garrison Savannah moved comfortably into second place and was then left in front much sooner than his jockey desired when Celtic Shot hit the third last fence hard.

The Fellow, who had raced wide throughout, was now the nearest challenger with Desert Orchid heading the chasing pack. Round the final bend and into the straight Garrison Savannah was still moving with a powerful rhythm. He gained a precious length with another extravagant leap at the second last fence but The Fellow was beginning to close as he approached the final fence. Desperate measures were needed now. Seeing a long stride Mark Pitman drove his horse at the birch like a man inspired. The response was a final, fearless, flowing jump that gained another priceless half length.

"I had to ask him an impossible question there," Mark Pitman told me later on BBC TV. "If he had not come up for me they would still be digging me out now."

For a moment it seemed Garrison Savannah, wearing vivid blue blinkers, would win comfortably. Then lack of a recent run began to tell; his step faltered on the steep ascent to the winning post at the very moment that The Fellow began a thrilling late charge on the stands side.

The Pitmans, mother and son, had endured a numbing defeat with Toby Tobias in similar circumstances twelve months earlier. Mark's father Richard, too, riding Pendil in the 1973 Gold Cup, had experienced the crushing disappointment of being caught on that same pitiless hill by The Dikler.

Now it seemed that history would be repeated as The Fellow sprinted up to join the weary leader. Few in the crowd knew who had won as the pair flashed past the post separated by almost the width of the course. Old Desert Orchid was an honourable third on his final visit to the Festival. A photo-finish was announced. The principal jockeys shook hands in a common bond of sportsmanship as they waited anxiously for the judge's decision.

Jenny Pitman, whose skill and patience had brought Garrison Savannah back to fitness after months of uncertainty, was overcome with emotion. "I kept thinking, how can this be happening all over again. I felt as if I was dead. I was barely conscious," she confessed later.

A deathly hush fell over the vast crowd as the result was announced. Garrison Savannah had just prevailed. Examination of the photo-finish print revealed that he had held on by perhaps three inches. Mark Pitman punched the air repeatedly in a spontaneous display of jubilation and relief. As he returned to the hallowed winner's enclosure he proudly saluted his father sitting in his commentary position high above the paddock. It was a gesture and a result that helped erase the scars of Pendil's defeat etched in the minds of both men.

When the young jockey jumped joyously from Garrison Savannah's back Jenny Pitman hugged him so tightly you wondered if she would ever release him. It was an embrace that every mother in the land would understand. The constant uncertainty of the jumping game was vividly demonstrated by the subsequent grim experience of Mark Pitman that fateful day. Within two hours the young jockey was on his way to hospital by ambulance after a ghastly fall in a hurdle race on his mother's final runner at the meeting. A cracked pelvis was diagnosed.

Jubilant Mark Pitman salutes his father Richard watching from his commentary position

At first it seemed his season might be over, yet when Jenny Pitman decided to send Garrison Savannah to Aintree for the Seagram Grand National her son, lying painfully in hospital, announced his intention of returning in time to ride him there. Now we all know that jump jockeys exhibit a rare toughness of spirit but this statement sounded, at best, a forlorn pipe-dream. It is history now that horse and rider made their date with destiny at Liverpool on April 6th, this time both helped by acupuncture.

Garrison Savannah was outstandingly well handicapped in the Grand National. As a Gold Cup winner he would never again be so leniently treated and, crucially, he had not taken a lame step since the Festival. The decision to run him at Liverpool carrying only 11 st. 1 lb was an entirely professional one but the lessons of the past suggested his task was formidable. Only Golden Miller had achieved the elusive double in the same year, 1934, though he also failed on three more occasions. Of the eight others that tried, Easter Hero, carrying 12½ st., had come closest with second place in 1929 in a record field of sixty-six runners.

Garrison Savannah was only the fourth horse to attempt the feat since the war. Ridden with aggressive confidence by Mark Pitman and constantly gaining ground with breathtakingly accurate jumping, he was always prominent, led at the twenty-third fence and held an advantage of at least six lengths, perhaps more, from Seagram landing over the final fence. Surely, we thought, he was on his way to matching the record of the immortal Golden Miller.

The long, endless run-in at Liverpool has been the scene of so many dramatic twists of fate and now it provided one more. At the elbow Seagram began to close menacingly with rapid strides. Suddenly, hauntingly, Garrison Savannah was faltering, the last of his strength ebbing away in the rain-softened ground. In less time than it takes to tell, Seagram, the jaunty little chestnut from Devon, swept past the exhausted leader barely a hundred yards from the line. Such was the strength of his thunderous late burst that at the post Seagram had won by five lengths.

Golden Miller's record was still intact but it had been a close-run thing. When you consider the severity of Garrison Savannah's muscle problems through the winter and the bone-crunching injury to his jockey in mid-March their combined assault on the Grand National was truly an essay in resilience.

TOTE CHELTENHAM GOLD CUP.   March 14th 1991.   £98,578.   *Good.*

1	Garrison Savannah	8 12 0	M. Pitman	16–1
2	The Fellow	6 12 0	A. Kondrat	28–1
3	Desert Orchid	12 12 0	R. Dunwoody	4–1
4	Cool Ground	9 12 0	L. Harvey	7–1
5	Kildimo	11 12 0	R. Stronge	66–1
6	Nick The Brief	9 12 0	R. Supple	12–1
7	Celtic Shot	9 12 0	P. Scudamore	5–2 Fav
8	Yahoo	10 12 0	N. Williamson	100–1

Sh. head, 15.   Owned Autofour Engineering.   Trained Mrs J. Pitman. Bred J. McDowell.   6m. 49.8 seconds.   Also 10 Arctic Call (J. Osborne) P.U., 11 Carrick Hill Lad (M. Dwyer) P.U. and Twin Oaks (N. Doughty) P.U., 16 Norton's Coin (G. McCourt) Fell, 33 Party Politics (A. Adams) P.U. and 250 Martin D'Or (J. N. Joly) P.U.   14 Ran.   Tote win: £15.00.

Garrison Savannah: b.g. 1983 (Random Shot–Merry Coin)

WINNERS OF THE CHELTENHAM GOLD CUP

1924	Red Splash	5yo	F. Rees	F. Withington	5–1
1925	Ballinode	9	T. Leader	F. Morgan	3–1
1926	Koko	8	J. Hamey	A. Bickley	10–1
1927	Thrown In	11	Mr H. Grosvenor	O. Anthony	10–1
1928	Patron Saint	5	F. Rees	H. Harrison	7–2
1929	Easter Hero	9	F. Rees	J. Anthony	7–4
1930	Easter Hero	10	T. Cullinan	J. Anthony	8–11
1931	No Race				
1932	Golden Miller	5	T. Leader	A. Briscoe	13–2
1933	Golden Miller	6	W. Stott	A. Briscoe	4–7
1934	Golden Miller	7	G. Wilson	A. Briscoe	6–5
1935	Golden Miller	8	G. Wilson	A. Briscoe	1–2
1936	Golden Miller	9	E. Williams	O. Anthony	21–20
1937	No Race				
1938	Morse Code	9	D. Morgan	I. Anthony	13–2
1939	Brendan's Cottage	9	G. Owen	G. Beeby	8–1
1940	Roman Hackle	7	E. Williams	O. Anthony	Evens
1941	Poet Prince	9	R. Burford	I. Anthony	7–2
1942	Medoc II	8	H. Nicholson	R. Hobbs	9–2
1943	No Race				
1944	No Race				
1945	Red Rower	11	D. L. Jones	Ld Stalbridge	11–4
1946	Prince Regent	11	T. Hyde	T. Dreaper	4–7
1947	Fortina	6	Mr R. Black	H. Christie	8–1
1948	Cottage Rake	9	A. Brabazon	M. V. O'Brien	10–1
1949	Cottage Rake	10	A. Brabazon	M. V. O'Brien	4–6
1950	Cottage Rake	11	A. Brabazon	M. V. O'Brien	5–6
1951	Silver Fame	12	M. Molony	G. Beeby	6–4
1952	Mont Tremblant	6	D. Dick	F. Walwyn	8–1
1953	Knock Hard	9	T. Molony	M. V. O'Brien	11–2
1954	Four Ten	8	T. Cusack	J. Roberts	100–6
1955	Gay Donald	9	A. Grantham	J. Ford	33–1
1956	Limber Hill	9	J. Power	W. Dutton	11–8
1957	Linwell	9	M. Scudamore	C. Mallon	100–9

1958	Kerstin	8	S. Hayhurst	C. Bewicke	7–1
1959	Roddy Owen	10	H. Beasley	D. Morgan	5–1
1960	Pas Seul	7	W. Rees	R. Turnell	6–1
1961	Saffron Tartan	10	F. Winter	D. Butchers	2–1
1962	Mandarin	11	F. Winter	F. Walwyn	7–2
1963	Mill House	6	G. W. Robinson	F. Walwyn	7–2
1964	Arkle	7	P. Taaffe	T. Dreaper	7–4
1965	Arkle	8	P. Taaffe	T. Dreaper	30–100
1966	Arkle	9	P. Taaffe	T. Dreaper	1–10
1967	Woodland Venture	7	T. Biddlecombe	F. Rimell	100–8
1968	Fort Leney	10	P. Taaffe	T. Dreaper	11–2
1969	What A Myth	12	P. Kelleway	H. Price	8–1
1970	L'Escargot	7	T. Carberry	D. L. Moore	33–1
1971	L'Escargot	8	T. Carberry	D. L. Moore	7–2
1972	Glencaraig Lady	8	F. Berry	F. Flood	6–1
1973	The Dikler	10	R. Barry	F. Walwyn	9–1
1974	Captain Christy	7	H. Beasley	P. Taaffe	7–1
1975	Ten Up	8	T. Carberry	J. Dreaper	2–1
1976	Royal Frolic	7	J. Burke	F. Rimell	14–1
1977	Davy Lad	7	D. Hughes	M. O'Toole	14–1
1978	Midnight Court	7	J. Francome	F. Winter	5–2
1979	Alverton	9	J. J. O'Neill	M. H. Easterby	5–1
1980	Master Smudge	8	R. Hoare	A. Barrow	14–1
1981	Little Owl	7	Mr A. J. Wilson	M. H. Easterby	6–1
1982	Silver Buck	10	R. Earnshaw	M. Dickinson	8–1
1983	Bregawn	9	G. Bradley	M. Dickinson	100–30
1984	Burrough Hill Lad	8	J. Francome	Mrs J. Pitman	7–2
1985	Forgive 'N Forget	8	M. Dwyer	J. Fitzgerald	7–1
1986	Dawn Run	8	J. J. O'Neill	P. Mullins	15–8
1987	The Thinker	9	R. Lamb	W. A. Stephenson	13–2
1988	Charter Party	10	R. Dunwoody	D. Nicholson	10–1
1989	Desert Orchid	10	S. Sherwood	D. Elsworth	5–2
1990	Norton's Coin	9	G. McCourt	S. Griffiths	100–1
1991	Garrison Savannah	8	M. Pitman	Mrs J. Pitman	16–1